MENTAL ILLNESS AND SOCIAL POLICY

The American Experience

MENTAL ILLNESS AND SOCIAL POLICY

THE AMERICAN EXPERIENCE

Advisory Editor
GERALD N. GROB

OUTLINES

OF

IMPERFECT AND DISORDERED

MENTAL ACTION.

BY

THOMAS C. UPHAM

ARNO PRESS
A NEW YORK TIMES COMPANY
New York • 1973

Reprint Edition 1973 by Arno Press Inc.

Reprinted from a copy in
  The University of Illinois Library

MENTAL ILLNESS AND SOCIAL POLICY:
  The American Experience
ISBN for complete set: 0-405-05190-5
See last pages of this volume for titles.

Manufactured in the United States of America

———◆———

Library of Congress Cataloging in Publication Data

Upham, Thomas Cogswell, 1799-1872.
    Outlines of imperfect and disordered mental action.

    (Mental illness ans social policy: the American
experience)
    Reprint of the ed. published by Harper, New York.
  1. Psychology, Pathological. 2. Inefficiency,
Intellectual. I. Title. II. Series.
[DNLM: WM U660 1868F]
RC454.U63 1973   616.8'9   73-2426
ISBN 0-405-05235-9

IMPERFECT AND DISORDERED

MENTAL ACTION

OUTLINES

OF

IMPERFECT AND DISORDERED

MENTAL ACTION.

BY

THOMAS C. UPHAM,

PROFESSOR OF MENTAL AND MORAL PHILOSOPHY IN
BOWDOIN COLLEGE.

NEW YORK:

HARPER & BROTHERS, PUBLISHERS,

329 & 331 PEARL STREET,

FRANKLIN SQUARE.

1868.

PREFACE.

In undertaking to prepare the present volume, I was strongly influenced by a conviction of the practical importance of the subject. It is perhaps true, that the public mind is but little informed, certainly much less than it should be, in relation to the true doctrines of regular or normal mental action; but it is, undoubtedly, much more ignorant of the philosophy of defective and disordered mental action. Nor is it surprising that this should be the case, when we consider that but very few writers, even of those who have professedly devoted themselves to mental inquiries, have particularly investigated this portion of the Philosophy of Mind. It has, in fact, been almost totally neglected, except by a few learned and philosophical writers of the medical profession, who, in the discharge of their professional duties, could not well avoid giving some attention to this subject. But the books of these writers, of great value as they undoubtedly are, are for the most part taken up with the consideration of disordered mental action as it is connected particularly with the physical system, and with various practical directions having relation to the treatment of insane persons. These works were not designed for popular circulation; nor, as a matter of fact, has this been the case.

Under these circumstances, it naturally suggested

itself to the proprietors of the Family Library that something might be prepared on this subject which would be both interesting and useful. In undertaking this task, although I had for some time directed my attention to inquiries of this nature, I deeply felt my inability to do justice to a subject hitherto considered so doubtful in its principles, and universally acknowledged to be exceedingly complicated in its relations. Believing, however, that such a work might be practically useful, and that, in fact, it was much needed, I was willing to do what I could in the somewhat narrow limits which the plan of the Family Library allowed me. I have therefore laid down the outlines of this great subject in the manner which facts and nature seemed to me to dictate, and with a sincere regard to what seemed to me to be the truth. As the work is designed for popular reading as much and even more than for men of science, I have endeavoured to be simple and natural in the plan of inquiry as well as in style. I commit it to the reader in the hope that he will accept whatever merit the work has, and regard it leniently in whatever it may fall short of his reasonable expectations.

THOMAS C. UPHAM.

Bowdoin College, Oct., 1839.

CONTENTS

INTRODUCTION.

DISORDERED ACTION OF THE EXTERNAL INTELLECT.

CHAPTER I.

NATURE OF SENSATION AND PERCEPTION.

CHAPTER II.

DISORDERED SENSATION AND PERCEPTION.

(I.) THE SENSES OF SMELL AND TASTE.

CHAPTER III.

DISORDERED SENSATION AND PERCEPTION.

(II.) THE SENSE OF HEARING.

CHAPTER IV.

DISORDERED SENSATION AND PERCEPTION.

(III.) THE SENSE OF TOUCH.

CHAPTER V.

DISORDERED SENSATION AND PERCEPTION.

(IV.) THE SENSE OF SIGHT.

B

CHAPTER VI.

EXCITED OR DISORDERED CONCEPTIONS.

CHAPTER VII.

SPECTRAL ILLUSIONS OR APPARITIONS.

CHAPTER VIII.

DISORDERED STATE OF THE POWER OF ABSTRACTION.

CHAPTER IX.

DISORDERED ATTENTION.

CHAPTER X.

ON DREAMING.

CHAPTER XI.

SOMNAMBULISM.

DISORDERED ACTION OF THE INTERNAL INTEL-LECT.

CHAPTER I.

DISORDERED SUGGESTION.

CHAPTER II.

DISORDERED CONSCIOUSNESS.

CHAPTER III.

DISORDERED ACTION OF RELATIVE SUGGESTION OR JUDGMENT.

CHAPTER IV.

CHAPTER V.

DISORDERED ACTION OF THE MEMORY.

CHAPTER VI.

IMPERFECT AND DISORDERED ACTION OF THE REASONING POWER.

CHAPTER VII.

DISORDERED ACTION OF THE IMAGINATION.

CHAPTER VIII.

NATURE AND CAUSES OF IDIOCY.

DERANGEMENT OF THE SENSIBILITIES.

CHAPTER I.

DISORDERED ACTION OF THE APPETITES.

CHAPTER II.

DISORDERED ACTION OF THE PROPENSITIES.

(I.) PROPENSITY OF SELF-PRESERVATION.

CHAPTER III.

DISORDERED ACTION OF THE PROPENSITIES.

(II.) PROPENSITY TO ACQUIRE OR ACQUISITIVENESS.

CHAPTER IV.

DISORDERED ACTION OF THE PROPENSITIES.

(III.) AMBITION, OR THE DESIRE OF POWER.

CHAPTER V.

DISORDERED ACTION OF THE PROPENSITIES.

(IV.) IMITATIVENESS, OR THE PROPENSITY TO IMITATION.

CHAPTER VI.

DISORDERED ACTION OF THE PROPENSITIES.

(v). THE DESIRE OF ESTEEM.

CHAPTER VII.

DISORDERED ACTION OF THE PROPENSITIES.

(VI.) SOCIALITY, OR THE DESIRE OF SOCIETY.

CHAPTER VIII.

DISORDERED ACTION OF THE AFFECTIONS.

CHAPTER IX.

DISORDERED ACTION OF THE MORAL SENSIBILITIES.

CHAPTER X.

CASUAL ASSOCIATIONS IN CONNEXION WITH THE SENSIBIL-TIES.

DISORDERED ACTION OF THE WILL.

CHAPTER I.

NATURE OF THE WILL.

CHAPTER II.

IMBECILITY OF THE WILL.

CHAPTER III.

DISORDERED ACTION OF THE WILL IN CONNEXION WITH OTHER POWERS.

INTRODUCTION.

CHAPTER I.

OUTLINES OF MENTAL PHILOSOPHY.

§ 1. *Extent and importance of the subject to be examined.*

THE reader will notice that I have entitled this Treatise, Imperfect and Disordered Mental Action. A title designedly made thus general, in order to include all the varieties of imperfect and alienated action of which (and they are almost without number) the human mind is the subject. Our inquiries are not meant to be limited to those more aggravated forms of mental disorder which infringe upon moral accountability, and which are commonly had in view, when what is called Insanity or Madness comes under discussion. We propose to take a more extensive view of the subject; and indulge the hope, that, in thus extending the plan of remark, the Treatise may be found to be more interesting and useful to the common reader at least, if not to the philosopher.

I can hardly consider it necessary to delay for

the mere purpose of attempting to illustrate the importance of the subject which it is now proposed to examine.   It commends itself at once to every sober and reflecting mind, as intimately and seriously connected with the well-being of men.   Every man ought to have some knowledge of the general structure and action of the mind, and of its irregular as well as its regular action.   Nor will it be enough that he has some general knowledge of the more aggravated cases of insanity, such as are characterized by a total confusion of the powers of thought, and sometimes by ungovernable ferocity.   There are cases of partial mental disorder, less perceptible to the unpractised eye, which come nearer home. There are mental aberrations and shades of aberration ;   there are mental imperfections and shades of imperfection, short of a total overthrow of the spiritual fabric, which, although they have seldom had a place in any Treatise designed to be generally accessible, it is nevertheless important, for various reasons, to understand.   A person may not be insane, in the ordinary sense of the term insanity, and yet may be the subject of various modifications of mental disorder, which have no inconsiderable bearing upon his usefulness and happiness.   He is merely called by his neighbours an " odd man," a " hairbrained man," a " violent man," a " visionary man," or by some other name, indicative, in their view, of some peculiarity of mental structure, although, by no means, of insanity, in the ordinary import of that term.   And yet such specialities of intellect and temper, inconsiderable as they may appear, ought

to have their place in the philosophy of the mind's
disordered action.

But there are other cases, much more marked in
their nature, and more decisively injurious in their
consequences.   We refer to those instances of
mental disorder where the mind is not merely dis-
composed, not merely temporarily set ajar, but in
ruins.   No sight is so afflicting, so overwhelming,
as that of a mind fundamentally, and, perhaps, permanently unsettled.   What, then, can be more important than to understand the facts and causes of
its ruin, and the principles on which a restoration
may be possible !

§ 2. *Necessity of some Preliminary or Introductory statements.*

Before, however, entering directly upon this important subject, it may, for various reasons, be desirable to attempt a brief examination of some matters
of a somewhat general nature which are closely
connected with it.

I.—In the first place, it seems to me just and reasonable to say, that we cannot have a correct knowledge of insanity or unsoundness of mental action,
without some knowledge of the laws and principles,
which are involved in a sane or sound action.   It is
necessary, therefore, as a preliminary matter, to give
a concise view of the Outlines of the Philosophy of
the Mind.

II.—In the second place, it is well known that
there is a close connexion between the body and the
mind, especially between the brain and the mind.

And such are the various influences and results of this connexion, that it is impossible to explain fully the aberrations to which the mind is subject without some reference to it. Here, then, although frequent references will be subsequently made to it from time to time, is obviously another preliminary topic.

III.—In the third place, it seems proper, before we go into the facts and details of the Work, to lay down the basis, at least, of a philosophical Classification. In the early history of any department of science, when the facts in relation to it have not been collected in sufficient number, or have not been subjected to a sufficiently careful examination, this course would perhaps be premature. But the facts, or what might properly be termed the Statistics of Insanity, have been so greatly multiplied, and that, too, under the supervision of men eminently fitted for the task, that this cannot properly be said in the present case.

§ 3. *The idea of Insanity of Mind predicated on that of Sanity.*

The three distinct topics which have now been mentioned will be introduced and examined as Preliminary views ; and, consequently, will not occupy a place in the body of the work, except incidentally and concisely. In accordance with these intimations, I shall now, in the present chapter, proceed to give the Outlines or general principles, on which the mind appears to be constituted. If we have a right understanding of things in this particular ; in other words, if we know what the regular action of the

mind is, we shall be more likely to appreciate correctly the statements, which we shall have occasion
to make of its irregular or disordered action. The
fact is, that every appropriate or sound action of the
mind (at least this is so generally the case as to admit of no exception worthy of notice here) is susceptible of degenerating into a defective or alienated
one. The philosophy of insanity, therefore (using
the term here in the broadest sense, as including all
the various forms both of defective and irregular
mental action), is parallel with that of sanity ; it occupies the same wide field ; it goes side by side.
To know, therefore, what the mind is in its insane
action, we must know what it is in its sane action ;
in other words, we must know something of the general principles of Mental Philosophy, properly so
called. But this knowledge, in its minuter details
at least, and in its illustrations, must be obtained
from other books. It cannot reasonably be expected, in such a Treatise as the present, to furnish anything more than some general outlines, which we
now propose to do.

§ 4. *Outlines of the Constitution of the Mind.*

The human mind exists in the three great de
partments of the intellect or understanding, the sensibilities, and the will. I am aware that this view
of the mind's constitution has not always been taken
by writers on Mental Philosophy ; but there is great
reason to believe that it is substantially a correct
one. It would be pleasing, and perhaps profitable,
to enter into a consideration of the proofs by which

this fundamental arrangement is sustained. But our limits will not permit this; and we can only refer the reader, in general terms, to those works on Mental Philosophy, where such a discussion would find a more appropriate place. Nevertheless, in view of the multiplied sources of evidence applicable to the inquiry, we have no hesitation in saying that we consider this great distinction as sufficiently established, and as constituting the true point of departure in all investigations into the mind.

Taking it for granted that this fundamental distinction exists, we proceed to say that it is the office of the understanding (what may be called, perhaps, the perceptive or cognitive department of the mind) to give us knowledge. The product of its action is INTELLECTION, not PASSION. The result of the action of the sensibilities, on the contrary, is found in those states of mind which are denominated emotions and desires, and in those combinations of these elementary feelings, which constitute the benevolent and malevolent affections. The office of the will, which is called later into action, and seems to hold a higher position, is mandatory and executive. Volitions, which are the results of the will's action, have no perceptive power, nor are they, in themselves, impregnated with any emotive or affective element. They are not only subsequent in time to the states of mind just mentioned, but are invested, as has just been intimated, with the supervisory and executive duty of carrying them into effect.

§ 5. *Further considerations on the same subject.*

The mind may be regarded as departmental (that is, as susceptible of leading generic distinctions), not only in reference to its results, but also in its law of movement, or, more explicitly, in its successive order of action. It is true that the mental departments, to a certain extent, rest upon, and are implicated with, each other ; but still their connexion and action are always consistent with a prescribed and definite law of progress. The order of movement is that in which the departments have already been enumerated, viz. : the intellect, the sensibilities, and the will ; commencing in the intellect, continued, under various forms and modifications, in the sensibilities, and terminating in what Richard Baxter (in a Treatise almost forgotten, but not without merit) has denominated the "volitive" faculty. The intellectual developement, in distinction from the sensitive and volitive, is obviously first in the order of nature. On this point we do not suppose that there can possibly be any great difference of opinion. As a general thing, certainly, there can be no action of the sensibilities without a previous action of the understanding. If we put forth any sensitive act ; if we exercise any desire or passion, it is, of course, involved in the very expressions, that there is and must be some object of desire or of passion, which is the subject of our knowledge ; in other words, upon which the intellect, in its perceptive or cognitive action, has been employed. There can be no question, therefore, that in a history of the mind's action our inquiries ought to begin with the intellect,

C

§ 6. *Of the Intellect, particularly the External Intellect.*

In considering the intellect first, as it is proper we should do, we must keep in mind the great division of the intellect, which is more or less hinted at by writers (and which certainly has its foundation in nature), viz., into the external and the internal intellect.

Under the head of the external intellect we include, especially and chiefly, those intellectual susceptibilities which are brought into action in direct and immediate connexion with the external world, particularly sensation and external perception. Without this connexion, which nature has obviously established, there is no reason to suppose that these powers would ever become operative. Intellectual states of external origin depend for their existence, therefore, upon the antecedent existence, and, with one exception, upon the actual presence, of external objects. If the mind were insulated and cut off from the outward and material world, or if the outward world had no existence, we could not taste, we could not touch, nor hear, nor see. All those mental states, which we express, when we speak of the diversities of touch, and smell, and taste, of sound and sight, are immediately dependent on the existence and presence of something, which is exterior to the intellect itself. And it is the intellect, so far as it is brought into action in this way, which we characterize by a convenient, though not, in all respects, a felicitous phraseology, as the external in tellect.—It is not necessary, however, as has already been intimated, to restrict the import of the phrase to these states of mind exclusively ; since there is at least one other state of mind which is so based upon antecedent sensations and perceptions as to become intimately and specifically, though not directly, connected with external objects ; and which, therefore, may properly be arranged under the same general head.

§ 7.   Of the Conceptive Power and Conceptions.

In accordance with the intimation at the close of the last section, we proceed to say that under this general head, viz., of the external intellect, we may properly include the conceptive power, or that power, not by which we originate things or discover them absolutely for the first time, but by which we recall or revive to the mind those impressions which we have previously received through the medium of the senses.   Conceptions, therefore, which are the results of the exercise of this power, is the name of re-existing sensations and perceptions, when the outward causes and objects of such sensations and perceptions are no longer present.   It is particularly in this respect, that conceptions differ from ordinary sensations and perceptions, viz., the absence of their outward causes and objects.   When, for instance, the rose, the honeysuckle, or other odoriferous body is presented to us, the effect which follows in the mind is termed a sensation.   When we afterward think of that sensation (as we sometimes express it); when the sensation is recalled, even though very imperfectly, without the object which originally caused it being present, it then becomes, by the use of language, a CONCEPTION.

And it is the same in any instance of perception, considered as distinct from mere conception. When, in strictness of speech, we are said to perceive any-thing, as a tree, a river, a building, or a mountain, the objects of our perceptions are in all cases be-fore us. But we may form conceptions of them; they may be recalled and exist in " *the mind's eye* ;" they may be conceptively brought near and made internally existent, however remote they may be in fact, both in time and place. Nevertheless, as this re-existence and restoration is, in the strict and spe-cific sense of the terms, based upon what had pre-viously been addressed to the outward senses, there is certainly reason for including the conceptive power and its results under the general head of the exter-nal intellect.

§ 8. *Of the External Intellect in connexion with peculiarities of character.*

It may be proper to remark here, that the view of the mind which separates the external from the in-ternal intellect, furnishes some assistance in forming a correct estimation of those varieties of intellectual character, which frequently present themselves to our notice. There are some men who have great pow-ers of external perception ; who readily perceive and appreciate all the varieties and peculiarities of extension, form, colour, and magnitude ; who, in a word, can accurately and promptly estimate whatever has tangibility and visibility ; but in whom the powers of comparison, judgment, and reasoning, and, in general terms, all those capacities, which are internal and reflective, are greatly deficient. It is undoubtedly the case, that these men often give the impression, at first sight, of great ability ; nor is it true that they are wanting in ability of a certain kind. But it is rather practical than philosophical ability ; ability suited rather to the appreciation of the exterior and the visible manifestations of things than of what may be called their subjectivity, or the more remote and intimate principles ; ability better adapted to the every-day business of common life than to the speculations of the closet and the intricacies of science. This peculiarity of mental structure has frequently been noticed ; and no system of Mental Philosophy, which derives its doctrines from a careful observation of nature, will be likely to deny its existence.

§ 9. *Of the Internal Intellect, or the Intellect as it is brought into action, independently of the direct agency of the Senses.*

The mind is first brought into action through the mediation and assistance of the senses. It is by means of the senses that we become acquainted with outward things, with whatever is visible and tangible, and has outline and form. Accordingly, the first great theatre of mental movement is the external world. This is the source from which the mind may be considered as drawing its earliest nutriment, and from which, in the first instance, it takes its character

But the development of the external intellect is followed, particularly where there are opportunities of mental cultivation, by a new movement, which is strictly internal. In other words, the soul, when once called into action by means of its connexion with external things, finds sources of knowledge in itself, entirely distinct from the outward sources of hearing, touch, and the like. There are inward powers of perception, constituting, as it were, hidden fountains of knowledge, which open themselves and flow up in the mind's remote and secret places. There is, therefore, philosophically considered, an internal as well as an external intellect; a perceptive power, which reaches to invisible and intangible existences and relations, as well as a perceptivity, which is merely occupied with what is presented to touch and sight, and the other senses.

I am aware that some mental philosophers, who have enjoyed more or less note in the literary world, have objected to this doctrine, particularly Hobbes, Condillac, and Helvetius; but it is supported by others certainly of not inferior weight; by Reid, Stewart, and Brown, and the Scotch school generally; by Cousin, and all the writers of the Platonic and Kantian school; by the leading phrenological writers; and, as it seems to me, by Mr. Locke. The authority of the more recent writers, those who have had the best opportunities to form a correct opinion, is decidedly in favour of it. And if it could be said that philosophy, as it exists in books, does

not favour it, still, have we not indubitable grounds
for saying that philosophy, as it exists in nature,
does? And what shall we say of that philosophy,
which is at variance with nature?

§ 10. *Of the Nature of Original Suggestion.*

Under the head of the Internal Intellect are properly included, as leading powers (or perhaps we
should more properly say, as leading sources of
knowledge), Original Suggestion, Consciousness,
Relative Suggestion or Judgment, and Reasoning.

I.—By means of Original Suggestion we become
possessed of various ideas, which we cannot ascribe
directly to the senses on the one hand, nor to an
act of the judgment or of the reasoning power on
the other; ideas which, in the language of Dr. Reid,
are not gotten by comparison, "and perceiving
agreements and disagreements, but immediately inspired by our constitution." Mr. Stewart also recognises the existence of this mental power. In
his Philosophical Essays he speaks of certain mental phenomena as attendant upon the objects of our
consciousness, and as SUGGESTED by them. The
notions of TIME, NUMBER, MOTION, MEMORY, SAME-
NESS, PERSONAL IDENTITY, PRESENT EXISTENCE,
&c., he ascribes neither to the external world on the
one hand, nor to the internal mental operations, of
which we are conscious, on the other, except so far
as they are the *occasions* on which the mind brings
them out or SUGGESTS from its own inherent energy. Of the notion of DURATION, for instance, he
would say, I do not see it or hear it, or feel it, nor

become acquainted with it by means of any other of
the senses ; nor am I conscious of it, as I am of
believing, of reasoning, of imagining, and of other
mental exercises ; but it is SUGGESTED by the mind
itself; it is an intimation absolutely essential to the
mind's nature and action. That is to say, it is an
intimation, or conception rather, which the mind,
constituted as it is, cannot fail to originate.

§ 11. *Consciousness another form of Internal mental action.*

II.—The term Consciousness expresses another
of the forms of internal mental action. By the
common usage of the language, the term consciousness is appropriated to express the way or method,
in which we obtain the knowledge of those objects
which belong to the mind itself, and which do not,
and cannot, exist independently of some mind. The
words remembering, imagining, and reasoning, are
terms expressive of real objects of thought ; but evidently the objects for which they stand cannot be
supposed to exist independently of some mind, which
remembers, imagines, and reasons. Of these, therefore, he may properly be said to be conscious. And
in all other cases where we apply the term under
consideration, consciousness is limited, in the testimony which it gives, to mere mental action and the
modifications of action ; and does not properly extend to anything which has existence, extraneous to
the conscious subject or soul itself.

Consciousness seems to sustain the same relation
to the attributes of mind which sensation does to

those of matter. In both cases we have direct knowledge; that is to say, knowledge without the necessary intervention of other facts. In the case of Sensation, whenever an object is presented to us, we have a new state of mind at once, and necessarily. So in Consciousness, whenever a new state of mind exists, we recognise its existence at once, without any accessory aid. We cannot help doing it.

Consciousness is a ground or law of BELIEF. And the belief attendant on the exercise of it, like that which accompanies the exercise of Original Suggestion, is of the highest kind. It appears to be utterly out of our power to avoid believing, beyond a doubt, that the mind experiences certain sensations, or has certain thoughts, or puts forth particular intellectual operations, whenever, in point of fact, that is the case. We may be asked for the reason of this belief, but we have none to give, except that it is the result of an ultimate and controlling principle of our nature ; and hence, that nothing can ever prevent the convictions resulting from this source, and nothing can divest us of them.

In the course of this Work we shall have occasion to bring forward some instances where the power of consciousness (whether we call it the power, or, as some would prefer, the mere *fact* of consciousness, is not, perhaps, in the present discussions, very essential) appears to be disordered. The examination of Insanity, as it presents itself under this particular head, will furnish some cases, which are interesting in a high degree.

§ 12. *Of Relative Suggestion or Judgment.*

III.—Another of those powers, coming under the general head of the Internal Intellect, is Relative Suggestion. It is well known that the mind has the power, as we commonly express it, of bringing its thoughts together, of placing them side by side, of comparing them. These expressions, although they are for the most part of material origin, indicate nevertheless an important fact in the mental action. When it is said that our thoughts are brought together, that they are placed side by side, and the like, the meaning undoubtedly is, that they are immediately successive to each other. And when it is further said that we compare them, the meaning is, that we perceive or feel their relation to each other in certain respects.

The mind, therefore, has an original susceptibility or power corresponding to this result; in other words, by which this result is brought about; which is sometimes known as its power of RELATIVE SUGGESTION, and at other times the same thing is expressed by the term JUDGMENT, although the latter term is sometimes employed with other shades of meaning. " With the susceptibility of relative suggestion" (says Dr. Brown, Lect. 51), " the faculty of *judgment,* as that term is commonly employed, may be considered as nearly synonymous; and I have accordingly used it as synonymous in treating of the different relations that have come under our review." Degerando, in his Treatise on the Origin of Human

Knowledge (pt. ii., chap. ii.), has a remark nearly to the same effect.

We arrive here, therefore, at an ultimate fact in our mental nature ; in other words, we reach a principle so thoroughly elementary that it cannot be resolved into any other.   The human intellect is so made, so constituted, that, when it perceives different objects together, it immediately and necessarily has a knowledge of some of the mutual relations of those objects.   It considers them as equal or unequal, like or unlike, as being the same or different in respect to place and time, as having the same or different causes and ends, and in various other respects.

§ 13. *Of the Nature of the Reasoning Power.*

IV.—Another of the internal powers is Reasoning.   An expression by which we are to understand the mental process or operation, by means of which we deduce conclusions from two or more propositions premised.   For our knowledge of the operations of the reasoning power we are indebted to consciousness, which gives us our direct knowledge, not only of this, but of all other mental processes.   It is hardly necessary, therefore, to add, that reasoning is not identical with, or involved in, consciousness.   If consciousness gives us a knowledge of the act of reasoning, the reasoning power, operating within its own limits and in its own right, gives us a knowledge of other things.   It is a source of perceptions and knowledge, which we probably could not possess in any other way.

Considered as sources of knowledge, none of the forms of intellectual action which have been mentioned are identical with each other. Each occupies its appropriate sphere, and has its specific and appropriate results. Without the aid of Original Suggestion, it does not appear how we could have a knowledge of our existence; without Consciousness we should not have a knowledge of our mental operations; without Relative Suggestion or Judgment, which is also a distinct source of knowledge, there would be no Reasoning; and, unassisted by Reasoning, we could have no knowledge of the relations of those things which cannot be compared without the aid of intermediate propositions. The reasoning power, accordingly, is to be regarded as a new and distinct fountain of thought, which, as compared with the other sources of knowledge just mentioned, opens itself still farther in the recesses of the internal intellect; and as it is later in its developement, so it comes forth with proportionally greater efficiency. It not only discloses to us those separate relations, which are so complicated and remote, that relative suggestion, or judgment in its elementary form, cannot reach them; but sustains the higher office of bringing to light the great principles and hidden truths of nature; revealing to the inquisitive and delighted mind a multitude of fruitful and comprehensive views, which could not otherwise be obtained.

This power too, pre-eminent and important as it is acknowledged to be, is not exempt from an impairment and alienation of its action. Indeed, Cullen and Locke, and we know not how many other leading writers, seem to have regarded it as the great seat of mental disorder.

§ 14. *Remarks on the Imagination.*

V.—Another leading power which, when we accurately consider its nature, seems properly to be arranged under the general head of the Intellect, is the Imagination.   We shall have occasion hereafter to recur again to the nature and intellectual process of imaginative action, when it comes in place to consider the disorders to which this important faculty is subject.   All we propose to do here is briefly to point out the relation existing between the imagination and the reasoning power.   D'Alembert somewhere intimates very distinctly, that this relation is a very close one ; and suggests farther, in illustration of his views, that Archimedes, the geometrician, of all the great men of antiquity, is best entitled to be placed by the side of Homer.   If such a relation exists, it furnishes one reason at least in support of the classification, which arranges the imagination, in connexion with the reasoning power, under the general head of the Intellect.

Some of the particulars, in which the imaginative and deductive powers are closely related, are these. They both imply the antecedent exercise of the power of abstraction ; they are both employed in framing new combinations of thought from the elements already in possession ; they both put in requisition, and in precisely the same way, the powers of association and relative suggestion.   Nevertheless, they

are separated from each other, and characterized by
the two circumstances, that they operate in part on
different materials, and that their objects are different. Reasoning, as it aims to give us a knowledge
of the truth, deals exclusively with facts more or less
probable. Imaginàtion, as it aims chiefly to give
pleasure, is at liberty to transcend the limits of the
world of reality, and, consequently, often deals with
the mere conceptions of the mind, whether they correspond to reality or not. Accordingly, the one as-
certains what is true, the other what is possible ; the
office of the one is to inquire, of the other to create.

§ 15. *Of other important Intellectual Principles.*

In addition to the intellectual susceptibilities which
have been mentioned, there are others which, in a
full account of the mental powers, would be entitled
to an important place ; such as Association, Memory, and Abstraction. The power of Abstraction,
in consequence of the applicability of its exercise
either to external or internal objects, might be arranged under either of the two great divisions of the
intellect. Association and memory, as they have a
very intimate relation to the reasoning and imaginative powers, would, with a high degree of propriety,
present themselves for consideration in immediate
connexion with those powers ; and, accordingly, be
arranged under the head of the Internal Intellect
rather than of the External. These important powers of the mind our limits will not permit us particularly to notice.

It is not to be inferred, however, from the circumstance of their not being considered here, that they will not hereafter receive their appropriate place and their full share of notice. Whatever may be true in respect to the power of abstraction, certain it is that no view of insanity would be adequate which should fail to point out the phenomena presented by a disordered condition of association and memory.

§ 16. *Of the Sensibilities in Distinction from the Intellect.*

The second great division of the mind is that of the Sensibilities. The action of the sensibilities is subsequent in time to that of the intellective nature. As a general thing, there is and can be no movement of the sensibilities ; no such thing as an emotion, desire, or feeling of moral obligation, without an antecedent action of the intellect. If we are pleased or displeased, there is necessarily before the mind some object of pleasure or displeasure ; if we exercise the feeling of desire, there must necessarily be some object desired, which is made known to us by an action of the intellect. So that if there were no intellect, or if the intellectual powers were entirely dormant and inactive, there would be no action of the emotive part of our nature and of the passions.

The department of the sensibilities is itself susceptible of being resolved into some subordinate yet important divisions ; particularly the natural and moral sensibilities. The department of the natural sensibilities considers objects chiefly as they have a

relation to ourselves.   The department of the moral
sensibilities, taking a wider range, contemplates objects as they relate to all possible existences.   The
one looks at things in the aspect of their desirable-
ness, the other fixes its eye on the sublime feature
of their rectitude.   The one asks what is GOOD,
the other what is RIGHT.

It will, perhaps, throw light upon the distinction
which we suppose to exist in the sensibilities, if
we call to mind that the natural (or pathematic
sensibilities, as they are sometimes called) exist
in brute animals the same as in man.   Brute animals are susceptible of various emotions ; they
have their instincts, appetites, propensities, and affections, the same as human beings have, and perhaps even in a higher degree.   They are pleased
and displeased ; they have their prepossessions and
aversions ; they love and hate, with as much ve-
hemence at least as commonly characterizes human passion.

But if we look in the lower animals for the other
and more elevated portion of the sensibilities, it is
not there.   And here, we apprehend, is the great
ground of distinction between men and brutes.   The
latter, as well as human beings, appear to understand
what is good, considered as addressed simply to the
natural affections ; but man has the higher knowledge of moral as well as of natural good.

§ 17.   *Other and more Subordinate Divisions of the
Sensibilities.*

The natural or pathematic sensibilities resolve

themselves again into the yet more subordinate division of the Emotions and Desires. These two
classes of mental states follow each other in the order in which they have been named ; the emotions
first, which are exceedingly numerous and various ;
and then the desires. The DESIRES are, in their
own nature, essentially fixed and uniform, and are
chiefly modified in their combination with emotions.
The various modifications which the desires assume,
appear in the distinct shape of Instincts, Appetites,
Propensities, and Affections. And it is here that we
find a very interesting and important department of
the mind, especially in connexion with insanity.

The moral sensibilities divide themselves in a
manner analogous to the classification which exists
in the natural. The first class of mental states
which presents itself to notice under this general
head, is that of Moral Emotions ; corresponding in
the place which they occupy in relation to the intellect, as well as in some other respects, to the natural emotions. The moral emotions are followed by
another class of moral feelings, which may be designated as obligatory feelings, or feelings of moral
obligation ; which hold the same relation to the
moral emotions, which the desires do to the natural
emotions. If we had not moral emotions (that is to
say, feelings of moral approval and disapproval), it
would not be possible for us to feel under moral
obligation in any case whatever, the latter state of
the mind being obviously dependent on the former.

D

§ 18. *Of the Will, and its Relation to the other Powers.*

Of the three leading divisions of the mind, which are supposed to embrace the whole mental structure, that of the Will naturally comes last. The natural course of investigation in Mental Philosophy obviously commences in the understanding, and is prosecuted through the sensibilities upward to the will. We shall not undertake here to go into a philosophical explanation of the nature of this power, but merely indicate in a few words the relation which it sustains to the other departments.

The will may be considered as occupying, in some important sense, a higher and more authoritative position. In other words, as we have already had occasion to intimate, it sustains, as compared with the other great mental departments, the part of the controlling and executive power of the mind. Action, in some form or other, was undoubtedly the great object which was had in view in the creation of the mind ; and although it cannot be denied that the preparatives of action (we mean now, action which has an object exterior to the mind) exist in the intellect and in the sensibilities, the presiding element of action, its effective or consummating power, is unquestionably lodged in the will. Whatever other powers he might possess, if man were destitute of the power of exercising volitions, and could not realize the results involved in such an exercise, he would, in the present state of existence at least, be an inefficient and useless being.

We admit that the intellect and the sensibilities, in their various forms of action, constitute the antecedents to volition. They are to be regarded as the established prerequisites of the internal voluntary movement, as furnishing the basis of motives, on which the subsequent operations of the will depend. But, without the will to carry into effect the antecedent suggestions of the intellect, and to arbitrate among the conflicting elements of the sensibilities, the mind would present an appearance but little better than that of a complete chaos. It is the will which, in the executive sense of the terms at least, if not in the advisory and consultative, sits the witness and arbitress over all the rest. It is essential alike to the action and accountability, the freedom and order of the other parts of the mind. They seem to revolve around it as a common centre ; kept in their place by its power, and controlled by its ascendency.

In closing this sketch of the Outlines of the Mind, it may be proper to remark, that the doctrines of this chapter are essentially those which are given in the Elements of Mental Philosophy, published a number of years since by the author of this treatise. In some of the statements, almost as a matter of necessity, the same expressions are employed. The analysis which has been given has necessarily been concise ; and, consequently, makes no pretensions to completeness and perfection. For a more full and explicit account of the writer's views of the leading doctrines of Mental Philosophy, the reader is referred to the work just mentioned.

CHAPTER II.

CONNEXION BETWEEN THE MIND AND BODY.

§ 19. *The Origin of many mental disorders to be found in the Connexion between the mind and the body.*

WE proceed now to another general topic, which may properly be embraced in this Introduction. It is undoubtedly true, that, in a great majority of cases, the human mind conforms in its action to the predominant principles of its own nature. In other words, it acts, in all ordinary instances, as its Creator designed it to act. But, unhappily, this is not always the case. The fact that there may be disorder or insanity of mind, implies that the mind sometimes suffers a disastrous deviation from the laws which commonly regulate it. Undoubtedly, the causes of these deviations are very various, and will repeatedly present themselves to our notice, and receive more or less of comment in the course of the present work. In connexion with this topic, however, viz., the causes of disordered mental action, we take this opportunity to say, that the origin, as we apprehend, of no small portion of mental disorder (stating the matter in the most general terms) is to be found in the connexion existing between the mind and the body This leading cause of irregu-

lar action, considered in its most general aspect,
may properly be made a distinct subject of inquiry.
It is in its general aspect, and not in its particulars,
that it has a place in this Introduction.

We do not deny, it will be noticed, that there may
be, as there undoubtedly are, other causes of mental
irregularity. We do not agree with some respectable writers in considering Insanity as being, in its
basis, exclusively a physical disorder. We have no
hesitancy in admitting the doctrine that there may
be other causes of mental irregularity, more remote
from common observation, and more intimately connected with the mind's interior nature and secret
impulses. But this view of the subject, nevertheless, does not preclude a distinct and particular attention to a cause of mental disorder so obvious,
and, by general consent, so powerful as that which
we now particularly refer to. Whatever may be
true of sources of disorder in the internal relations
of the mind, there is no dispute that they may be
abundantly found in its external relations. In other
words, expressing the matter in few and plain terms,
it is hardly possible for the body to be disordered,
without the fact of physical disorder having an influence on the mental movement.

Accordingly, it will be the object of the remarks
embraced in this chapter, and as introductory, in
some degree, to the statements to be made hereafter, to show, by some facts and illustrations, the
connexion existing between the body and mind, and
the influence they reciprocally exert. This topic is
one of so much importance, that it ought to be thor-

oughly understood. And it seems a proper one, in its general form at least, to occupy a place in these introductory remarks.

§ 20. *The Mind constituted on the Principle of a Connexion with the Body.*

In endeavouring to illustrate the subject of the intimate connexion and the reciprocal influence of the mind and body, we naturally remark, in the first place, that the mind is evidently constituted on the principle of such a connexion.—The human mind, as we have already had occasion distinctly to observe, exists in the threefold nature or threefold division of the Intellect, Sensibilities, and Will. These great departments of the mind, although the limits which separate them are distinctly marked, have, nevertheless, an intimate connexion with each other. The action of the will, for instance, depends upon the antecedent action of the sensibilities ; and that of the sensitive nature is based upon the antecedent action of the intellect ; so that the commencement of action in the other parts of the mind seems to depend upon the antecedent action in the purely intellectual part.

The inquiry then arises, In what way is the Intellect first brought into action ? And, in answering this inquiry, we are led to remark, that the action of the intellect (the understanding, as Mr. Locke calls it) is twofold, external and internal. Accordingly, we not unfrequently employ the convenient phrases, External Intellect and Internal Intellect. By the phrase external intellect, as we have already had

occasion to explain, we mean the intellect, as it acts
in immediate or nearly immediate connexion with
the external world. And it is in this department of
the mind that we find the beginnings, the initiation
of all mental action. But it is well understood (so
much so, we suppose, as not to be a matter of controversy) that the action, which takes place here,
takes place in connexion with BODILY action. The
external intellect does not act, nor is it capable of
acting, although the mind is so constituted that the
movement of all the other parts depends upon movement here, without the antecedent affection of the
outward or bodily senses. Hence the remark at
the commencement of this section, that the mind is
constituted on the principle of a connexion with the
body. Hence the propriety of the remark, too, that
the action of the mind cannot be satisfactorily explained, neither its sane action nor its insane action, without a careful consideration of this connexion.

§ 21. *Illustration of the subject from the effects of
old age.*

The existence of the connexion between the mind
and body, and of their influence upon each other,
appears, in the second place, from the effects which
are witnessed in old age. The effects of old age,
it is true, are first experienced in the bodily system.
The outward senses become blunted and dim ; the
eye, considered as a merely material organ, loses its
keenness of sight ; the ear its quickness of hearing ;
the palate its nice discriminations of taste ; and in

various other ways the whole bodily system shows
the rapid diminution of its activity and power. But
it is well known, since it is a matter of every day's
observation, that these effects are not restricted to
that part of the human system where they first show
themselves. The mind, also, is unfavourably affected at the same time, and through the influence of
the same causes.

These results, it is true, are not experienced, to a
great extent, in the Internal intellect, or that division
of the intellect which operates in the discovery of
truth, independent, in a great measure, of the outward senses; but they are seen and felt, in a high
degree, in that department of the mind which we
have proposed to designate, in consequence of its
depending in its action on the external senses, as
the External Intellect. This portion of the mind
seems at once to fall with the outward organization
and the material instrumentality upon which it rested.

§ 22. *The Connexion of the body and mind farther shown from the effects of diseases.*

In addition to what has been said, it may be remarked further, in confirmation of the same general
views, that violent corporeal diseases in youth and
manhood, before any decays take place from age,
often affect the powers of thought. Persons have
been known, for instance, after a violent fever, or
violent attacks of some other form of disease, to
lose entirely the power of recollection. Thucydides,
in his account of the plague of Athens, makes mention of some persons who had survived that disease;

but their bodily sufferings had affected their mental constitutions so much, that they had forgotten their families and friends, and had lost all knowledge of their own former history.—It is a singular fact, also, that the result of violent disease is sometimes quite the reverse of what has now been stated. While in one case the memory is entirely prostrate, we find in others that, under the influence of such attacks, the memory is suddenly aroused, and restores the history of the past with a minuteness and vividness unknown before. But both classes of cases confirm what we are now attempting to show, viz., the ex istence of a connexion between the mind and body, and a reciprocal influence between them.

§ 23. *Shown also from the effects of stimulating drugs and gases.*

If there be not a close connexion between the body and mind, and if there be not various influences propagated from one to the other, how does it happen that many things of a stimulating nature, such as ardent spirits and opium, strongly affect the mind when taken into the system in considerable quantities? But, without delaying upon the effects of drugs of this description, which, unhappily, can hardly fail to be noticed every day, we would instance particularly the results which are found to follow from the internal use of the nitrous oxide gas. This gas, when it is received into the system, operates, in the first instance, on the body. The effect is a *physical* one. In particular, it quickens the circulation of the blood, and also, as is commonly

E

supposed, increases the volume of that fluid. But its effects, which are first felt in the body, are afterward experienced in the mind, and generally in a high degree. When it is inhaled in a considerable quantity, the sensations are more acute ; the conceptions of absent objects are more vivid ; associated trains of thought pass through the mind with increased rapidity; and emotions and passions, generally of a pleasant kind, are excited, corresponding in strength to the increased acuteness of sensations and the increased vividness of conceptions.

There is another gas, the FEBRILE MIASMA, which is found, on being inhaled, to affect the mind also, by first affecting the sanguineous fluid. But this gas diminishes, instead of increasing the volume of blood ; as is indicated by a small, contracted pulse, and an increasing constriction of the capillaries. As in the case of the nitrous oxyde gas, the mental exercises are rendered intense and vivid by the febrile miasma ; but the emotions which are experienced, instead of being pleasant, are gloomy and painful. The trains of thought which are at such times suggested, and the creations of the imagination, are all of an analogous character, strange, spectral, and terrifying.*—We may add as a general remark here, that, whenever the physical condition of the brain, which is a prominent organ in the process of sensation and external perception, is affected, whether it be from a more than common fulness of the bloodvessels or from some other cause, the mind itself will be found to be affected also, and often-times in a high degree.

* See Hibbert's Philosophy of Apparitions, pt. ii., ch. i.

§ 24. *Influence on the Body of Excited Imagination*
and Passion.

The powers of the mind are not only liable to be
powerfully affected by certain conditions of the corporeal system, but the body also, on the other hand,
even to the functions of the vital principle itself, is
liable to corresponding affections, superinduced by
certain conditions of the mind. When the passions,
for instance, are excited, particularly that of fear,
the body at once feels the influence; and instances
have occurred where, under the influence of the last-
named passion, even death itself has followed. In
the city of New-York, a few years since, a little
child was left in the evening in the care of a maid-
servant, the mother having gone out. As the child
was disposed to be troublesome and to cry, after
being placed at the usual time in bed in another
room, the domestic resorted to the expedient of qui-
eting it by making and placing before it the image
of some frightful object. The fears of the little
child were greatly excited; and when, in the latter
part of the evening, the mother returned and went
to the room, she found it dead; its eyes being open
and fixed with a singularly wild and maniac kind of
stare on the frightful image, which the girl had so
cruelly placed before it. In the time of the American Revolution, as the transaction was related by an
officer who was present, a soldier who had committed some crime was condemned to be shot.
He was finally pardoned, without a knowledge of
the pardon being communicated to him, since it was

thought advisable that he should be made to suffer as much as possible from the fear of death. In accordance with this plan, he was led at the appointed time to the place of execution; the bandage was placed over his eyes ; and the soldiers were drawn out, but were privately ordered to fire over his head. At the discharge of their muskets, although nothing touched him, the man fell dead on the spot.

" A criminal was once sentenced in England to be executed, when a college of physicians requested liberty to make him the subject of an experiment connected with their profession. It was granted. The man was told that his sentence was commuted, and that he was to be bled to death. On the appointed day, several physicians went to the prison, and made the requisite preparations in his presence ; the lancet was displayed; bowls were in readiness to receive the blood ; and the culprit was directed to place himself on his back, with his arms extended, ready to receive the fatal incision. When all this was done, his eyes were bandaged. In the mean time, a sufficient quantity of lukewarm water had been provided ; his arm was merely touched with the lancet, and the water, poured slowly over it, was made to trickle down into the bowl below. One of the physicians felt his pulse, and the others frequently exchanged such remarks as, ' He is nearly exhausted ; cannot hold out much longer ; grows very pale,' &c. ; and, in a short time, the criminal actually *died* from the force of imagination."*

* As the statement is given in the Work entitled **Popular Su** perstitions.

§ 25. *Connexion of the Mental Action with the Brain.*

From what has been said, we suppose it has been made sufficiently clear, that there is a close and important connexion existing between the mind and the body, and that they are reciprocally the subjects of various influences resulting from this connexion. In what has been hitherto said, however, we have considered the subject in the most general point of view. In other words, we have had no other object than the announcement and establishment of the general fact. We have now to add further, that this doctrine is particularly true as far as the brain is concerned. Without admitting the doctrine that the mind is identical with the brain, or even that the mind finds in the brain a congeries of organs specifically suited to the development of each of its separate faculties, we nevertheless hold it to be certain, not only that there is a reciprocal connexion and influence between the two, but that such connexion and influence exist in a remarkably high degree : so much so that it is absolutely necessary to advert to it in any attempt to explain the mental action, especially disordered mental action.

It may be proper, therefore, to make some general statements in regard to the brain, although we are not left at liberty, by our proposed course of investigation, to enter minutely into that subject.

The brain, although it is susceptible of various subordinate divisions, such as the cerebrum and the cerebellum, may in general terms be described as

that globular mass of nervous matter, which is lodged
in and occupies the cavity of the cranium or scull.
It is of an irregular figure, exhibiting on its surface
a great number of projections and depressions, cor
responding in some cases to irregularities in the
scull, but which are to be ascribed in part also to
convolutions and cavities in the brain itself. The
more important divisions of the cerebral mass are,
FIRST, into the cerebrum, which occupies the whole
of the upper part of the cranium, and the little brain
or cerebellum, which in size is about one eighth or
ninth part of the cerebrum, and is situated under its
posterior lobes ; and, SECONDLY, the longitudinal
division into two equal and symmetrical halves,
termed hemispheres. The spinal cord, or, as it is
frequently termed, the spinal marrow, is a cylindrical
body of nervous matter proceeding from the lower
part of the brain, with which it is connected through
the medium of a medullary mass, called the MEDULLA
OBLONGATA. Like the brain, it is enclosed in mem·
branes, and is of the same substance. It extends
through, and occupies, the vertebral canal. A number of white cords, called nerves, proceed from the
base of the brain and from the spinal marrow to
different parts of the system. They are composed
of medullary matter, and are contained in membra-
neous sheaths. Some of them communicate with,
or, more properly, *constitute*, at their termination, the
different organs of sense.

§ 26. *Of the Brain, considered as a part of one great Sensorial Organ.*

The nerves, the spinal cord, and the brain, connected together as they are, consisting essentially of the same substance, and contributing, each in its own way and degree, to the same results, may properly be regarded as forming one great SENSORIAL ORGAN. It is by means of the assistance furnished by the sensorial organ (under which expression we include also the subordinate organs of taste, smell, sight, touch, and hearing) that the mind is first brought into action. On this organ, the *sensorial,* as thus explained, an impression, originating from the presence and application of some external body, must be made, before there can be sensation and external perception. Without the presence of some external body, and without the assistance furnished by the sensorial parts of the system, there is reason to believe that the powers of the mind would never be effectively called into action. It is here, in connexion with this conjunction of body and mind, that we discover the beginnings of mental movement. An impression, for instance, is made on that part of the sensorial organ called the auditory nerve, and a state of mind immediately succeeds which is variously termed, according to the view in which it is contemplated, either the sensation or the perception of sound. An impression is made by the rays of light on that expansion of the optic nerve, which forms what is called the RETINA of the eye, and the intellectual principle is brought into that new posi-

tion, which is termed visual perception, or a percep
tion of sight.   And the same of other cases.

It will be noticed, that we speak of the new state
of mind, the sensation or external perception, as immediately consequent on the application of the outward body to the external senses.   But it is necessary to add, in order to have a correct view of the
case, that the outward impression is rapidly propagated to the brain (so very rapidly that it may well
be considered as a single act) before the mental
state results.   So that we may properly regard the
brain, so far as the mere corporeal process is concerned, as the ultimate seat of sensation.   It is there
that the bodily impression is felt last.   If the impression fails to be felt in the brain, the mental state
fails also.   Of this there is very easy and satisfactory proof.   If, for instance, the nerve, which connects the outward sense with the brain, be divided
or be greatly compressed, so as to cut off the communication between them, it is well known that the
mind will not be affected by the pressure and application of outward objects as it would otherwise be.
In other words, there will be no sensation.

§ 27. Relation of these Views to the General Subject.

Now we may well inquire whether this view ot
the connexion existing between the mind and the
great sensorial organ, particularly the brain, must
not necessarily have an intimate relation to the subject of insanity.   Is it possible that this great and
important organ can, as a general thing, be disor-

dered, or even be disordered merely in some of its parts, without occasioning some degree of disturbance in the mental action? On the contrary, are we not to seek for the origin of a considerable portion of mental disorders in the fact of the disturbed and disordered state of this part of the physical system?

We do not suppose, as we have already had occasion to intimate, that the causes of mental disorder are exclusively physical. There are intellectual and moral causes, as well as those more obvious and, perhaps, more common ones, which are located in the physical structure. Let a man indulge in the frequent exercise of the principle of resentment; let the resentful principle grow stronger and stronger, as it will not fail to do by this indulgence; and ultimately it will exercise an authority inconsistent with the just action of the other parts of the mind; and the person will bear about him, superinduced by mental and not by physical causes, the undoubted marks of insanity. At the same time, we are entirely confident that every system of Disordered Mental Action must be very imperfect which does not recognise distinctly the relation existing between the sensorial organ and the mind, and the important and unquestionable fact that the disordered condition of the former frequently results in a corresponding disordered state of the latter.

CHAPTER III

GENERAL ARRANGEMENT OF THE SUBJECT

§ 28. *The Classification of Insane mental action should be predicated on that of Sound mental action.*

WE wish to embrace one other topic, and only one, in this Introduction. It will be our object in the present chapter to give a concise view of the general plan which we propose to pursue in the investigation of the subject before us. The general outline which has been given of the Philosophy of the Mind, helps us very much here. In truth, it indicates very distinctly the course which ought to be taken. We have already had occasion to remark, that the Philosophy of Insanity (using the term in the broad sense) is parallel with that of Sanity ; and we mean to intimate by this, not only that they occupy the same wide field, and proceed side by side in the more general sense, but that they are parallel with each other, and are mutually correspondent in their subordinate divisions.

In writing this Treatise on Insanity, we propose, therefore, to pursue the same course, to follow the same order of investigation, as if we were endeavouring to prepare a Treatise on the Philosophy of the Mind. The plan, accordingly, is clearly indicated in what has already been said in relation to the Outlines of Mental Philosophy. We feel the more satisfaction in taking this course, because the writers on this subject seem, as a general thing, to have failed more in the matter of arrangement than they have in the detail of facts, or in the philosophical reflections to which their facts have given rise. Perhaps, however, we ought not to speak of their Works as a failure, even in this respect; if it be true, as it undoubtedly is, in respect to some of them, that their great and leading object was, not to frame a system, but merely to collect facts and to ascertain the statistics of Insanity, preparatory to the labours of others, who, they anticipated, would arise in due time to impress order and philosophic symmetry upon the mass of valuable but chaotic materials. They laboured well in their vocation, and have merited high praise. So true is this, that all which seems to be wanting at the present time is to take the materials, which are furnished ready at hand in great abundance, and arrange them according to the relations they sustain to the immutable principles of Mental Philosophy.

§ 29. *Defects in early Classifications and Improvements of them.*

The plan of this work will perhaps appear to some as a novel one, and as wanting, more than ought to be the case, in the supports of authority. But, in point of fact, the plan, in its leading features, has already been sanctioned to some extent by some writers of no small name. In the time of Mr. Locke.

and during all antecedent periods, so far as we
know, it was a common doctrine, that insanity is
exclusively predicable of the perceptive or intellectual part of man, and does not exist in the affections.
In other words, it consists in a lesion or injury of
the intellect, and not of the heart. Pinel (an honourable name even among those who have been
most distinguished as the benefactors of their race)
proposed the extension of the doctrine of insanity,
so as to include the moral or affective part of man's
nature as well as the intellectual. The proposition
was regarded at first as a startling one. Nor does
Pinel appear to have understood distinctly, and in its
details, what may properly be included under the
head of the moral or affective faculties. Nevertheless, he illustrated and confirmed his doctrine in its
general form by such an array of facts, gathered
from his widely diversified experience, that it has
ever since been accredited by the leading writers.
The sagacity of Pinel, sanctioned by the facts which
came under his notice, led him to conclude that the
doctrine of insanity ought not to be limited to the
intellect. We may now go farther, and say that it
ought not to be limited to anything short of the
length and breadth, and the heighth and depth of the
whole mind. It is a source of pleasure, therefore,
to notice that a recent German writer, Professor
Heinroth, has taken this ground. As it has not
been in our power to gain access to Prof. Heinroth's work, we are indebted for what little we know
of it to the recently published and very valuable
Treatise of Dr. Prichard on Insanity. " *The disor.*

.lers of the mind, according to this writer" (says
Dr. Prichard), *" are only limited in number and in
kind by the diversities which exist in the mental fac-
ullies."* He gives us to understand farther, thaͭ
Prof. Heinroth divides the mental operations intc
three different departments, viz., the Understand
ing, the Feelings or Sentiments, and the Will. Dr.
Prichard had adopted a somewhat different arrangement before the Work of Heinroth came into his
hands ; nor did he find sufficient reason for altering
his arrangement in the views which were presented
in that work. But he has the candour to say expressly, that " no systematic arrangement of mental
disorders can be contrived more complete than that
of Professor Heinroth." And again, " His scheme
is the most complete system that can be formed ;
and I have laid the outline of it before my readers,
as it may tend to render more distinct their conception of the relations of the different forms of insanity
to each other." Dr. Prichard gives a short account
of the minor divisions of Heinroth's classification,
which we do not consider it necessary to repeat, as
it furnishes no important suggestion (although, if we
had the original work before us, perhaps it would be
otherwise) which we shall deem it necessary to
adopt in what follows.

§ 30. *The Inquiry naturally begins with the External Intellect.*

The first step to be taken will be to give an account of insanity or unsoundness of mental action,
as it exists intellectually ; that is to say, as it exists

in the Intellect or Understanding   And here we are to keep in view the natural order of the mind's action.   If we begin with the intellect, it does not follow that we may begin with any portion of it indiscriminately.   This would evidently be inconsistent with the details at least of philosophic arrangement.   We commence, therefore, with the External Intellect, or that portion which, in consequence of its connexion with external things, is first brought into action.   Accordingly, it will be our object, in the first place, to give some account of Disordered Sensation and of Disordered External Perception, which will open at once a broad and interesting field of inquiry.

In this part of the subject we shall find, for the most part, that the disordered mental action has its basis in disordered physical action, particularly in an irregular or abnormal condition of the nervous system.   And here, perhaps, more than anywhere else, it will be necessary to keep in mind the general principles in relation to the connexion between the mind and body which have been brought forward in the preceding chapter.

In treating of sensation and external perception, it will be proper to consider the senses, which are the instruments of this form of mental action, separately from each other, at least as far as it can conveniently be done, and also with reference to some definite principle of arrangement.   Under the head of Disordered Visual Sensations, the interesting subject of Apparitions will appropriately have a place. Furthermore, there are some states and powers of

the mind, which from their nature may be ranked
either under the head of the external or the internal
intellect, being susceptible of existing as attributes
or manifestations of the mind in both forms. We
refer particularly to the power which is denominated
abstraction, and to the state of mind which some
writers have hesitated in describing as a distinct
mental power, but which is recognised under the
name of Attention. *We may find it convenient to
give some account of disordered action as it is found
to exist in connexion with these mental powers or
states under this head.

§ 31. *Proceeds from the External to the Internal Intellect.*

As we advance farther in the investigation before
us, we shall find that the intellect may be disordered, not only in its operation through the senses and
its connexion with the external world, but also in its
internal action. Original Suggestion, Consciousness, Relative Suggestion, Reasoning, together with
the collateral and subordinate powers of Association
and Memory, may all, in various ways and degrees,
be disturbed in their operation. These will all be
considered in their proper place and order ; and although it will be our object to be as concise as possible, many interesting facts, gathered from various
sources, will be presented to the reader's notice. .

Under the preceding head, that of the external intellect, the causes of disturbed action, as we have
already intimated, will be found for the most part in
the disordered state of the physical system, particu-

larly the sensorial organ. Under the present head, although physical causes will not be excluded, there will be others more frequently occurring, which are more strictly of an intellectual and moral nature. It may be remarked here, however, in general terms, that the doctrine of the causation of insanity, whether external or internal, is involved as yet, in many respects, in no small degree of obscurity.

§ 32. *Is continued in the Sensibilities and the Will.*

From the internal intellect we proceed, in the order which nature evidently points out, to the Sensibilities ; beginning with the natural or pathematic, in distinction from the moral sensibilities. The first great division of the natural sensibilities, as we have already had occasion to remark, is that of the Emotions, which is followed by the distinct class of mental states called Desires. Under the head of Desires we have the distinct mental principles (complex in their nature, including both desires and emotions) which are known in treatises of Mental Philosophy under the distinct names of Appetites, Propensities, and Affections. It is in connexion with the natural sensibilities, as existing particularly under these last complex forms, that we propose to prosecute this investigation. It is true that emotions and desires, even in their simple and unmixed form, are not exempt from insanity ; but, so far as this is the case, nothing more will apparently be necessary than to remark upon the subject incidentally. In their complex form—in other words, a they appear under the distinct and important modifications of the Appetites, Propensities, and Affections, they will deserve and receive a more particular notice.

This view of the subject will naturally be followed by some statement of mental derangement, as it is connected with the Moral Sensibilities. And the whole subject will be closed by a concise view of the insanity of the Will.

§ 33. *Of popular adaptation, combined with philosophical precision.*

A view of Insanity, conducted in the manner which has now been proposed, would seem to present some claims to be considered a philosophical view; which would not be the case if the inquiry were conducted without a regard to fixed principles, having their foundation in nature. Such is our plan; and this plan we affirm to be truly a philosophical one. At the same time, we wish to combine with a scientific form so much of personal and practical illustration, and that, too, presented in such simplicity of style, as shall render the work accessible and interesting to the common reader. It is generally conceded to be a fact, that instances of insanity are multiplying. Certain it is that they are frequent, if they are not actually increasing in number. Many are the families whose happiness is interrupted by the inroads of mental disorder; and no individual, whatever may be his present soundness of mind, is at liberty to consider himself as permanently exempt from its accessions.

It is desirable, therefore, that a treatise on this

F

subject, while it takes a philosophical view, should, at the same time, be adapted to popular apprehension. The public should have the means of knowing something of the nature of these dreaded attacks, either that they may guard against their occurrence, or rightly estimate them when they have come. Furthermore, the philosophy of insanity, using the term in a general sense, is, in fact, a portion, "part and parcel," of the philosophy of the human mind; although, with scarcely an exception, it has been excluded from the leading works on Mental Philosophy. And as such, saying nothing of other considerations, it ought to have a place in every system of general and popular instruction; and, consequently, ought to be adapted, so far as can be done consistently with philosophical precision and truth, to this important object.

IMPERFECT AND DISORDERED

MENTAL ACTION.

DIVISION FIRST.

DISORDERED ACTION OF THE INTELLECT.

PART I.

DERANGEMENT OF THE EXTERNAL INTELLECT.

DISORDÈRED ACTION

OF THE

EXTERNAL INTELLECT

CHAPTER I.

NATURE OF SENSATION AND PERCEPTION.

§ 34. *Remarks on the Nature of Sensation.*

IN accordance with the plan which has been laid down, we proceed to prosecute our inquiries, in the first place, in connexion with the external intellect, or that portion of the intellect which is brought into action in more immediate and intimate proximity with external objects. And under this general head, the first form of intellectual action which presents itself to our notice is that of Sensation. Perhaps it may be proper to remark here, that the term SENSATION has a twofold application. We sometimes use it as expressive of a mental power, and sometimes as expressive merely of the result of the power; in other words, of the mental state or act. The condition, under which this state or act exists, and by which chiefly it is known, is the presence of

some external object, operating upon some organ of
sense.   In other words, a sensation is a simple state
of mind, immediately successive to a change in some
organ of sense, or at least to a bodily change of some
kind, which is caused by the presence of some external body.

Accordingly, while we speak of the sensations of
heat and cold, of hardness and softness, and the like,
we do not ordinarily apply this term to joy and sorrow, hatred and love, and other emotions and passions, which, although they are states of the mind,
either simple or complex, originate, nevertheless,
under different circumstances.

§ 35. *All Sensation is properly and truly in the Mind.*

In order to understand more fully the nature of
sensation, we may properly advert a moment to the
common opinion, that sensation has its true position
in the body, and actually takes place there, particularly in the organs of sense.   The sensation of
touch, as people seem to imagine, is in the hand,
which is especially regarded as the organ of touch,
and is not truly internal ; the smell is in the nostrils,
and the hearing in the ear, and the vision in the eye,
and not in the soul.   But it will at once occur that
the outward organs of smell, hearing, and vision are
nothing more nor less than mere forms and modifications of matter.   And that matter, from its very
nature, is not and cannot be susceptible of perception and feeling.   It would be inconsistent with all
our notions of materiality to consider thought and

feeling as attributes of it. All we can say with truth and on good grounds is, that the organs of sense are accessory to sensation and necessary to it, but the sensation or feeling itself is wholly in the mind.

"A man" (says Dr. Reid) "cannot see the satellites of Jupiter but by a telescope. Does he conclude from this that it is the telescope that sees those stars? By no means; such a conclusion would be absurd. It is no less absurd to conclude that it is the eye that sees, or the ear that hears. The telescope is an artificial organ of sight, but it sees not. The eye is a natural organ of sight, by which we see, but the natural organ sees as little as the artificial."

But we presume it is not necessary to enter much at length into the consideration of this topic. We readily admit the general connexion existing between the body and the mind, and the still more intimate and important connexion existing between the mind and the sensorial organ; but we should carefully guard against the admission of views which seem to imply, what is a very differing thing, the sameness or identity of the mind with any mere material modification.

§ 36. *Of the Actual Process in cases of Sensation.*

But while we admit the existence of an intimate connexion between the action of the mind and the antecedent action of some physical organ in all cases of sensation, we do not deny that there is, in some respects, a degree of obscurity attending it. Per haps all we can say with safety in the matter is this.

Some object capable of affecting the outward organ must first be applied to it in some way, in consequence of which a modification or affection of the organ actually takes place. Subsequently to the change in the organ, either at its extremity and outward development, or in the brain, with which it is connected, and of which it may be considered as making a part, a change in the mind, or a new state of the mind, immediately takes place. In the statement so far we are sustained by acknowledged facts.

But when we inquire how it is, or why it is, that a new state of a material organ causes a new state of the mind ; or, in other words, that an affection of the mind naturally and necessarily follows an affection of some part of the body, we touch upon one of those ultimate limits of intellectual action which seem to reject any farther analysis. All we know, and all we can state with confidence, is the simple fact that a mental affection is immediately subsequent to an affection or change, which is physical. It is in this way that we find ourselves constituted. Such is the appointment of the Being who has made us.

§ 37. *Of the Meaning and Nature of Perception.*

As intimately connected with the subject of Sensation, we now proceed to that of Perception. Sensation and Perception (we speak now, it will be noticed, of external, and not of internal perception) have much in common with each other.—Perception, using the term in its application to outward objects, differs from sensation as a whole does from a part. It embraces more. It may be defined, therefore, an affection or state of the mind which is immediately successive to an affection of some organ of sense, and which is referred by us to something external as its cause.

It will be recollected that the term SENSATION, when applied to the mind, expresses merely the state of the mind without reference to anything external, which might be the cause of it, and that it is the name of a truly simple feeling. Perception, on the contrary, is the name of a complex mental state, including not merely the internal affection of the mind, but also a reference to the exterior cause. Sensation is wholly within ; but Perception carries us, as it were, out of ourselves, and makes us acquainted with the world around us. If we had but sensation alone, there would still be form, and fragrance,.and colour, and harmony of sound, but it would all seem to be wholly internal. Perception, availing itself of the facts of sensation, connects with them the ideas of causality and externality, and thus reveals to us the visible and tangible realities of the outward world.

§ 38. *Of the Connexion between Sensation and Perception.*

The mental powers, Sensation and Perception, are considered together in the present chapter, because they are closely connected, and, in consequence of this connexion, throw light upon each other. Perception is the natural result of Sensation. It is that to which sensation tends, and without which, as its natural result, sensation would be almost of no value. Although susceptible of being philosophically distinguished, they are yet so closely implicated with each other that they are, in a great degree, practically one.

It is particularly necessary to consider them together in the examination of the subject of Insanity. It is true that we may philosophically make a distinction in the aspects of the mental disorder which are presented in the two cases. And yet they are so closely connected, that the examination of them entirely apart from each other would lead to embarrassment. The insanity of external perception involves and substantiates that of sensation. The one does not exist without the other; and the former is the developement and indicator of the latter. These remarks are to be kept in view in connexion with the observations which are to follow.

CHAPTER II.

DISORDERED SENSATION AND PERCEPTION.

(I.) THE SENSES OF SMELL AND TASTE.

§ 39. *Circumstances attending Disordered Sensations.*

HAVING remarked, so far as seemed to be necessary, on the general nature of Sensation and External Perception, we are now prepared to say farther, in the first place, that sensation, even when considered as distinct from perception, is susceptible of a disordered or alienated action. In the verification of this statement two views are to be taken. FIRST. It is evidently a law of our nature, that the inward sensation, whenever it exists, shall correspond to the condition of the outward or bodily organ. Consequently, a disordered or irregular movement of the organ necessarily communicates itself to the inward or mental state. Perhaps our meaning may not be exactly apprehended here. What we mean to assert is simply this, viz., that the sensation, in consequence of receiving its character from the diseased organ, is not such a sensation as would have existed in a different state of the organ. The product of the action of a sound organ, provided there is no irregular or abnormal affection of the mind itself, is a sensation of a well-defined and specific character. Such a sensation is a sound or normal one. On the other hand, one that exists under the opposite circumstances, is an unsound or abnormal one. This, if we rightly understand the matter, is to be regarded as the result of the natural and permanent relation between the organ and the mental state.

SECOND. A view directly the opposite of this may be taken, in explanation of the same result. That is to say, if the organ of sense is sound, but the mind is in a disordered state, the sensation may be unsound or abnormal for this reason also, viz., of unsoundness of mind. The mind, being disordered in itself, is not in a situation to receive the natural or true impression, which the action of the organ would otherwise give. It may be either so depress ed in its power of action as not to be deeply enough affected, or it may be so highly susceptible as to receive a wrong impression in the other direction. It may be too vivid or too weak, or fail, in some other respects, in the natural and precise correspondence to the outward affection. We make these general statements here, and leave it to the reader himself to make an application of them, in connexion with the facts to be adduced hereafter.

§ 40. *Disordered Perceptions consequent on Disordered Sensations.*

Perception, as we have already had occasion to intimate, is something additional to sensation, and inclusive of it. Accordingly, the perception will be as the sensation is. If the sensation be actually disordered, it will be found to be the case that the perception will partake of the disorder, and will be unreal, visionary, and deceptive. Perception always has reference to some outward cause; we mean here outward, even in reference to the organ of sense. And when the perceptive power is not disordered, we perceive things, to the limits of that power, just as they are. But it will be recollected that sensation is an intermediate step, preparative to the result of perception. Consequently, if the sensation is disordered, the relation existing between the subsequent perception and the outward cause of perception is disturbed. And, under these circumstances, the perception cannot be expected to correspond, and will not, in fact, correspond to the reality and truth of things. It becomes, what has just been asserted, unreal and visionary. In other words, it imposes upon our belief, by indicating, with such distinctness as to secure our assent, the existence and presence of objects which are not present, and often not real. It surrounds us with a world of mere illusions.

In accordance with these views, we find it to be the case that there are various kinds of diseased or disordered sensations and perceptions, corresponding to the particular outward organ of sense, whatever it is, which happens to be disordered. These sensations and perceptions (for they are so closely connected that it is not only difficult, but, for nearly all practical purposes, quite unnecessary to separate them) we propose now to examine. And, in doing this, we shall find it not only the most satisfactory, but the most convenient method, to pursue the inquiry in connexion with each of the organs of sense separately. Accordingly, as it is practically of but little consequence with which of the organs we begin, we shall commence our remarks with those which, from their results or some other cause, are generally considered the lowest in importance and rank, and proceed to those which, in their connexion with the operations of the mind at least, appear to be more important.

§ 41. *Of Disordered Sensations and Perceptions, connected with the Organ of Smell.*

In accordance with the suggestion which has just been made, we may properly begin with the Sense of Smell. The medium through which we have the sensations and perceptions of smell, is the organ which is termed the olfactory nerve, situated principally in the nostrils, but partly in some continuous cavities. When any odoriferous particles, sent from external objects, affect this organ, there are certain states of mind produced which vary with the nature of the odoriferous bodies. The facts of the existence and of the nature of these states of mind are made known by our consciousness. And as the intimations and the leading facts of Consciousness are unquestionably common to all persons, we take it for granted that no one is ignorant either of the existence of the sensations and perceptions of smell, or of their general nature.

Among other things, it is well known that, in a sane or sound mind, acting in connexion with a sound state of the outward organ, the perceptions of smell, and the sensations which, as their antecedents, are involved in them, always have a definite and well-known character; and which, in accordance with this character, we properly describe as sane or *sound* sensations and perceptions. But if either the mind, considered in itself, be disordered, or if such be the case with the outward organ, in connexion with which the mind acts, the sensations and perceptions, under such circumstances, will be found to vary, in a greater or less degree, from the standard of soundness. In other words, they will have the character of disorder, unsoundness, or alienation. That such unsound sensations and perceptions, connected in their origin with the sense of smell, sometimes exist, is sufficiently verified by facts.

Some of these facts we shall now proceed to mention, although it may not be proper to delay, since there are other views of mental disorder of greater importance, in order to bring forward instances and illustrations at great length.

§ 42. *Statements Illustrative of the Preceding Section.*

There is a remark in the valuable Treatise on Mental Derangement of Dr. Andrew Combe, which, not improbably, his own personal observations had verified to this effect, that " the senses of taste, hearing, sight, and SMELL may be perverted ; and then odours are felt and tastes perceived which no healthy organs can recognise."* Speaking of insane persons, Dr. Neville remarks, " Some are tormented wherever they go by bad smells, and may be seen compressing their nostrils in order to escape the annoyance from which they suffer."† Buffon, in his Natural History of Man, has given an account of a priest of Guyenne, by the name of Blanchet, who had experienced a violent attack of insanity, and who himself, after his recovery, made a statement in writing of the peculiar sensations he had during the continuance of his disorder. Blanchet states, in general terms, that his senses became so exceedingly quick and delicate as to subject him alternately to exquisite pleasure or the greatest suffering. The sense of smell, as well as the other senses, was disordered. He says expressly " I

---

* Observations on Mental Derangement, Boston, ed., p. 216.
† Neville's Insanity, London ed., p. 24.

seemed at times to perceive odours and delicious perfumes, whose exquisite savours neither nature nor the art of the chymist could equal. At other times, insupportable odours, nauseous and bitter tastes drove me almost to desperation. Even the sense of touch was affected with these extremes of pleasure and pain."

The celebrated Esquirol mentions the case of a young female under his care in the Hospital La Salpétrière, whose sense of smell was disordered. She would frequently request the removal of the cause of some disagreeable odour. At other times she spoke of enjoying the most fragrant perfumes, although in neither case was there any odoriferous body near. "It is a circumstance worthy of remark" (says Dr. Adams, who has referred to this individual in a recent valuable article on Psycho-Physiology), "that she had lost the sense of smell so as to be insensible of the presence of natural odours, while the disordered state of her brain was giving her the most vivid impressions of odours when none were present to impress the organ of smell."*

Dr. Burrows mentions the case of a sea-captain, who, in consequence of being wrecked, was compelled to suffer the extremities of famine. "The latter part of the time, when his health was almost destroyed by privation and long suffering, a thousand strange images affected his mind ; every particular sense was perverted, and produced erroneous impressions ; fragrant perfumes had a fetid odour, and all objects appeared of a greenish or yellow

* American Biblical Repository, No. xxxiv.

hue."* Dr. Conolly mentions the case of a woman who experienced simultaneous illusions of sight, smell, and hearing. "All kinds of animals seemed to be scampering before her; the smell of brimstone, and the continual sound of singing voices, conspired to trouble her."†

Here, then, are cases, as we understand the subject, of really disordered mental action; very trifling ones, perhaps, in themselves considered, but still actually existing. The mind does not, in these cases, correspond to the intentions and the undisturbed tendencies of its own nature; it is impelled by a wrong bias; and, under this unnatural impulsive influence, is the subject of an operation which, to say the least, is not a sound one.

§ 43. *Of Disordered Sensations and Perceptions connected with the Sense of Taste.*

The mental action which takes place in connexion with the organ of Taste next proposes itself for consideration. It is the tongue, covered with its numerous papillæ, which essentially forms this organ, although the papillæ are found scattered in other parts of the cavity of the mouth. The application of any sapid body to this organ immediately causes in the organ itself a change, an alteration, or an affection; and this is at once followed by a mental affection or a new state of the mind. In this way we have the sensations and perceptions, to which we give the various names sweet, bitter, sour, acrid, &c.

* Burrows's Commentaries on Insanity, p. 320.
† Conolly's Indications of Insanity. p. 114.

G

The sensations and perceptions of Taste, as well as those of Smell, may be disordered.

FIRST. If, in consequence of actual bodily disease, an organ of sense is brought, without the presence of an outward object, into that particular state into which it is ordinarily brought by the application of its appropriate external object, the same sensation, attended also with its resulting perception, will arise in the mind in the former case as in the latter. In other words, the person will seem actually to smell, or taste, or hear, as much so as if some object of smell, taste, or hearing were actually present. The sensation will be so well defined, and the perception, of which it is the basis, so distinct, that the belief will be controlled ; and he will have no doubt of the real existence and presence of odoriferous, sapid, and other external objects, corresponding to the inward sensations and perceptions, unless he is aware of the peculiar state of the outward organ, and is in that way kept from error.

SECOND. If the disordered action which we have supposed to exist in the outward organ, or external sensorial developement, should be found to exist exclusively in that part of the great sensorial organ which we denominate the Brain, the effect upon the mind will be the same. That is to say, the person will have the sensation or perception precisely as if the object were present. The case of the woman in the Hospital La Salpétrière, mentioned in the preceding section, is an instance in point. It appears that, while the outward organ of smell had so lost its power as to render her insensible of the presence of natural odours, and also when no odoriferous bodies were present to impress the organ, if it had been susceptible of impressions, there were, nevertheless, distinct and very vivid impressions of odours, which may probably be ascribed, as is suggested by Dr. Adams, to a disordered action existing exclusively in the brain.

THIRD. Furthermore, it will be kept in recollection, that there is not only an action of the body upon the mind, but also of the mind upon the body. The influence in the two cases may properly be regarded as reciprocal, though not, perhaps, in an equal degree. Hence it is possible (and, in some instances, is undoubtedly the fact) that a very excited and unnatural state of the mind may, unaided by the presence of an outward body, produce in some part of the sensorial organ the precise state or affection which the presence of such a body would produce. And the natural consequence of this state of things will be a reaction upon the mind itself, and the production of false sensations and perceptions; that is, of sensations and perceptions without anything external corresponding to them.

The conceptive power, for instance, sometimes becomes unnaturally excited; so much so as to control our belief. In other words, we may have such distinct conceptions of smells, tastes, sounds, and the like, that we cannot help fully believing in their actual existence and presence, and that we are truly the subjects of them. At such a time, certainly, the mind will be likely to have an influence on the outward organ, and to bring it into a position

precisely corresponding to the internal vivid concep
tion.

These explanatory views, although they are intro
duced in connexion with the sense of taste, are ap
plicable to the disordered action of all the senses.

§ 44. *Illustrations of the foregoing Views in con-*
nexion with Disordered Taste.

To apply these views to the sense of Taste. It
is well known that insane persons not unfrequently
ascribe some peculiarity of taste to objects which
does not belong to them, and which they would not
ascribe to them if the sensorial organ in all its parts,
and the mind also, were in a perfectly sound state.
The priest of Guyenne, mentioned in a former section, gives us to understand, that in his case the
sense of taste, as well as the other senses, had its
vicissitudes of pleasure and pain. Sometimes the
savours were exquisite, exceeding the capabilities of
nature and art. Sometimes nauseous and bitter
tastes drove him almost to desperation. In the
statement of Dr. Combe, introduced in the section
illustrative of disordered smells, we are informed, in
general terms, that the sense of TASTE, as well as
the senses of smell, hearing, and sight, may be perverted ; and that then tastes may be perceived which
no healthy organs can recognise.

Dr. Neville, in some remarks upon insane persons, makes the following statement, which involves
some facts illustrative of the subject under consideration. " The feeling by which we are admonished
of the necessity of taking meat and drink, is very

commonly either blunted or very much exalted. Many insane persons never show the slightest signs of feeling either hunger or thirst. They voluntarily pass days without food, and would sometimes perish of inanition, were they not compelled to feed ; others, on the contrary, seem insatiable in their appetites ; and their whole minds are, apparently, concentrated on the pleasures of the table."* Dr. Good mentions the case of a young woman who was wholly destitute, or nearly so, of the power of discriminating either the smell or taste of objects. In this instance, as in most others, it is probable that the disorder existed primarily (although it is possible it might have been internal and mental) in the outward organ, and thence communicated itself to the internal sensations and perceptions. Whatever may have been the true cause, the resulting states of mind could not be regarded otherwise than as really disordered.

Instances similar in their results to those which have been mentioned might be multiplied from the writings of individuals who have had charge of institutions for the insane, or have enjoyed other favourable opportunities of judging. The general principles which have been laid down, and the facts which have been mentioned, will probably enable the intelligent reader to understand the subject, so far as it is connected with the lower senses of smell and taste, without going farther into particulars.

* Neville's Insanity, p 27

CHAPTER III.

DISORDERED SENSATION AND PERCEPTION.

(II.) THE SENSE OF HEARING.

§ 45. *Of Disordered Sensations and Perceptions in connexion with the Hearing.*

IN the prosecution of this part of our general subject, we proceed to remark farther, that there may be imperfect and disordered sensations connected with the sense of Hearing. The causes of disordered auditory sensations and perceptions, like those of other mental acts connected with the senses, are threefold ; distinct in their nature, but yet susceptible (and this is, perhaps, generally the fact) of acting in combination.

In the first place, disordered auditory states of mind may arise from a disordered condition of the auditory nerve. It is well known, as we have already had occasion to intimate, that an unusually strong or inordinate affection of any of the organs of sense may be followed by actual sensations, when the usual outward cause of such sensations is no longer present. If the eye be fixed for any length of time upon some bright object—the sun, for instance—the optic nerve is found to be powerfully and unfavourably affected. And when we turn our eye from the bright object, we find that its image, in consequence of the excited state of the retina, still emains. In other words, the retina, owing to the great power of the first impression, continues to be affected in the same way as when the object was before it. And the mind, consequently, is in a corresponding state ; that is, it seems to see the object, although it is no longer present. So, when the auditory nerve has been for a long time affected by a loud and continuous sound, the physical affection remains after the sound (that is, the outward cause of the sound) has ceased. The movement of the tympanum, which was so powerfully affected in the first instance, has not ceased ; and, so long as this is the case, the mind is affected in the same manner as if the outward cause of sound existed.

§ 46. *Facts Illustrative of Disordered Auditory Sensations and Perceptions.*

These are cases, it is true, of merely occasional or temporary disorder of the physical organs ; but facts of this kind evidently go to show that there is a *possibility*, at least, of these organs being permanently disordered. And other classes of facts evince, beyond all question, that this possibility is sometimes realized. Accordingly, persons (probably in conse quence of the organ having been unduly affected at some previous time, and thus thrown into an unnatural position) are sometimes troubled with a ringing noise, which seems to them the sound of bells. At another time they hear, for hours and days together, the rumbling of carts or the explosions of cannon. At other times, again, their ears are affected with what they imagine to be the voices and songs of celestial beings. There is an account given in a foreign Medical Journal (the Medico-Chirurgical Repertory of Piedmont) of a young lady who attended for the first time the music of an orchestra, with which she was exceedingly pleased. She continued to hear the sounds distinctly and in their order for weeks and months afterward, till, the whole system becoming disordered in consequence of it, she died.

In some instances there is an unpleasant feeling in the tympanum of the ear, as if it were greatly distended or stretched tight, attended with an increased sensation of sound, so that very small sounds appear like thunder. A letter to Dr. Rush from one of his patients, whose nervous system had become much deranged, has these expressions: "I am, as it were, all nerve; the least noise is like a shock ot thunder; so that for seven years I have been in the constant habit of stopping both ears with wax." "A mere catarrh" (says Dr. Conolly, Insanity, p. 238) "will sometimes cause one ear to convey a different sound from that conveyed by the other; the same note, but in a different key; or the same words, but as if from two voices, one an octave higher than the other."

§ 47. *Of the Brain in connexion with Diseased Auditory states of Mind.*

From what has been said, it seems to be clear that the auditory nerve sometimes becomes morbidly affected to such a degree, that there is an internal sensation of sound without any corresponding external cause whatever. The medium of communication which the mind employs is in fault. The machinery of the instrument of external perception is disordered; and, as a natural consequence, the mind loses its power of answering promptly and correctly to the external reality and aspect of things.

We proceed to remark, in the second place, that the same results will follow if a diseased action should be found to exist, not in the outward organ, viz., the auditory nerve, but in the part of the brain which is particularly connected with it. Esquirol, in the article Démonomanie, in the Dictionnaire des Sciences Medicales, gives some account of the disordered mental action of a woollen spinster, who was under his care in the La Salpétrière Hospital, which seems to confirm this view. Among other things, he mentions her return from a long walk at a certain time. Becoming fatigued, she lay down upon the ground to rest. " In a short time *she felt a motion in her head, and heard a noise like that of a spinning-wheel.*"* It is certainly a reasonable supposition here, that the affection was in the brain rather than in the outward organ. The illusory sound like that of a spinning-wheel resulted, in all probability, from the circumstance of the brain's assuming the same position or the same movement, into which it had been customarily brought by the real sound of the wheel when she was at her work.

Nevertheless, the two cases are intimately connected with each other. It is generally difficult to decide with certainty whether the original cause of

* Dictionnaire des Sciences Medicales, tom. viii., p. 302.

H

disordered auditory sensations exists in a diseased state of the brain or of the auditory nerve. Probably, in a majority of cases, the diseased action exists in both of these parts of the great sensorial organ at the same time.

The facts which have already been given in the preceding section will serve to illustrate this cause of mental disorder, viz., a disordered action of the brain, as well as that first mentioned. And some other facts of a similar nature may properly be added here.

Persons who are subject to disordered auditory sensations frequently hear their names called. "We are accustomed" (says Dr. Rush, speaking of names) "to hear them pronounced more frequently than other words ; and hence the part of the ear which vibrates with the sound of our names moves more promptly, from habit, than any other part of it." And this, we may well suppose, is especially the case if the organ of hearing be disordered. Sometimes short sentences are heard, generally having relation to the subject upon which the mind happens to be exercised at the moment. We learn from Washington Irving, that Christopher Columbus was at one time subject to deceptive auditory sensations He relates that, in the midst of his gloom, when he had abandoned himself to despair, Columbus heard a voice calling to him in the following terms : "Oh, man of little faith ! fear nothing ; be not cast down. I will provide for thee. The seven years of the term of gold are not expired ; and in that and in all other things I will take care of thee." It is possible, however, in the case of Columbus, that the deceptive sensations may have arisen from a peculiarly excited state of mind, without the accessory fact of a disturbed organ.   A view of the subject which requires, in its place, a more particular notice.

It is here, in connexion with these facts and views, that we find an explanation, in part at least, of those singular soliloquies which are sometimes carried on by insane persons.   Acting under the impression that they are actually spoken to, they utter the corresponding replies; and thus a sort of interlocutory conversation is carried on, a part only of which is audible, except to the vitiated ear of insanity.

§ 48. *Third Cause of Disordered Auditory Sensations and Perceptions.*

We come now to a THIRD cause of the disordered states of mind which we are considering.   The sensorial organ may be sound in all its parts, and yet the mind may, in its own nature, be so disordered as to produce these vitiated and abnormal results.   It is an acknowledged truth (and we hope to be excused for repeating it), that strong affections of the mind may cause new modifications of the bodily part, as certainly and effectually as that, on the other hand, violent affections of the body may have their result in the mind.   Accordingly, a person in a high degree of mental excitement may have such a distinct conception of a human voice, of the sound of a musical instrument, or of some other sound, that the auditory nerve, in consequence of the sympathy between the mind and the body, will become affect-

H 2

ed precisely as if an external cause of sound existed. And then the sound, that is, the internal sensation of sound, follows.

Persons, for instance, sitting alone in a room, are sometimes interrupted by the supposed hearing of a voice which calls to them. But, in truth, it is only their own internal conception of that particular sound, which, in consequence of some inordinate mental excitement, happens, at the moment, to be so distinct as to cause a modification of the auditory nerve, such as is common in cases of actual hearing, and thus imposes itself on them for a reality. And this may be done, it will be remembered, when there is no actual disease of the physical organ.

This is probably the whole mystery of what Boswell has related as a singular incident in the life of Dr. Johnson, that, while at Oxford, he distinctly heard his mother call him by his given name, although she was, at the very time, in Litchfield. The same principle explains also what is related of Napoleon. Previously to his Russian expedition, he was frequently discovered half reclined on a sofa, where he remained several hours, plunged in profound meditation. Sometimes he started up convulsively and with an ejaculation. Fancying he heard his name, he would exclaim, " Who calls me?" These are the sounds, susceptible of being heard at any time in the desert air, which started Robinson Crusoe from his sleep when there was no one in his solitary island but himself.

> " The airy tongues that syllable men's names,
> On shores, in desert sands, and wildernesses."

Perhaps it ought to be added, as a matter of *possibility* at least (and the principle involved in the remark will apply equally well to any other organ of sense), that the conception of sound may at times be so distinct as to control a person's belief, and thus assume the appearance of reality, without any corresponding position of the auditory nerve. It is, unquestionably, an established principle in mental philosophy, that the belief may sometimes be controlled in that way. And, whenever this is the case, whatever is believed to be affects us in the same manner as if it had an actual existence. Such, however, is the powerful influence of the mind over the body, it is probable, that, in nearly all such cases of highly excited conception, attended with belief, the physical organ puts itself in harmony with the internal mental state.

§ 49. *The Disordered auditory Sensations of the poet Cowper.*

The mental hallucinations to which the poet Cowper was subject appeared, among other forms, in that of deceptive or illusive sensations of hearing. All the causes of this form of mental disorder seem to have existed in his case. It has never been doubted that his nervous system was very much disordered ; and it is certainly no improbable supposit.on, that the irregular and diseased action was experienced in the brain, as well as in the outward developements of the sensorial organ. And then his mind, too, was intensely conceptive and imaginative, to a degree that almost overstepped the limits of sanity. Is it surprising, then, that he should have heard voices when there was nothing present which had the power of sound?

He does not himself, however, appear to have suspected the psychological or the physiological causes of the voices which he from time to time heard; but regarded them as actual communications from invisible beings. In a letter to one of his correspondents, he says, "I awoke this morning with these words relating to my work loudly and distinctly spoken:

" ' *Apply assistance in my case, indigent and necessitous.*'

" And about three mornings since with these:

" ' *It will not be by common and ordinary means.*'

" It seems better, therefore, that I should wait till it shall please God to set my wheels in motion, than make another beginning only to be obliterated like the two former. I have also heard these two words on the same subject:

" ' *Meantime, raise an expectation and desire of it among the people.*' "

At the commencement of another letter we find the following remarkable statement: "My experience since I saw you affords, on recollection, nothing worthy to be sent to Olney, except the following notice, which I commit to writing, and communicate as a kind of curiosity rather than for any other reason; though Milton, who is at present an interesting character to us both, is undoubtedly the subject of it. I waked the other morning with these words distinctly spoken to me:

" ' *Charles the Second, though he was, or wished to be accounted a man of fine tastes and an admirer of the arts, never saw, or expressed a wish to see, the man whom he would have found alone superior to all the race of men.*' "

Mr. Southey has recently published an interesting life of this distinguished poet, in which he relates the above instances, and others similar to them.

CHAPTER IV.

DISORDERED SENSATION AND PERCEPTION.

(III.) THE SENSE OF TOUCH.

§ 50. *Disordered Sensations and Perceptions connected with the Sense of Touch.*

THE sense of Touch may properly present itself next in order. The principal organ of this sense is the hand. Nevertheless, it ought not to be considered as limited to that part of our frame, but as diffused over the whole body. It is not surprising, however, that the hand should principally arrest our attention as the organ of this sense, since it is furnished with various articulations ; is easily moveable by the muscles ; and can readily adapt itself to the various changes of form in the objects to which it is applied.

The sense of touch, like the other senses, may be disordered in itself and in its sensorial connexions (we have reference here particularly to the brain), and, as a natural consequence, in its mental results. As various principles already laid down are applicable here, we shall proceed, without delaying upon the general views which the subject presents, to mention some incidents and facts which may tend to illustrate this form of alienation. It may be proper to add, however, that the natural results of the sense of touch are more various than those of the other senses ; and that, as would naturally be expected, there is no less diversity in the morbid results. They relate not only to form and extension, but to hardness and softness, heat and cold, pleasure and pain, and whatever else may in any way pertain to that sense.

§ 51. *Facts Illustrative of Tactual Disorders.*

Dr. Abercrombie mentions a case, originally recorded in the Memoirs of the Medical Society of London, of a gentleman " who, after a paralytic attack, had such a morbid state of sensation that cold bodies felt to him as if they were intensely hot. When he first put on his shoes, he felt them very hot ; and, as they gradually acquired the temperature of his feet, they appeared to him to cool." He mentions also the case of a soldier, a very strong man, and able for all his duties, who had so completely lost the feeling of his right arm and leg, that he allowed the parts to be cut, or red-hot irons to be applied to them, without complaining of any pain.[*]

Mr. Southey, in his Life of Wesley (vol. ii., chap. xviii.), gives an interesting account of a zealous and

---

[*] Diseases of the Brain, p. 275, 6.

devoted itinerant preacher by the name of Haime. The case of this man, as Mr. Southey himself intimates, is worthy of notice in a physical and psychological, as well as in a religious point of view. At one time he suffered greatly from extreme religious depression, which brought him, to say the least, to the very borders of insanity. Some of the physical sensations which this pious man experienced at this time seem to me to illustrate the subject now before us. We give the statement in his own words. " So great was the displeasure of God against me, that he in a great measure took away the sight of my eyes. I could not see the sun for more than eight months. Even in the clearest summer day it always appeared to me like a mass of blood. At the same time, I lost the use of my knees. I could truly say, ' Thou hast sent fire into my bones.' I was often as hot as if I were burning to death. Many times I looked to see if my clothes were not on fire. I have gone into a river to cool myself; but it was all the same ; for what could quench the wrath of his indignation that was let loose upon me ? At other times, in the midst of summer, I have been so cold that I knew not how to bear it. All the clothes I could put on had no effect ; but my flesh shivered, and my very bones quaked."

Dr. Burrows, in his Commentaries on Insanity, narrates a remarkable case having relation to this subject in the following terms : " A gentleman, aged thirty-six, insane, with a strong hereditary predisposition to suicide, contrived, during the temporary absence of his keeper, though his legs were fastened together, to kick a hole in the fireguard and thrust his feet into a quick fire, which he made more fierce by tearing up a book and thrusting the leaves in. He was found a few minutes after, sitting very composedly in this position. His toes and part of one foot were severely burned; the other escaped with a smart scorching. In the burned foot inflammation, extensive and deep eschars, and mortification, with sloughing of the muscles and tendons, followed. And, finally, all the bones of the toes, and some of the metatarsal bones, sloughed away. The cure of this foot occupied more than a year; the scorched one soon got well. But neither during the combustion of the toes, nor for months afterward, upon removing the diseased parts or dressing the wound, was any pain expressed. But when the mind improved and the desire of suicide diminished, which it did long before the wound healed, he complained violently of the pain he suffered from it or when it was dressed."[*]

This case seems to show (and it is what the analogy presented by the irregular action of the other senses would lead us to expect) that disordered tactual sensations do not depend exclusively upon a disordered condition of the bodily organ; but also, and perhaps in an equal degree, upon an irregular or abnormal action of the mind. In many cases there is probably a combined sensation, the corporeal combining itself with the mental. A case mentioned in Dr. Brewster's Work on Natural Magic is one of this character, presenting the results

[*] Burrows's Commentaries on Insanity, Part ii., Com. ii , p 290

of a morbid state of the body operated upon by an inordinately excited state of the mind. It is the account of a lady who was subject to spectral illusions, of whom it is expressly said that she possesses a "naturally morbid imagination, so strongly affecting her corporeal impressions that the story of any person having suffered severe pain, by accident or otherwise, will occasionally produce acute twinges in the corresponding part of her person. An account, for instance, of the amputation of an arm, will produce an instantaneous and severe sense of pain in her own arm."

§ 52. *Other cases illustrative of Disordered Sensations and Perceptions.*

There are some cases of tactual disorder still more striking than those which have been mentioned. It is not unfrequently the fact, that persons have very peculiar tactual sensations existing, not in a particular part merely, but over the whole body. One, for instance, has a sensation which conveys to him the idea of great bodily enlargement or diminution. Another has a sensation of lightness, as if he were composed of feathers. Another experiences a feeling of weight, as if he were made of lead. And others, again, have a strong and indescribable sensation, which they indicate by saying, it seems to them as if they were made of glass or of some other substance.

Some very marked cases of insanity have a connexion with the facts which have now been alluded to. The organ of touch, for instance, throughout the physical system is so disordered as to give a person the distinct sensation of brittleness or of being made of glass. The sensation, we will suppose, is so distinct and so strong as to control this person's belief; and that he actually believes himself to be made of glass. This, certainly, is possible. The state of mind, it will be recollected, which is called belief, is not, strictly speaking, a voluntary one ; but has its laws, which necessarily determine it. And we cannot be surprised, therefore, that, under the circumstances supposed, he should have a full persuasion that he is physically in this condition. In other words, he is, in his own view and practically, a man of glass, and regulates his conversation and his conduct in consistency with this fundamental error. We have here a full and marked case of insanity ; one which is universally acknowledged to be so ; but which, in its origin, appears to be founded exclusively upon a disordered condition of the sense of touch. And the same of other cases.

§ 53. *Application of these views to the Witchcraft Delusion in New-England.*

The statements of this chapter will help to explain one of the leading features of the witchcraft delusion, which prevailed in New-England about the year 1690. The feature we refer to was this. The unfortunate subjects, as they were supposed to be, of diabolical arts, often complained that they were pricked with pins, or pierced with knives, or struck with blows. And all by the means and through the agency of some invisible hand. The simple fact probably was, that they were merely the subjects of disordered or alienated sensations and perceptions of the touch. They felt something, undoubtedly. And the sensation was very much such a one as would have followed the prick of a pin, the wound from a knife, or the infliction of a blow. But there was, in fact, nothing more than what can be easily explained on natural and philosophical principles. There is no need to suppose the introduction of invisible and external agency. Dr. Cotton Mather, who is the principal historian of those remarkable events, furnishes one fact that throws some light upon this point. Speaking of the bewitched persons, he says: "They often felt the hand that scratched them, while yet they saw it not; but, when they thought they had hold of it, it would give them the slip. Once the *fist* beating the man was discernible, but they could not catch hold of it."*

We admit, however, that the principles of this chapter are not sufficient to explain all the facts which are said to have occurred in that remarkable period of delusion. We shall hereafter, probably, have occasion, in connexion with other forms of disordered mental action, to refer to the subject again.

* Mather's Magnalia, book vi., ch. 7.

CHAPTER V.

DISORDERED SENSATION AND PERCEPTION.

(IV.) THE SENSE OF SIGHT.

§ 54. *Of the Outward or Physical Organ of the Sensations and Perceptions of Sight.*

FOLLOWING the plan of inquiry which we have marked out, we proceed now to the consideration of disordered mental action as it exists in connexion with the sense of sight. The organ of this sense is the eye. The medium on which this organ acts are rays of light, everywhere diffused, and always advancing, if they meet with no opposition, in direct lines. The eye, which may be regarded as a sort of telescope, having its distinct parts, and discovering throughout the marks of admirable wisdom, not only receives externally the medium on which it acts, but carries the rays of light into itself; and, on principles purely scientific, refracts and combines them anew. If they were to continue passing on precisely in the same direction, they would produce merely one mingled and indistinct expanse of colour. In their progress, however, through the crystalline humour, they are refracted or bent from their former direction, and are distributed to certain focal points on the retina, which is a white, fibrous expansion of the optic nerve. As soon as the rays of light have been distributed on their distinct portions of the retina, and have formed an image there, they are immediately followed by the sensation or perception which is termed sight.

§ 55. *Disordered Visual Sensations and Perceptions.*

Whenever we seem to see things which we do not see ; in other words, whenever the visual perception is not in accordance with the outward reality, we naturally and properly speak of such a sensation or perception as a disordered one. The causes of such disordered visual results are various.

I. The FIRST which we shall mention is one entirely analogous to the cause of disordered sensations in other cases, viz., an unnatural and morbid sensibility of the retina of the eye, either the whole of the retina or only a part. This cause, it is true, is in some degree conjectural, in consequence of the retina being so situated as to render it difficult to make it a subject of observation and experiment. But knowing, as we do, that the nervous system generally is liable to be diseased, and that the disease of a particular portion is commonly productive of results having relation to the object or uses of that portion, we may for this reason, as well as for what we know directly and positively of the occasionally disordered affections of the optic nerve, give it a place in the explanations of the subject now before us. In these cases the optic nerve is a source of action to itself. It is so excitable, so morbidly sensitive, that it repeats its antecedent states, as it were, automatically, when the natural causes or those states are no longer present.

II. The SECOND cause is the mental state itself acting sympathetically upon the visual organ. We know, when the object of sight is directly before the eye, that there is a new state, an affection of the optic nerve ; and it is probable, in consequence of the sympathy between the mind and body, that. when, in the absence of a visible body, we merely think or conceive of one, there is always a very slight sympathetic affection of the retina, analogous to what exists when the visible object is actually present. In a perfectly healthy state of the body, including the organ of visual sense, this affection of the retina is of course very slight. But under the influence of a morbid sensibility, the mere conceptions of the mind, if they happen to be particularly vivid, may at times impart such an increased activity to the whole or a part of the retina as to give existence to disordered or illusory sights.

§ 56. *The preceding Views confirmed by the Analogy of the other Senses.*

It is the same in the case of visual as of auditory sensations. The vibrations of the morbidly sensitive nerve of the ear will cause sensations of sound within, wholly independent of any external cause. The auditory nerve may either, in the first place, be a source exclusively of action to itself, or may be, in the second place, under the influence chiefly of sympathy from the mind ; but in either case it acts irrespective of an outward sonorous cause. So in regard to the optic nerve and the portions of the sensoiial organ immediately connected with it. It may be so morbidly sensitive as to act of itself, and to give re-existence, from the mere force of habit, to the pictures that were formerly impressed upon it. And particularly the mere thought or conception of a visible object may affect it, by the power of sympathy, as really and in the same way as if such visible object were actually present to the sight. And thus the individual who is the subject of these excited or morbid affections, whether they are exclusively physical, or physical and mental together, may be regarded as possessing the power in himself of originating and sustaining the representation or pictures of objects, although no such objects are present. In other words, as these results depend upon a morbid state of his physical or mental system, or of both combined, rather than upon any deliberate act of his will, he may properly be regarded as the subject of disordered visual sensations, more commonly known as spectral illusions.

We will only add, in confirmation of what has been said in reference to the possible and actual affection of the retina, that in one of the most interesting cases of disordered visual sensations which have been published, the person who was the subject of them expressly states, that, for some hours preceding their occurrence, she had a peculiar feeling in the eyes, which was relieved as soon as they had passed away.*

* Brewster's Natural Magic, Letter III.

I

§ 57. *Illustrations of the Subject from the use of Opium.*

There are some articles, such as ardent spirits in their various forms, opium, and the febrile miasma gas, as we have already had occasion to remark in a former chapter, which, on being introduced into the system, and especially when taken repeatedly and in considerable quantities, are found powerfully to affect the mind. And the effect on the mind appears to be produced by means of an intermediate influence, as we should naturally expect it would be, upon the sensorial organ. All the various sensations and perceptions, those which originate in the sense of sight no less than others, may be more or less disordered in this way.

It appears from the work entitled the Confessions of an English Opium-eater, that the author of it was inordinately addicted to the use of opium ; so that, in the end, not only his health was affected, but his intellect was thrown into an unnatural and disorderly posture. The nerve of vision became so disordered that it at once assumed the position which his thoughts indicated, whatever that might be. So that his eye, in discordance with its natural laws of action, constantly peopled the surrounding vacant space with visions and phantasms of terror or of beauty. He informs us, among other things, that at night, when he lay in bed, vast processions passed along in mournful pomp. But his visions do not appear to have been limited to representations of a mournful character. Whatever he happened to think upon, whether it were landscapes, or palaces, or armies in battle array ; in a word, whatever was a subject of thought, and was capable of being visually represented, formed themselves into images or phantasms of the eye, and swept before him in order and distinctness, no less marked and imposing than if the real objects themselves had been present.

§ 58. *Disordered Action may exist in connexion with more than one Sense at the same time.*

Sometimes (and not unfrequently) the mental disorder, which exists by means of the senses, extends to two or more of the senses at the same time. Such seems to have been the fact in the case of that remarkable visionary, Blake, the English painter. " Did you ever see a fairy's funeral, madam ?" he once said to a lady who happened to sit by him in company. " Never, sir !" was the answer. " I have," said Blake, " but not before last night." He then proceeded to state as follows :

" I was walking alone in my garden. There was great stillness among the branches and flowers, and more than common sweetness in the air. *I heard a low and pleasant sound*, and knew not whence it came. At last I saw the broad leaf of a flower move, and underneath I saw a procession of creatures of the size and colour of green and gray grasshoppers, bearing a body laid out on a roseleaf, which they buried with songs, and then disappeared."* It would seem from this statement, and from other things which are related of him, that this re-

* Macnish's Philosophy of Sleep, p. 229.

markable person was the subject of disordered auditory as well as visual sensations.

We might multiply instances and illustrations under this head, but perhaps it is needless. The subject, as it presents itself to notice here, is closely connected with the disordered action of the conceptive power; so much so, that the farther examination of it at present would necessarily imply the anticipation of some things which are to be said hereafter. There remain, however, one or two incidental topics.

§ 59. *Of Disordered Perceptions in connexion with excited Religious Feeling.*

As having a relation with what has been said under the general subject of alienated Sensations and Perceptions, it may be proper briefly to refer to some facts that have attracted notice in connexion with strongly excited religious feeling. Not unfrequently, individuals at such times have been the subjects of perceptions which were unnatural and illusory. Nor have the illusions been limited to one sense merely.

One, for instance, has beheld angels ascending to heaven, or descending on the ladder of Jacob; or has seen the river of the water of life, clear as crystal. Another has heard the voices of invisible beings singing the song of Moses and the Lamb. Another, again, has seen the Saviour in the most trying moments of the crucifixion; and has no more doubt of having truly and visually beheld him, than the disciple Thomas when he thrust his hand into his side.

We are aware that this subject is one of a delicate nature, and on which we are greatly liable to be misunderstood. Accordingly, we do not hesitate frankly to express our conviction that there is such a thing as spiritual communications; special influences of the Holy Spirit; joys unspeakable, flowing from a celestial source; a living mental intercourse with heaven. At the same time, it is not the less true that there may be sights seen which are not spiritual, but corporeal, and voices heard which are not from above. Is it not dangerous to rest one's hopes and belief of possessing a truly religious character on things of this kind? Without rudely setting at defiance any feelings and opinions which may happen to exist on this subject, we may still take the liberty to inquire whether the strong bodily sensations which have sometimes been felt, and the sights which have been seen, and the voices which have been heard, cannot very often, as in instances already remarked upon, be traced to some disorder of the physical system? Or, admitting that the body is sound and under no special excitement, whether they may not be merely our own thoughts, strengthened by reflection rendered intense by desire?

> " Alas! we listen to our own fond hopes,
>   Even till they seem no more our fancy's children,
>   We put them on a prophet's robe, endow tnem
>   With prophet's voices, and then Heaven speaks in them,
>   And that which we would have be, surely shall be."

The salvation of the soul is too weighty a concern to be risked on such an uncertain foundation; especially as we have the Word of life, which points out the marks of a truly religious state, yet without making mention, as far as we are able to perceive, of dreams, and sounds, and visions, as included among those marks.

§ 60. *Concluding Remarks on Disordered Sensation and Perception.*

Such are some of the aspects and varieties of mental disorder, which are presented under the general head of Disordered Sensation and Perception. The facts which have been mentioned may appear inconsiderable in themselves, but they are important in their totality. A man might perhaps escape the imputation of insanity, in the ordinary acceptation of the term, who happened not to smell aright; but if in addition to that, he did not taste aright, nor touch aright, nor hear aright, nor see aright; if he put sweet for bitter, and bitter for sweet; if he heard audible voices in the midst of utter stillness; if he peopled the vacant space around him with mere imaginary visibilities; if all, or even half of this, were true, it does not appear, whatever might be true of the imputation of absolute insanity, how he could well lay claim to the possession of entire soundness of mind.

It is true, there are forms and modifications of disordered mind more deeply seated and more formidable than these which we have now been contemplating. But it cannot be denied that these, though nearer the surface of the mind, and more easily manageable than others, are yet of sufficient importance to require a particular notice. They give to the whole mind an anomalous aspect; they perplex the outward conduct, and diminish a person's happiness and usefulness.

———

CHAPTER VI.

EXCITED OR DISORDERED CONCEPTIONS.

§ 61. *On the General Psychological Nature of Conceptions.*

WE proceed now to the consideration of another form of disordered mental action, viz., EXCITED OR DISORDERED CONCEPTIONS. Conceptions, the states of mind to which our attention is now directed, are those ideas which we have of any absent objects of sensation and perception. When a sapid body or an odoriferous body is presented to its appropriate organ of taste or smell, the effect which follows in the mind is termed a SENSATION. When we afterward think of that sensation, as we sometimes express it; in other words, and more properly, when the sensation is recalled, even though very imperfectly, without the object which originally caused it being present, it then becomes, by the use of language, a CONCEPTION.

And it is the same in any instance of perception. When, in strictness of speech, we are said to perceive anything, as a flower, a tree, or a building, the

objects of our perceptions are in all cases before us
But we may form conceptions of them ; they may
be recalled and exist in the " mind's eye," however
remote they may be in fact, both in time and place.
Accordingly, these mental states are distinct from
every other ; they have their specific or characteristic nature and traits ; and, in various points of view,
are unquestionably deserving of especial attention.
Nevertheless, it will not be necessary particularly to
delay upon them in this place. In their natural or
ordinary form they will generally be found to have
a place in treatises on Mental Philosophy, where
they are sufficiently explained. It will answer our
purpose to refer to a single trait more. It is this.
These states of mind are susceptible of variations in
their degree of strength or vividness ; and the consequence is, that they sometimes assume modifications which, especially in the form of INORDINATELY
EXCITED or DISORDERED CONCEPTIONS, very properly have a place in a treatise on Disordered Mental
Action.

§ 62. *There may be Disordered Conceptions connected with the Action of all the Senses.*

There may be conceptions based upon the antecedent operation of any or of all the senses. There
may be conceptions of smell, of taste, of sounds, of
touch, as well as of sight. The facts which we
have already found it necessary to introduce, in connexion with the disordered action of sensation and
perception, show this to be the case. Conceptions
of sound may be so vivid as to affect our belief, and

thus, without the least affection of the auditory nerve, convert the mere semblance of audition into a virtual reality. In other cases, the conception, even when less excited, may call into action, in virtue of the sympathetic connexion between the mind and body, the diseased organ, and thus produce essentially the same result, when there is in neither case any external cause of sound. And the same of other cases of sensation and perception depending upon other organs. In fact, the present subject has already been in part, and necessarily, anticipated. And this being the case, we shall feel ourselves more at liberty to confine our remarks here, as we propose to do, to disordered conceptions of Sight. These, in consequence of the great importance of the visual organ, and the frequency of the deceptions connected with it, claim especial attention.

§ 63. *Of the less permanent Excited Conceptions of Sight.*

There are conceptions of sight (disordered, perhaps, in the sense of being inordinately excited) which are not permanent, but have merely a momentary existence. (I.) These are noticed, in the first place, in children, in whom the conceptive or imaginative power, so far as it is employed in giving existence to creations that have outline and form, is generally more active than in later life. Children, it is well known, are almost constantly projecting their inward conceptions into outward space, and erecting the fanciful creations of the mind amid the realities and forms of matter, beholding houses, men, towers, flocks of sheep, clusters of trees, and varieties of landscape in the changing clouds, in the wreathed and driven snow, in the fairy work of frost, and in the embers and flickering flames of the hearth. This, at least, was the experience of the early life of Cowper, who has made it the subject of a fine passage in the poem of "The Task :"

> " Me oft has fancy, ludicrous and wild,
>   Soothed with a waking dream of houses, towers,
>   Trees, churches, and strange visages express'd
>   In the red cinders, while, with poring eye,
>   I gazed, myself creating what I saw."

Beattie too, after the termination of a winter's storm, places his young minstrel on the shores of the Atlantic, to view the heavy clouds that skirt the distant horizon :

> " Where, mid the changeful scenery ever new,
>   Fancy a thousand wondrous forms descries,
>   More wildly great than ever pencil drew,
>   Rocks, torrents, gulfs, and shapes of giant size,
> And glittering cliffs on cliffs, and fiery ramparts rise "

II. Again, excited conceptions which are not permanent are frequently called into existence in connexion with some anxiety and grief of mind, or some other modification of mental excitement. A person, for instance, standing on the seashore, and anxiously expecting the approach of his vessel, will sometimes see the image of it, and will be certain, for the moment, that he has the object of his anticipations in view, although, in truth, there is no vessel in sight. That is to say, the conception, idea, or image of the vessel, which it is evidently in the power of every one to form who has previously seen one, is rendered so intense by feelings of anxiety as to be the same in effect as if the real object were present, and the figure of it were actually pictured on the retina. It is in connexion with this view that we may probably explain a remark in the narrative of Mrs. Howe's captivity, who in 1775 was taken prisoner, together with her seven children, by the St. Francois Indians. In the course of her captivity, she was at a certain time informed by the Indians that two of her children were no more ; one having died a natural death, and the other being knocked on the head. "I did not utter many words" (says the mother), "but my heart was sorely pained within me, and *my mind exceedingly troubled with strange and awful ideas* [meaning conceptions or images]. I often imagined, for instance, that *I plainly saw* the naked carcasses of my children hanging upon the limbs of trees, as the Indians are wont to hang the raw hides of those beasts which they take in hunting."

§ 64. *The Conceptive Power may be placed in a wrong position by habit.*

The conceptive power, by the aid of which we have the internal or mental recognition of sensible objects which are not present, may, like the other powers, be greatly strengthened. A person, for instance, who has been accustomed to drawing, retains a much more perfect notion of a building, landscape, or other visible object than one who has not. A portrait painter, or any person who has been in the practice of drawing such sketches, can trace the outlines of the human form with very great ease ; it requires hardly more effort from them than to write their names. This increase of conceptive power is far from always being advantageous. On the contrary, it may sometimes be carried so far as to affect the mind in other respects very unfavourably. The faculty may be made to possess an exaggerated intensity of action, resulting in its interference with the due exercise of other parts of the mind. "We read" (says Dr. Conolly), "that when Sir Joshua Reynolds, after being many hours occupied in paint-ing, walked out into the streets, the lamp-posts seemed to him to be trees, and the men and women moving shrubs."

There are persons, who are entirely convinced of the folly of the popular belief of ghosts and other nightly apparitions, but who cannot be persuaded to sleep in a room alone, nor go alone into a room in the dark. This is owing to the fact of their having early formed conceptions of invisible and unearthly beings ; conceptions which have gradually been ren-dered more vivid and intense by repetition. Ac-cordingly, when they happen out at night, their minds are employed in giving existence to such imaginary beings ; and their ideas of them are so vivid as to control their belief; and, consequently, they are the subjects, at such times, of a considera-ble degree of disquiet and even terror.

"It was my misfortune" (says Dr. Priestly) "to have the idea of darkness, and the ideas of invisible malignant spirits and apparitions, very closely con-nected in my infancy ; and to this day, notwithstanding I believe nothing of those invisible powers, and, consequently, of their connexion with darkness or anything else, I cannot be perfectly easy in every kind of situation in the dark."

In all persons this faculty may be trained to an increased degree of strength, by the same process which gives facility and strength of action to other mental powers, viz., by constant repetition or practice; in other words, by the formation of a habit. And this increase of energy may, by possibility at least, be so great as to render it proper to consider the power, under such circumstances, as existing in an unnatural or disordered state.

§ 65. *Of Permanently Disordered Conceptions.*

We thus, by the considerations which have been brought forward, approach, and, to some extent, verify the doctrine which it is our object here to announce, viz., that the conceptive faculty may be truly disordered; and that, too, not merely for a short time, under a temporary excitement, but *permanently*. Those who are not subject to this peculiarity of mind have but little idea of the very high degree of vividness which may attach to the mental states. When the conceptive power is inordinately and permanently excited, the forms and outlines, the hues and combinations of outward objects exist in the intellect like living things, in the freshness and distinctness of reality.

And this is not all. There is a relation, more or less intimate, among all the powers of the mind. Whenever, for instance, we have a perception of things, our belief is controlled; in other words, we naturally and necessarily have a belief in the existence of the things which are perceived. And, in like manner, whenever in the vividness of conceptions there is a near approach to the acknowledged and necessary vividness of the perceptive states of the mind, there is a similar tendency to an affection of the belief. This tendency is realized; in other words, the belief is fully controlled, if the vividness in the two cases is nearly the same.

Now the mere inordinate vividness implies a disordered state of the mind; but, if this be combined with the coexistence of a belief in the actuality of the things conceived of, the disorder is very much increased. It is then that the subject of this unhappy state of things may be said, with something more than a mere metaphorical import of the terms, to live in the midst of a world of his own creating. The mind, exercising itself upon the materials which the outward world has furnished, reproduces distinct images of things, and, substantiating their reality by the authority of belief, recognises things that are not as in no ways different from things that are. Hence, there are constant mistakes. Things unreal are mistaken for things real. And hence, also, there is frequently a great perplexity of the judgment and the reasoning power. This is obvious, because the judgment and the reasoning power necessarily implicate the ultimate verification of their results with the certainty and reality of their premises; and the source of confidence in the premises has, in a great degree, failed. Not to mention other incidental evils, which are likely to connect themselves with this peculiar state of mind.

§ 66. *Of disordered Conceptions, combined with a disordered State of the outward Organs.*

Now if we connect this state of mind, which is sufficiently unfavourable in itself, with a disordered condition of the external senses, the evil will, if possible, be still farther increased. If, for instance, the conception of visible objects be very vivid, and, at the same time, the organ of sight be morbidly susceptible, the vivid conception will be likely, by mere sympathy, to place the optic nerve in the position of actual vision. And the immediate consequence is, that, to all intents and purposes, there is at once a visual perception; and the conception and the perception become merged in each other. Under such circumstances, is it surprising that men should see a variety of phantasms, and find the world peopled with invisible beings?

But it is our wish here to consider this state of mind separate, as much as possible, from mere disordered sensations and perceptions. It is true they are sometimes combined together, perhaps frequently. At the same time, if we wish to get at the sources of insanity and of the modifications of insanity, it seems necessary to give them a distinct consideration. They not unfrequently combine together in producing the same results; but there is no doubt that they may produce essentially the same results separately; and they have their distinct laws of action. Hence the necessity of treating of them under distinct heads.

§ 67. *Of the original Causes of inordinately excited Conceptions.*

It becomes here an interesting inquiry, upon what causes disordered conceptions depend? One of the causes of them is probably to be found, in the first place, in the mind itself; that is to say, in some other part of the mind disconnected from the conceptions themselves. A disordered state of the propensities and passions may, for instance, produce a disordered state of the conceptions. Take an individual who is of a very sanguine temperament (in whom that state of mind which is denominated Hope is predominant), and it will be found, I suppose, that his conceptions of those prospective objects at which he aims are much more distinct and vivid than those of another person in whom hope is deficient. We do not undertake to explain how the vividness of one state of mind communicates itself, as in this case, to another; but there will probably be no diversity of opinion as to the fact.

Take, again, an individual in whom the passion of fear exists in an inordinate degree. It is notorious that such a person will magnify difficulties and dangers. His agitated mind will give outline, and prominence, and distinctness to objects which scarcely attract the notice of another person. So intense are his conceptions, that his belief is, in a great degree, controlled by them; and, against the remonstrances of his reason, he peoples the darkness, and even the day itself, with imaginary conspirators against his person, and with thieves that lay in wait for his property.

(II.) And why may we not suppose, furthermore, that the conceptive faculty itself, independently of its connexion with the other mental powers, may some-times be disordered? The mind has its nature and its laws; and, although it cannot be diseased or disordered in the same way that a material exist-ence may be, yet sound philosophy does not forbid the supposition that it may possibly be susceptible of derangement in such way and degree as may be consistent with its own nature. Take, for instance, the susceptibility of Belief. The state of mind which we call belief has its laws, and may be re-garded as a universal attribute of the mental nature. In other words, all men have this susceptibility. Furthermore, in the great mass of mankind it exists nearly in the same degree, and exhibits the same manifestations. And yet it is well known that in some individuals it discovers an extreme quickness, an astonishing facility; so much so, that the persons in whom this peculiarity exists unhesitatingly receive every statement which is made to them, however improbable and contradictory. The susceptibility obviously exists in an unnatural and disordered state, which in its action results in annulling the beneficial tendencies of the other parts of the mind, and ren-ders the person, besides making him a commor. laughing-stock, useless, in a great degree, to socie-ty. This is, beyond all question, to be considered

K

as a disordered state of the mind ; but the disorder does not appear to result from the unnatural and disordered position and influence of other parts of the mind, nor from anything peculiar, so far as we can perceive, in the sensorial organization. The violation of nature is to be found *in the mental trait itself.* The disease (if we may be allowed to apply the term to mental existences) is connatural, not in the body, but the mind itself, and in that particular part of the mind.

We introduce this statement, it will be noticed, in illustration of the general doctrine that a disorder of the mind may be connatural ; that is to say, may really have its foundation in the constitution and facts of the mental, in distinction from the physical nature. And if the susceptibility of belief or any other mental attribute may be disordered *in itself,* why may not the conceptive power be disordered in itself also ? We suppose it, at least, to be possible.

§ 68. *Instance Illustrative of this Subject.*

We bring the remarks of this chapter to a close by introducing an instance where the Conceptive power seems to have been inordinately excited ; and where, also, the results appear to have been more marked than they would otherwise have been, in consequence of the sympathetic influence of the very vivid conceptions on the disordered physical system. "In March, 1829" (says Dr. Macnish, in his Philosophy of Sleep, chap. xv.), "during an attack of fever, accompanied with violent action in the brain, I experienced illusions of a very peculiar kind

They did not appear except when the eyes were shut or the room perfectly dark. And this was one of the most distressing things connected with my illness; for it obliged me either to keep my eyes open, or to admit more light into my chamber than they could well tolerate. I had the consciousness of shining and hideous faces grinning at me in the midst of profound darkness, from which they glared forth in horrid and diabolical relief. They were never stationary, but kept moving in the gloomy background. Sometimes they approached within an inch or two of my face; at other times they receded several feet or yards from it. They would frequently break into fragments, which, after floating about, would unite; portions of one face coalescing with those of another, and thus forming still more uncouth and abominable images. The only way I could get rid of those phantoms was by admitting more light into the chamber and opening the eyes, when they instantly vanished; but only to reappear when the room was darkened or the eyes closed.

"One night, when the fever was at its height, I had a splendid vision of a theatre, in the arena of which Ducrow, the celebrated equestrian, was performing. On this occasion I had no consciousness of a dark background, like to that on which the monstrous images floated; but everything was gay, bright, and beautiful. I was broad awake; my eyes were closed, and yet I saw, with perfect distinctness, the whole scene going on in the theatre: Ducrow performing his wonders of horsemanship; and the assembled multitude, among whom I recognised

several intimate friends ; in short, the whole proces..
of the entertainment, as clearly as if I were present
at it.   When I opened my eyes, the whole scene
vanished like the enchanted palace of the necro-
mancer; when I closed them, it as instantly returned.

" But, though I could thus dissipate the spectacle, I found it impossible to get rid of the accompanying music. This was the grand march in the
Opera of Aladdin, and was performed by the orchestra with more superb and imposing effect, and with
greater loudness, than I ever heard it before. It was
executed, indeed, with tremendous energy. This
air I tried every effort to dissipate, by forcibly endeavouring to call other tunes to mind, but it was in
vain.   However completely the vision might be dis-
pelled, the music remained in spite of every effort to
banish it.   During the whole of this singular state
I was perfectly aware of the illusiveness of my feelings, and, though labouring under violent headache,
could not help speculating upon them and endeavouring to trace them to their proper cause.   This
theatrical vision continued for about five hours ; the
previous delusions for a couple of days."

CHAPTER VII.

SPECTRAL ILLUSIONS OR APPARITIONS.

§ 69. *Of the General Nature of Spectral Illusions or Apparitions.*

THE doctrines, which have been advanced in connexion with our examination of disordered Sensations and Perceptions, and of disordered Conceptive States of the Mind, appear to furnish all the requisite elements for a satisfactory explanation of Spectral Illusions or Apparitions.

Spectral illusions or apparitions are appearances which seem to be real and external, but which, in truth, have merely an internal or subjective existence; occasioned sometimes by the disordered state of the outward organ of sense; sometimes by the unnatural or disordered state of the portion of the brain particularly related to the outward organ; sometimes by an unnatural or abnormal position of the conceptive power; and probably, for the most part, by the combined action of all these causes.

Apparitions are very various in their character; as much so as the various objects and combinations of objects, which from time to time come under the notice of the visual organ. Accordingly, there may be apparitions, not only of angels and departed spirits, which appear to figure more largely in the history of apparitions than other objects of sight, but of landscapes, mountains, rivers, precipices, festivals, armies, funeral processions, temples ; in a word, of all visual perceptions which we are capable of recalling.

There are unreal and visionary intimations, which have their origin in other senses, and which mingle with, and sometimes give a marked character to, the illusive scenes which are visually enacted ; but apparitions, in the proper sense of the term, have especial reference to those things, and those only, which can be visibly represented. It is in this sense of the term, in particular, that we propose to illustrate them ; although the subject, as in the conclusion of the last chapter, has already been, to some extent, anticipated. Furthermore, as there are some states of the body in connexion with which apparitions develope themselves more than at other times, we shall find an advantage in examining the subject in reference to these more marked occasions.

§ 70. *First Cause of the States of Mind termed Apparitions.—Neglect of Periodical Bloodletting.*

One of those more marked occasions on which those states of mind which are called Apparitions will be likely to develope themselves, is the neglect of periodical bloodletting. There may be the elements of these states of mind previously existing in the mental or bodily constitution, or in both, such as an unnatural tendency to excitement in the sensorial organ or in the conceptive power ; and yet this tendency may not result in the states of mind under consideration until some marked and specific occasion shall occur, such as has now been mentioned. The doctrine that spectral illusions or apparitions are likely to be attendant on a superabundance of blood, occasioned by the neglect of periodical blood-letting, seems to be illustrated and confirmed by the actual and recorded experience of various individuals, as in the following instance.

Nicolai, the name of the individual to whom the statements here given relate, was an inhabitant of Berlin, a celebrated bookseller. He was a man in whom the conceptive or imaginative power was naturally very excitable, and in a high degree inventive or creative. And what is a fact, which some will undoubtedly esteem it important to know, he was neither an ignorant man nor superstitious; but, on the contrary, possessed of much information, and capable of philosophical analysis. The following account of the illusive sights or apparitions which appeared to him is given in his own words:

"My wife and another person came into my apartment in the morning in order to console me, but I was too much agitated by a series of incidents, which had most powerfully affected my moral feeling, to be capable of attending to them. On a sudden I perceived, at about the distance of ten steps, a form like that of a deceased person. I pointed at it, asking my wife if she did not see it. It was but natural that she should not see anything; my question, therefore, alarmed her very much, and she immediately sent for a physician. The phantom

L 2

continued about eight minutes. I grew at length more calm, and, being extremely exhausted, fell into a restless sleep, which lasted about half an hour. The physician ascribed the apparition to a violent mental emotion, and hoped there would be no return; but the violent agitation of my mind had in some way disordered my nerves, and produced farther consequences, which deserve a more minute description.

" At four in the afternoon, the form which I had seen in the morning reappeared. I was by myself when this happened, and, being rather uneasy at the incident, went to my wife's apartment, but there likewise I was persecuted by the apparition, which, how ever, at intervals disappeared, and always presented itself in a standing posture. About six o'clock there appeared also several walking figures, which had no connexion with the first. After the first day the form of the deceased person no more appeared, but its place was supplied with many other phantasms, sometimes representing acquaintances, but mostly strangers ; those whom I knew were composed of living and deceased persons, but the number of the latter was comparatively small. I observed the persons with whom I daily conversed did not appear as phantasms, these representing chiefly persons who lived at some distance from me.

" These phantasms seemed equally clear and distinct at all times and under all circumstances, both when I was by myself and when I was in company, as well in the day as at night, and in my own house as well as abroad ; they were, however, less frequent when I was in the house of a friend, and rarely appeared to me in the street. When I shut my eyes these phantasms would sometimes vanish entirely, though there were instances when I beheld them with my eyes closed; yet, when they disappeared on such occasions, they generally returned when I opened my eyes. I conversed sometimes with my physician and my wife of the phantasms which at the moment surrounded me ; they appeared more frequently walking than at rest, nor were they constantly present. They frequently did not come for some time, but always reappeared for a longer or shorter period, either singly or in company; the latter however, being most frequently the case. I generally saw human forms of both sexes; but they usually seemed not to take the smallest notice of each other, moving as in a market-place, where all are eager to press through the crowd; at times, however, they seemed to be transacting business with each other. I also saw several times people on horseback, dogs, and birds.

" All these phantasms appeared to me in their natural size, and as distinct as if alive, exhibiting different shades of carnation in the uncovered parts, as well as different colours and fashions in their dresses, though the colours seemed somewhat paler than in real nature. None of the figures appeared particularly terrible, comical, or disgusting, most of them being of an indifferent shape, and some presenting a pleasing aspect. The longer these phantasms continued to visit me, the more frequently did they return, while, at the same time, they increased in

L

number about four weeks after they had first appeared. I also began to hear them talk ; these phantoms sometimes conversed among themselves, but
more frequently addressed their discourse to me ;
their speeches were commonly short, and never of
an unpleasant turn. At different times there appeared to me both dear and sensible friends of both sexes, whose addresses tended to appease my grief,
which had not yet wholly subsided : their consolatory speeches were in general addressed to me when
I was alone. Sometimes, however, I was accosted
by these consoling friends while I was engaged in
company, and not unfrequently while real persons
were speaking to me. These consolatory addresses consisted sometimes of abrupt phrases, and at
other times they were regularly executed."

§ 71. *Methods of Relief adopted in this case.*

These are the leading facts in this case, so far as
the mere appearance of the apparitions is concerned.
But as Nicolai, besides possessing no small amount
of acquired knowledge, was a person of a naturally
philosophic turn of mind, he was able to detect and
to assign the true cause of his mental malady. He
was, it is to be remembered, in the first place, a
person of a very vivid fancy, and hence his mind
was the more likely to be affected by any disease of
the body. A number of years before the occurren-
ces above related, he had been subject to a violent
vertigo, which had been cured by means of leeches;
it was his custom to lose blood twice a year, but
previously to the present attack this evacuation had

oeen neglected. Supposing, therefore, that the mental disorder might arise from a superabundance of blood and some irregularity in the circulation, he again resorted to the application of leeches. When the leeches were applied, no person was with him besides the surgeon; but, during the operation, his chamber was crowded with human phantasms of all descriptions. In the course of a few hours, however, they moved around the chamber more slowly; their colour began to fade, until, growing more and more obscure, they at last dissolved into air, and he ceased to be troubled with them afterward.*

§ 72. *Second Cause of Spectral Illusions or Apparitions.—Attacks of Fever.*

Violent fevers also, calling into action the hidden materials and elements of illusive sights, are found at times to constitute another leading occasion of Apparitions. The vivid conceptions which the sick person has, operate sympathetically upon his disordered physical system, until the mind, projecting, as it were, its own creations into the exterior space, peoples the room with living and moving phantoms. " Spectral illusions" (says Dr. Macnish) " are more frequently induced by fever than by any other cause."

* • Memoir on the Appearance of Spectres or Phantoms occasioned by Disease, with Psychological Remarks, read by Nico-.ai to the Royal Society of Berlin, on the 28th of February, 1799; as quoted by Hibbert, pt. i., ch. i.—Walter Scott, in his Demonology and Witchcraft, speaks of the apparitions of Nico-iai as a leading case in this department of human knowledge. He also expresses the opinion, that many others have had the same experience with Nicolai, but have been deterred by various causes from making it public.

There is a statement illustrative of this view of the subject in the fifteenth volume of Nicholson's Philosophical Journal, a part of which will be here repeated. The fever in this instance, of which an account is given by the patient himself, was of a violent character, originating in some deep-seated inflammation, and at first affecting the memory, although not permanently.

" Being perfectly awake" (says this person), " in full possession of memory, reason, and calmness, conversing with those around me, and seeing, without difficulty or impediment, every surrounding object, I was entertained and delighted with a succession of faces, over which I had no control, either as to their appearance, continuance, or removal.

" They appeared directly before me, one at a time, very suddenly, yet not so much so but that a second of time might be employed in the emergence of each, as if through a cloud or mist, to its perfect clearness. In this state each face continued five or six seconds, and then vanished, by becoming gradually fainter during about two seconds, till nothing was left but a dark opaque mist, in which almost immediately afterward appeared another face. All these faces were in the highest degree interesting to me for beauty of form, and for the variety of expression they manifested of every great and amiable emotion of the human mind. Though their attention was invariably directed to me, and none of them seemed to speak, yet I seemed to read the very soul which gave animation to their lovely and intelligent countenances. Admiration, and a sentiment of joy and affection when each face appeared, and regret upon its disappearance, kept my mind constantly riveted to the visions before it ; and this state was interrupted only when an intercourse with the persons in the room was proposed or urged," &c. The apparitions which this person experienced were not limited to phantasms of the human countenance ; he also saw phantasms of books, and of parchment and papers containing printed matter. Nor were these effects exclusively confined to ideas received from the sense of sight ; at one time he seemed to himself to hear musical sounds ; that is, his conceptions of sound were so exceedingly vivid, combined, probably, with the sympathetic concurrence of a disordered auditory organ, that it was, in effect, the same as if he had really heard melodious voices and instruments.

§ 73. *Third Cause of Apparitions.—Inflammation of the Brain.*

In the third place, spectral illusions or apparitions will be likely to be called into existence by means of inflammations and other diseases of the brain. We may infer, from certain passages which are found in his writings, that Shakspeare had some correct notions of the influence of a disordered condition of the brain on the mental operations. We allude, among others, to the passage where, in explanation of the apparition of the dagger which appeared to Macbeth, he says,

"A dagger of the mind, a false creation,
Proceeding from the heat-oppressed brain "

Whether the seat, or appropriate and peculiar residence of the soul be in the brain or not, it seems to be certain that this part of the bodily system is connected in a very intimate and high degree with the exercises of the mind; particularly with perception and volition. Whenever, therefore, the brain is disordered, whether by a contusion or by a removal of part of it, by inflammation or in other ways, the mind will, in general, be affected in a greater or less degree. It may indeed be said, that the immediate connexion in the cases which we now have reference to, is not between the mind and the substance of the brain, but between the mind and the blood which is thrown into that part of the system. It is, no doubt, something in favour of this notion, that so large a portion of the sanguineous fluid finds a circulation there; it being a common idea among anatomists, that at least one tenth of all the blood is immediately sent from the heart into the brain, although the latter is in weight only about the fortieth part of the whole body. It is to be considered also, that the effects which are wrought upon the mind by the nitrous oxide and the febrile miasma gas, are caused by an intermediate influence on the blood. On the other hand, it may be said that there cannot be a great acceleration of the blood's motion, or increase of its volume, without a very sensible effect on the cerebral substance. And, therefore, it may remain true that very much may be justly attributed to the increase of quantity and motion in the blood, and still the brain be the proximate cause of alterations in the states of the mind.

§ 74. *Facts having relation to the third Cause of Apparitions.*

But here we stand in need of facts, as in all other parts of this investigation. The following statement, selected from a number of others not less authenticated, can be relied on.* A citizen of Kingston-on-Hull had a quarrel with a drunken soldier, who attempted to enter his house by force at an unseasonable hour. In this struggle the soldier drew his bayonet, and, striking him across the temples, divided the temporal artery. He had scarcely recovered from the effects of a great loss of blood on this occasion, when he undertook to accompany a friend in his walking-match against time, in which he went forty-two miles in nine hours. He was elated by his success, and spent the whole of the following day in drinking, &c.

The result of these things was an affection, probably an inflammation, of the brain. And the consequence of this was, the existence of those vivid states of mind which are termed apparitions. Accordingly, our shopkeeper (for that was the calling of this person) is reported to have seen articles of sale upon the floor, and to have beheld an armed soldier entering his shop when there was nothing seen by other persons present. In a word, he was for some time constantly haunted by a variety of spectres or imaginary appearances ; so much so that he even found it difficult to determine which were real cus-

* See the Edinburgh Medical and Surgical Journal, vol. **vi.**, p. 288.

tomers and which were mere phantasms of his own mind. The remedy in this case was bloodletting, and some other methods of cure which are practised in inflammations of the brain. The restoration of the mind to a less intense and more correct action was simultaneous with that of the physical system.

§ 75. *Fourth Cause of Spectral Illusions or Apparitions.—Hysteria.*

It is farther to be observed, that people are not unfrequently affected with apparitions in the paroxysms of the disease known as HYSTERIA or hysterics. For the nature of this disease, which exists under a variety of forms, and is of a character so peculiar as to preclude any adequate description in the narrow limits we could properly allot to it, the reader is referred to such books as treat of medical subjects. This singular disease powerfully agitates the mind; and its effects are as various as they are striking. When the convulsive affections come on, the patient is observed to laugh and cry alternately, and altogether without any cause of a rational or moral nature ; so that he has almost the appearance of fatuity, or of being delirious. But spectral illusions or visionary sights are among its most striking attendants. The subjects of it distinctly see every description of forms; trees, houses, men, women, dogs, and other inferior animals, balls of fire, celestial beings, &c. We can, without doubt, safely refer to the experience of those who have been much conversant with instances of this disease in confirmation of this.

The existence of the states of mind under consideration might, without much question, be found, on farther examination, to connect itself with other forms of disease. The subject is certainly worthy, whether considered in relation to science or to human happiness, of such farther developements as it is capable of receiving.

§ 76. *Of Ghosts and other Spectral Appearances.*

In connexion with what has been said in this and some of the preceding chapters, it may not be out of place to add something in.explanation of ghosts and other spectral appearances, which occupy so conspicuous a place in popular superstitions. GHOSTS are partly APPARITIONS, taking that term as it has been illustrated, and in part mental illusions, arising from not viewing objects aright. In respect to all appearances of this nature, remark, I.— That they are seen most frequently in the dark, hardly any one pretending to have seen them in the day-time. And this is a circumstance altogether in favour of the idea that they are in nearly all cases, although they cannot all be referred to one cause, mere deceptions practised on us, either by means of the senses or by means of an excited internal conception, operating in some cases, perhaps, upon a disordered physical system. In the dark, as we are exposed to a greater variety of dangers than at other times, our feelings are in consequence excited in a greater or less degree, and, as there is a great dimness in the outlines of objects, they readily assume, when viewed under such circumstances, new, and various, and uncertain shapes.

II.—Let it be observed, as another circumstance commonly attending their visitations, that ghosts and other spectres are seen most frequently among people of very little mental cultivation, among the ignorant. Uninstructed minds are generally the most credulous. If there were truly any beings in nature of this sort, and they were anything more than imaginary appearances, persons who are well-informed and philosophic would stand a chance, equally good with others, of forming an acquaintance with them. From these two circumstances we seem to be justified in the supposition, that many of these imaginary beings are the creations of a credulous and excited mind, viewing objects at an hour when their outlines cannot be distinctly seen.

§ 77. *Other Circumstances characteristic of their recurrence.*

III.—It is to be remarked farther, that ghosts, whenever they present themselves, are found to agree very nearly with certain previous conceptions which persons have formed in respect to them. If, for instance, the ghost be the spirit of one with whom we have been particularly acquainted, he appears with the same lineaments, although a little paler, and the same dress, even to the button on his coat; the dress in general, however, is white, corresponding to the colour of the burial habiliments; so that they may be said to have a personal or individual, a generic, and, as some have maintained, a national character. " They commonly appear" (says Grose, who has written on this subject) " in the same dress they wore while living; although they are sometimes clothed all in white; but that is chiefly the churchyard ghosts, who have no particular business, but seem to appear PRO BONO PUBLICO, or to scare drunken rustics from tumbling over their graves. Dragging chains is not the fashion of English ghosts, chains and black vestments being chiefly the accoutrements of foreign spectres seen in arbitrary governments."

IV.—This additional circumstance remains also to be noticed, viz., wherever ghostly and spectral beings have come from the dead to the living, it has generally been found that they were among the particular friends, although sometimes of the enemies, of those whom they came to see. This is very natural. It is our friends and enemies whom we think most of; much more than of those to whom we are unknown, and towards whom our feelings are indifferent. A person, for instance, has lost a very near friend by death; his soul is greatly distressed; and amid the joys of life, which have now lost their charms, and amid its cares, to which he turns with a broken heart, he incessantly recalls the image so endeared to him. What wonder, then, that his imagination, which, in the light of the day, was able to keep before itself the picture of the departed, should, in the stillness and shades of midnight, when remembrances multiply, and feelings grow deeper and deeper, increase that picture to the size, and give to it the vivid form of real life! These circumstances justify

ᴜs in ascribing, for the most part, the existence of
that supposed class of beings called ghosts (and we
may include in the remark all spectres whatever) to
the two causes mentioned at the commencement of
this topic, viz., conceptions rendered inordinately in
tense, and objects actually seen, but under such circumstances as to be misrepresented to us.

§ 78. *Farther Illustrations and Remarks on the
same Subject.*

The principles laid down in this chapter illustrate
various incidents, hitherto considered very remarkable, which are to be found in history, both ancient and
modern. They help to illustrate, for instance, the
alleged appearance of Cæsar's ghost to Marcus
Junius Brutus on the plains of Philippi ; a circumstance which is the foundation of a passage in the
play of Julius Cæsar.

> "How ill this taper burns ! Ha! who comes here ?
> I think it is the weakness of mine eyes,
> That shapes this monstrous apparition.
> It comes upon me ; art thou anything ?
> Art thou some god, some angel, or some devil ?"

Brutus was not only greatly fatigued at the time
this terrific figure appeared to him, but his mind
was exceedingly anxious ; and we may therefore
well suppose that the spectral apparition was merely
an internal excited conception.

It is also worthy of inquiry whether these views
may not account, in part at least, for a singular
power of the Scotch Highlanders, called the second
sight. Especially as they live in a dark, lonely,

and mountainous country, and their feelings, in consequence, are not only likely to be quickened and
impetuous, like their own mountain torrents, but to
possess a cast of melancholy.   Such a state of feeling is favourable to the existence of inordinately excited conceptions or apparitions; and apparitions
(that is, the seeing of things which are not present)
is implied in the exercise of the second sight.

§ 79. *Remarks of Walter Scott on the subject of
Ghost-stories.*

As the interest of this subject is not limited to
novelists and the writers of romance, but is practically and widely important, we are induced to subjoin here a passage from a popular author, who is
perhaps, better qualified than almost any other writer to form a correct opinion on it.   " There are
many ghost-stories which we do not feel at liberty
to challenge as impostures, because we are confident that those who relate them on their own authority actually believe what they assert, and may have
good reason for doing so, though there is no real
phantom after all.   We are far, therefore, from aver-
ring that such tales are necessarily false.   It is easy
to suppose the visionary has been imposed upon by
a lively dream, a waking revery, the excitation of a
powerful imagination, or the misrepresentation of a
diseased organ of sight; and, in one or other of
these causes (to say nothing of a system of deception, which may, in many instances, be probable),
we apprehend a solution will be found for all cases
of what are called real ghost-stories.

" In truth, the evidence with respect to such apparitions is very seldom accurately or distinctly questioned. A supernatural tale is, in most cases, received as an agreeable mode of amusing society, and he would be rather accounted a sturdy moralist than an entertaining companion who should employ himself in assailing its credibility. It would, indeed, be a solecism in manners, something like that of impeaching the genuine value of the antiquities exhibited by a good-natured collector for the gratification of his guests. This difficulty will appear greater, should a company have the rare good fortune to meet with the person who himself witnessed the wonders which he tells ; a well-bred or prudent man will, under such circumstances, abstain from using the rules of cross-examination practised in a court of justice ; and if in any case he presumes to do so, he is in danger of receiving answers, even from the most candid and honourable persons, which are rather fitted to support the credit of the story which they stand committed to maintain, than to the pure service of unadorned truth. The narrator is asked, for example, some unimportant question with respect to the apparition ; he answers it on the hasty suggestion of his own imagination, tinged as it is with belief of the general fact, and, by doing so, often gives a feature of minute evidence which was before wanting, and this with perfect unconsciousness on his own part. It is a rare occurrence, indeed, to find an opportunity of dealing with an actual ghost-seer ; such instances, however, I have certainly myself met with, and that in the case of able, wise, candid, and resolute persons, of whose veracity I had every reason to be confident. But, in such instances, shades of mental aberration have afterward occurred, which sufficiently accounted for the supposed apparitions, and will incline me always to feel alarmed in behalf of the continued health of a friend who should conceive himself to have witnessed such a visitation.

" The nearest approximation which can be generally made to exact evidence in this case, is the word of some individual who has had the story, it may be, from the person to whom it has happened, but most likely from his family or some friend of the family. Far more commonly, the narrator possesses no better means of knowledge than that of dwelling in the country where the thing happened, or being well acquainted with the outside of the mansion in the inside of which the ghost appeared.

" In every point, the evidence of such a second-hand retailer of the mystic story must fall under the adjudged case in an English court. The judge stopped a witness who was about to give an account of the murder, upon trial, as it was narrated to him by the ghost of the murdered person. ' Hold, sir,' said his lordship ; ' the ghost is an excellent witness, and his evidence the best possible ; but he cannot be heard by proxy in this court. Summon him hither, and I'll hear him in person ; but your communication is mere hearsay, which my office compels me to reject.' Yet it is upon the credit of one man, who pledges it upon that of three or four persons, who have told it successively to each other,

that we are often expected to believe an incident in
consistent with the laws of nature, however agreeable to our love of the wonderful and the horrible."*

———

CHAPTER VIII.

DISORDERED STATE OF THE POWER OF ABSTRAC-
TION.

§ 80. *Remarks on the general Nature of this
Power.*

THE power of abstraction is not, properly speak
ing, an original and distinct source of knowledge ;
but it furnishes, nevertheless, one of the most important means, in virtue of which the knowledge
which we have may be separated from other knowledge, and contemplated in a new aspect.   It is the
perceptive power (the external perceptivity) which
gives the carpenter a knowledge of the log of wood,
upon which he finds himself employed ; but it is the
abstractive power which enables him to contemplate
this complex object in its parts, separating the various traits or qualities of length, breadth, hardness,
firmness, texture, colour, and the like, and making
them, in their state of intellectual insulation from
each other, the subjects of fixed and distinct examination.   It applies equally well to external and to

* Scott's Demonology and Witchcraft, Letter X.

internal objects; it separates and holds in its grasp
the invisible objects of mind, as well as the visible
and tangible objects of outward sense ; and hence,
if other things furnish no reason to the contrary, it
may, without impropriety, be considered under the
general head of the External Intellect as well as at
any subsequent place.

§ 81. *Farther considerations on the Nature of this
Power.*

In order to understand the nature of the abstractive power more fully, we proceed to say farther,
that in every case of abstraction there appears to be
a number of things involved.   In the first place, it
is implied that the object in respect to which the act
of abstraction is to take place, is complex; or, if the
object be not complex, that there is, at least, a combination of objects or parts of objects present to the
mind.   There is implied farther, that in every case
of abstraction there must necessarily be a determination, a choice, an act of the will.   This internal
voluntary movement must concern the complex object before the mind; or, if the object be not one,
the combination of objects before the mind, in some
specific and precise point of view, rather than another.   So that we may truly and justly be said to
have not only a desire, but a determination to consider or examine some part of the complex object
or objects before us more particularly than other
parts.   When the mind is in this manner directed
to any particular object out of many, or to any particular part of a single complex object, we find it to

M

be the fact, that the principle of association, or whatever principle it is which keeps the other objects or parts of objects in their state of union with it, ceases, in a greater or less degree, to operate and to maintain that union ; the other objects rapidly fall off and disappear, and the particular object or part of an object, towards which the mind is especially directed, remains the sole subject of consideration. That is to say, it is abstracted, or becomes, as it is represented and exists in the mind, an abstract idea. And if this be a correct statement of the matter, it will be seen that the abstractive power is not, properly speaking, a simple power, but implies a complex movement of the mental action.

It ought, perhaps, to be added here, that the abstraction or separation of the object may exist mentally when it cannot take place in the object itself. For instance, the size, the figure, length, breadth, colour, &c., of a building, may each of them be made subjects of separate mental consideration, although there cannot be an actual or real separation of all, or, perhaps, any of these things in the building itself.

§ 82. *Of Natural Defect in the Power of Abstraction.*

The power of abstraction, to a greater or less extent, is unquestionably one of the leading attributes of human nature. Many discussions have arisen in relation to it. Whether it is or is not a power possessed by brute animals, has been made a matter of inquiry ; but this is a point which it is not necessary

to discuss here. Whatever may be true of brute
animals, certain it is, at any rate, that man could not
be what he is without it; and that the want of it to
any great extent, and also its disordered action,
whatever phasis the irregularity may assume, must
be regarded as a great misfortune.

In some instances the abstractive power is simply defective ; it falls below that average amount of
energy which characterizes the great mass of mankind. It may not, however, be always easy to detect this deficiency. It shows itself, as a general
statement, in a dulness or hebetude of mind, in a
mingling and confusion of objects, which is sometimes mistaken for the mere want of external perception.

But perhaps we may be a little more specific, and
go a little more into particulars. The classification
of objects implies the exercise of abstraction. Its
exercise is implied, again, in the giving of general
names, and also in the formation and use of numbers. These are its common and almost necessary
results, saying nothing of the immense power which,
in its higher efforts, it gives to the human mind.
Hence the man, in whom this power is naturally deficient, fails very much in distinguishing one class of
objects from another, even if there is no marked defect in the external perceptive powers. He mistakes
and confounds the names of objects, as well as the
objects themselves. Incapable of separating the attributes of things, by which they are distinguished
one from another, he seems to behold them in a
dilated and unformed mass, as objects are seen in a

mist. In respect to the uses, powers, and relations
of numbers, and to all the truths and processes involved in mathematical formularies, he is utterly
at a loss; he stands aghast, and feels very much as
does the sailor, in the midst of a boundless ocean
without chart or compass.

§ 83. *Illustrations of natural Defect in this Power*

How often such instances of deficient abstractive
power occur, we are not able to say.   Undoubtedl
the weakness of some inefficient minds is to be considered as located here, which, as it is presented to
the unpractised eye of common observation, would
be ascribed to some other part of the mind; perhaps
to the perceptive powers, to memory, or to reasoning.   If such is the case, the instances of defective
abstractiveness, if such an expression may be allow-
able, are more frequent than is commonly supposed.

We have just had occasion to intimate that the
power of abstraction is called into exercise in the
formation, understanding, and application of numbers.   Something farther may properly be said here.
Before we can consider objects as forming a multitude, or are able to number them, it seems necessary to be able to apply to them a common name.
This we cannot do until we have reduced them to a
genus or species; and the slighest reflection will
sufficiently show that the formation of genera and
species necessarily implies the exercise of the abstractive power.   If the formation and the use of
numbers, and the knowledge of mathematical truths
and relations generally, rest upon the exercise of

the abstractive power, then we may, perhaps, find in truths of this nature the readiest and most decisive test of the original weakness or strength of that power. Where there is a great natural deficiency of the power in question, the mind recedes from the presence of diagrams and numerical processes as instinctively as the sensitive plant falls back from the roughest touch. The records of literary institutions too often show that such cases, though not always in the highest degree, have an existence. Extreme cases, however, sometimes occur.

Dr. Gall mentions a citizen of Paris, not altogether wanting in intelligence in other respects, who, to use his own language, " is so destitute of the talent of combining numbers, that it has always been impossible to make him comprehend that two and two make four, or that two and one make three."* What a difference (it would require no feeble calculus to estimate it) between the abstractive power of such a man, and that of Leibnitz and Newton!

§ 84. *Of excessive Facility and Profoundness in the Abstracting Power.*

Abstraction (although this is not all that is involved in the term) implies the direction of the attention to the particular abstracted objects before the mind, exclusive of other objects. This state of mind is, perhaps, in no case a perfect one. Other objects will, from time to time slightly obtrude themselves on the mind's notice ; disturbing, though not essentially interrupting, the chain of thought. And this

* Gall's Works, Boston ed., vol. v., p. 93.

seems to be the intention of nature, viz., that, even in profound abstraction, there should be something conservative, and that an individual, in thinking of the subject before him, should not absolutely forget what belongs to himself as a man. Accordingly, this faculty (for such we call it, although there are a number of things involved in it, making it a complex rather than a simple power) may undoubtedly be disordered by too great facility and profoundness. In such cases, as in all others, it is altogether probable that the abstractive power operates, in the first instance, under the direction of the will. The mind is directed towards a particular subject, and contemplates it in its own and in its relative abstractness, because the individual chooses or wills to do it. But the abstraction speedily becomes so intense, that the energy of the will seems, under these new circumstances, unequal to the control of the mental action. The restorative power seems to be quite in abeyance. The man remains profoundly adhesive, if we may be allowed the expressions, in the mud of his own contemplations ; apparently unable to get out himself, and insensible, to a most remarkable degree, to any suggestions and appliances which may come from any other source. For the time being, he is a lost man ; not only lost to the externalities of common decency and propriety, but lost to himself ; and ignorant, in another sense than that of the Apostle Paul, whether he is in the body or out of the body.

Such persons sometimes have the reputation of profound men. Profound men they undoubtedly are ; but it is generally much less evident that they are men of good common sense, or that they are practically useful. Their abstractiveness (a convenient single term to express the faculty in question) is out of proportion to the other powers of the mind, so that the other powers seem to be absorbed in this. In the language of Dr. Good, " all the external senses remain in a state of torpor ; so that the eyes do not see, nor the ears hear, nor the flesh feel ; and the miser may be spoken to, or conversation may take place around him, or he may even be struck upon the shoulders, without any knowledge of what is occurring."

§ 85. *Further Illustrations of this Topic.*

It is true that a man of a perfectly sound mind may, under some accidental circumstances (perhaps under the influence of some uncommon feelings of curiosity, or of joy, or of sorrow), be absorbed to that degree of intensity which has now been described. But when this is frequently the case ; when a man is liable, at any time and place, to be carried out of the reach of all ordinary facts and relations into the region of pure and unmitigated ideality, the description of a perfectly sound mind will not apply with perfect propriety. We do not mean to intimate that he is what, in common parlance, is termed a crazy man, and that he is, generally speaking, a proper subject of those precautions which craziness implies, but simply to say that the description of perfect soundness is inappropriate. The true balance of the mind is lost. He is what the people,

with a significant whisper, sometimes call an odd
man, perhaps a *very* odd man.

We know but little of the personal and private
history of Archimedes, the justly celebrated geometrician of Syracuse. But, so far as we have a
knowledge of him, he might, perhaps, be justly considered as at least a partial illustration of the views
which have been given. He was occupied with
some geometrical demonstration at the very time
when the Roman army took Syracuse, and so intently engaged in it that he was wholly insensible to
the scenes of confusion and suffering which ensued,
and to the shouts and outcries which everywhere re-
sounded. He was even calmly drawing the lines of
a diagram, when a soldier suddenly entered his room
and placed a sword to his throat. " Hold, friend"
(said Archimedes), " one moment, and my demonstration will be finished."

At any rate, whatever may have been true of the
Syracusan geometrician, such instances are undoubtedly to be found. It is unquestionably the
case, that there are men who have the power of voluntarily abstracting their minds from every other
subject, and fixing it intensely upon the subject before them, without possessing an equal power of
promptly recalling their attention to other objects
which may happen in the mean while to present a
reasonable claim upon their notice. Sir Walter
Scott, in the Romance of St. Ronan's Well, has
given, with his usual descriptive accuracy, a deline-
ation of one of this class, in the following terms :
" Bewildered amid abstruse researches, metaphysi

cal and historical, Mr. Cargill, living only for himself and his books, acquired many ludicrous habits,
which exposed the secluded student to the ridicule of
the world, and which tinged, though they did not altogether obscure, the natural civility of an amiable
disposition, as well as the acquired habits of polite-
ness which he had learned in the good society that
frequented Lord Bidmore's mansion.   He not only
indulged in neglect of dress and appearance, and all
those ungainly tricks which men are apt to acquire
by living very much alone ; but besides, and especially, he became probably the most abstracted and
absent man of a profession peculiarly liable to cherish such habits.   No man fell so regularly into the
habit of mistaking, or, in Scottish phrase, *misken-
ning* the person he spoke to, or more frequently inquired at an old maid after her husband, at a child-
less wife after her young people, at the distressed
widower after the wife at whose funeral he himself
had assisted but a fortnight before ; and none was
ever more familiar with strangers whom he had never seen, or seemed more estranged from those who
had a title to think themselves known to him.   The
worthy man perpetually confounded sex, age, and
calling ; and when a blind beggar extended his hand
for charity, he has been known to return the civility
by taking off his hat, making a low bow, and hoping
his worship was well."*

* St. Ronan's Well, chap. xvi.

§ 86. *Illustration from Bruyere's Manners of the Age.*

Bruyere sketches a character, under the name of Menalcas, which, in some of its points at least, corresponds to the views which have now been presented. " Menalcas (the character is supposed to have been drawn from life, viz., the Count de Brancas) goes down stairs, opens the door to go out, shuts it. He perceives that his nightcap is still on ; and, examining himself a little better, finds but one half of his face shaved, his sword on his right side, his stockings hanging over his heels, and his shirt out of his breeches. If he walks into the street, he feels something strike on the face or stomach. He can't imagine what it is, till waking and opening his eyes, he sees himself by a cartwheel, or under a joiner's penthouse, with the coffins about his ears. One time you might have seen him run against a blind man, push him backward, and afterward fall over him. Sometimes he happens to come up, forehead to forehead, with a prince, and obstructs his passage. With much ado he recollects himself, and has but just time to squeeze himself close to a wall to make room for him. He seeks quarrels and brawls, puts himself into a heat, calls to his servants, and tells them, one after another, everything is lost or out of the way, and demands his gloves, which he has on his hands ; like the woman, who asked for her mask when she had it on her face. He enters an apartment, passes under a sconce, on which his periwig hitches, and is left hanging. The courtiers look on him and laugh. Menalcas laughs too, louder than any of them, and turns his eyes round the company to see the man who shows his ears and has lost his wig. He says YES, commonly, instead of NO. And when he says NO, you must suppose he would say YES. When he answers you, perhaps his eyes are fixed on yours, but it does not follow that he sees you, nor any one else, nor anything in the world. All that you can draw from him, when he is most sociable, are some such words as these : *Yes, indeed, 'tis true, good, all the better, sincerely, I believe so, certainly, ah, oh, heaven,* and some other monosyllables, which are not spoken in the right place neither. He never is among those whom he appears to be with. He calls his footman very seriously, *Sir,* and his friend, *Robin.* He says your *Reverence* to a prince of the blood, and your *Highness* to a Jesuit. When he is at mass, if the priest sneezes, he cries out, ' *God bless you.*' He is in company with a judge, grave by his character, and venerable by his age and dignity, who asks him if such a thing is so. Menalcas replies, ' *Yes, madam.*' As he came up once from the country, his footmen attempted to rob him and succeeded. They jumped down from behind the coach, presented the end of a flambeau to his throat, demanded his purse, and he delivered it to them. Being come home, he told the adventure to his friends, who asked him the circumstances, and he referred them to his servants ' Inquire of my men,' said he, ' they were there.' "

§ 87. *Other instances illustrative of excessive Abstraction.*

We may, perhaps, in this connexion, although it is not without some degree of hesitation that we do it, refer to the case of Sir Isaac Newton, as a person in whom the abstractive power, sometimes at least, seems to have showed itself in excess. His mind, in the exercise of this power, seized the subject before it, insulated it, removed everything else to an unseen distance, and held it in its inextricable grasp firmly and alone; but, in doing this, the abstractive power seems to have absorbed all the other mental powers; and while the subject of his examination was so thoroughly brought within its control as to be in some sense lost in the mind, it might be said, with almost equal truth, that the philosopher was lost in the subject. His biographers assure us (and the facts which they detail sufficiently confirm their statements), that his thoughts at such times, as he sat for hours on his bedside without dressing himself, or in some other position equally indicative of their intensity, appeared to preserve no connexion with the ordinary affairs of life.

Still more striking was this singular trait in Dr. Robert Hamilton, the author of a celebrated "Essay on the National Debt," and esteemed a profound and clear-headed philosopher. A writer in the New Monthly Magazine, after speaking of the profound science, beautiful arrangement, and clear expression, characteristic of Dr. Hamilton's writings, goes on to say: "Yet, in public, the man was a shadow ; pulled off his hat to his own wife in the streets, and apologized for not having the pleasure of her acquaintance ; went to his classes in the college on the dark mornings, with one of her white stockings on one leg, and one of his own black ones on the other ; often spent the whole time of the meeting in moving from the table the hats of the students, which they as constantly returned ; sometimes invited them to call on him, and then fined them for coming to insult him. He would run against a cow in the road, turn round, beg her pardon, ' Madam,' and hope she was not hurt.   At other times he would run against posts, and chide them for not getting out of his way ; and yet his conversation at the same time, if anybody happened to be with him, was perfect logic and perfect music."

The case of the Rev. Dr. George Harvest, one of the ministers of Thames Ditton, and said to have been a man of uncommon abilities and an excellent scholar, is very similar.   " He was once" (so say the accounts of the peculiarities which distinguished him) " on the eve of being married to the bishop's daughter, when, having gone a gudgeon fishing, he forgot the circumstance, and overstayed the canonical hour, which so offended the lady that she indignantly broke off the match. If a beggar happened to take off his hat to him in the streets, in hopes of receiving alms, he would make him a bow, tell him he was his most humble servant, and walk on.   He has been known on Sundays to forget the days on which he was to officiate, and would

walk irto church with his gun under his arm, to ascertain what the people wanted there.   Once, when
he was playing at backgammon, he poured out a
glass of wine, and it being his turn to throw, having
the box in one hand and the glass in the other, and
being extremely dry, he swallowed down both the
dice, and discharged the wine upon the dice-board.

"His notorious heedlessness was so apparent
that no one would lend him a horse, as he frequently lost his beast from under him, or, at least, from
out of his hands, it being his frequent practice to
dismount and lead the horse, putting the bridle under his arm, which the horse sometimes shook off,
or the intervention of a post occasioned it to fall.
Sometimes it was taken off by the boys, when the
parson was seen drawing his bridle after him ; and
if any one asked him after the animal, he could not
give the least account of it, or how he had lost it."*

Instances of this kind might be easily multiplied.
It will be noticed, that in cases such as have been
enumerated, the leading trait is not mere weakness
of the mind, not that specific characteristic which is
known in writers on Insanity under the name of imbecility, not mere helplessness and wandering of the
attention ; but an excessive facility and profoundness of abstraction, which results in excluding all
notice of everything, whether of greater or less importance, excepting the particular subject which at
the moment happens to occupy the mind.   No matter what the nature of the subject is.   It may be of
great moment or of very trivial moment ; the crea-

* Macnish's Philosophy of Sleep, ch. xvii.

tion of a world or the birth of an insect.   It is all
the same to Menalcas.   Relatively to him, there is
nothing which, for the time being, comes at all into
comparison.   The proprieties of time and place; the
conventional decencies and civilities of society; the
claims of age, talents, and station ; the common
practical duties of life ; everything, in a word, is dis-
regarded, forgotten, involuntarily thrown out of account.

CHAPTER IX.

DISORDERED ATTENTION.

§ 88. *Of the general nature of attention.*

The mere fact of Attention or mental Concen-
tration is, unquestionably, a different thing from
Concentrativeness, or that elementary power (if
such there be, and whatever may be its nature) by
means of which we give attention.   Our inquiries,
in the first place, have relation to the fact of attention rather than the power.   Probably we come near
the common view of the matter by saying, in general
terms, that attention expresses the state of the mind
when it is steadily and strongly directed to the object, whatever it is, which happens to be before it.
As the mind, in the exercise of Attention, generally
directs itself to a particular object, exclusive of other

objects, it is not surprising that attention should sometimes be confounded with Abstraction. Attention, however, does not make it a chief or leading object, as Abstraction does, to consider things apart, and in a state of isolation from each other, but particularly to consider them fixedly and closely, whether they present themselves to the mind alone or in connexion with other objects. In other words, the grasp which the perceptive power fixes upon the object of its contemplations, whether considered as one or many, abstractly or complexly, is essentially an undivided, an unbroken one.

In what way the perceptive or intellective power is able to do this, it may not be an easy matter to determine with entire certainty. But the probability is, that it is owing to a distinct and specific act of the will, directing, condensing, and confining to a particular point, the movement of the percipient nature. So that in all cases of attention the act of the mind may be regarded as a complex one, involving not only the mere perceptions, or series of perceptions, but also an act of the will, founded on some feeling of desire or sentiment of duty. It is the act of the will, prompted, in general, by the feeling of desire or interest, which keeps the mind intense and fixed in its position. Nevertheless, as we generally have reference, when we speak of this subject, to the intellectual movement rather than to the volitive or voluntary energy which may be supposed to lay back of it, it is not without reason that we propose to consider it under the head of the intellect rather than under any subsequent division. And, as

Attention, like Abstraction, is as predicable of the External Intellect as of the Internal, it may as well be considered under the former subordinate division as under the latter.

§ 89. *Of differences in the Degree of Attention.*

It is worthy of notice, that we often speak of Attention as great or small, as existing in a very high or a very slight degree. When the view of the mind is only momentary, and is unaccompanied, as it generally is at such times, with any force of emotion or energy of volitive action, then the attention is said to be slight. When, on the contrary, the mind directs itself to an object or series of objects with earnestness, and for a considerable length of time, and refuses to attend to anything else, then the attention is said to be intense.

Some persons possess a command of attention in a very high degree. There have been mathematicians who were able to investigate the most abstruse and complicated problems amid every variety and character of disturbance. It is said of Julius Cæsar, that, while writing a despatch, he could at the same time dictate four others to his secretaries ; and, if he did not write himself, could dictate seven letters at once. The same thing is asserted also of the Emperor Napoleon, who had a wonderful capability of directing his whole mental energy to whatever came before him.*—Many other striking instances of this kind, illustrating the immense energy of attention which is characteristic of some individuals, might be introduced here if it were necessary.

* Elements of Mental Philosophy, vol. ii., § 153, 3d ed.

N

§ 90. *Of Absence of Mind, or inability to fix the Attention.*

But this view of the subject, viz., great strength or energy of attention, is of less consequence to us, in our present inquiries, than the opposite. In some men there seems to be an utter inability to detain the intellect, for any length of time, upon a given topic. Every new object which presents itself, every new idea which arises in the mind, claims the attention, slight as it is, which had just before been given to some other object or some other thought. The mind may be considered as in a state of constant transition from object to object, almost without motive and without purpose.

Such a state of the mind is, in the highest degree, unfortunate. It is fatal to the acquisition of knowledge. If the eye of the student, who is the subject of it, is fixed upon his book, it is probable that his thoughts are altogether removed from any connexion with the thoughts and reasonings of his author. To all practical purposes, the faculties of a person in this situation are obliterated and lost. Of what use are perceptive powers, and judgment, and powers of reasoning, if, in consequence of weakness of the will, or for any other cause, it is impossible to direct them, for any length of time, to any definite and practicable purpose? Such a person is unable to make any favourable impression on the community ; he is even unable to manage the concerns of his own family ; and is likely to be a source of great anxiety and trouble to all with whom he is immediately connected.

§ 91. *Illustration of inordinately weak or disordered Attention.*

An interesting case, illustrative of this mental disorder, is to be found in the writings of Sir Alexander Crichton. The case is repeated in Dr. Good's Study of Medicine (vol. iv., class iv., ord. i.); and it is in the words of this last-mentioned and highly valuable writer that we give it here. Of the individual whose character he is describing, he says: " In his disposition he was gentle and calm, but somewhat unsociable. His absence of mind was extreme, and he would sometimes willingly sit for a whole day without moving. Yet he had nothing of melancholy belonging to him ; and it was easy to discover by his countenance that a multiplicity of thoughts were constantly succeeding each other in his imagination, many of which were gay and cheerful ; for he would heartily laugh at times, not with an unmeaning countenance, but evidently from mental merriment. He was occasionally so strangely inattentive, that, when pushed by some want which he wished to express, if he had begun a sentence, he would suddenly stop short after getting half way through it, as though he had forgotten what else to say. Yet, when his attention was roused, and he was induced to speak, he always expressed himself in good language, and with much propriety ; and if a question were proposed to him which required the exercise of judgment, and he could be made to attend to it, he judged correctly.

" It was with difficulty he could be made to take

any exercise ; but was at length prevailed upon to drive his curricle, in which Sir Alexander at times accompanied him.   He at first could not be prevailed upon to go beyond half a mile ; but in succeeding attempts he consented to go further.   He drove steadily, and, when about to pass a carriage, took pains to avoid it ; but when at last he became familiarized with this exercise, he would often relapse into thought, and allow the reins to hang loose in his hands.   His ideas seemed to be for ever varying.   When any one came across his mind which excited anger, his horses suffered for it ; but the spirit they exhibited at such an unusual and unkind treatment made him soon desist, and re-excited his attention to his own safety.   As soon as they were quieted, he would relapse into thought ; if his ideas were melancholy, the horses were allowed to walk slow ; if they were gay and cheerful, they were generally encouraged to go fast.

" Something may in this case, perhaps, be owing, as supposed by Sir A. Crichton, to an error in the mode of education ; but the chief defect seems to have been in the attentive faculty itself, and its labouring under a natural imbecility which no mode of education could entirely have removed."

In connexion with the remark just made, Dr. Good, from whom we take this statement, goes on to assert the important doctrine which we have repeatedly had occasion to advance, that the various powers of the mind may be weak and diseased in themselves.   In other words, they may be diseased originally and in their own nature, and independently of other causes. At least, it is thus that we understand him.

§ 92. *Cases of sudden failure of the Attention.*

It is sometimes the case, that the power of Attention fails suddenly, in minds where it had existed with a considerable degree of energy up to the very time of its failure. Previous to this period, the individual was capable of directing his attention, with at least the ordinary degree of quickness and effect, to any subjects which might present themselves. But from that time the power vanishes ; the mind wanders abroad, independent of all control ; but perhaps the evil is only temporary.—A striking instance and illustration of what has just been said is to be found in the Psychological Magazine. The individual was a Mr. Spalding, a gentleman well known in Germany for his literary acquirements. The statement not only had reference to his own personal experience, but was drawn up and published by himself. It is as follows :

" I was this morning engaged with a great number of people, who followed each other quickly, and to each of whom I was obliged to give my attention. I was also under the necessity of writing much ; but the subjects, which were various, and of a trivial and uninteresting nature, had no connexion the one with the other. My attention, therefore, was constantly kept on the stretch, and was continually shifting from one subject to another. At last it became necessary that I should write a receipt for some money I had received on account of the poor. I seated myself and wrote the first two words, but in a moment found that I was incapable of proceeding, for I could not recollect the words which belonged to the ideas that were present in my mind. I strained my attention as much as possible, and tried to write one letter slowly after the other, always having an eye to the preceding one, in order to observe whether they had the usual relationship to each other ; but I remarked, and said to myself at the time, that the characters I was writing were not those which I wished to write, and yet I could not discover where the fault lay. I therefore desisted ; and partly by broken words and syllables, and partly by gestures, I made the person who waited for the receipt understand he should leave me. For about half an hour there reigned a kind of tumultuary disorder in my senses, in which I was incapable of remarking anything very particular, except that one series of ideas forced themselves involuntarily on my mind. The trifling nature of these thoughts I was perfectly aware of, and was also conscious that I made several efforts to get rid of them and supply their place by better ones, which lay at the bottom of my soul. I endeavoured, as much as lay in my power, considering the great crowd of confused images which presented themselves to my mind, to recall my principles of religion, of conscience, and of future expectation ; these I found equally correct and fixed as before.

" There was no deception in my external senses, for I saw and knew everything around me ; but I could not free myself from the strange ideas which existed in my head. I endeavoured to speak, in order to discover whether I was capable of saying anything that was connected; but, although I made the greatest efforts of attention, and proceeded with the utmost caution, I perceived that I uniformly spoke other words than those I intended. My soul was at present as little master of the organs of speech as it had been before of my hand in writing. Thank God, this state did not continue very long, for in about half an hour my head began to grow clearer, the strange and tiresome ideas became less vivid and turbulent, and I could command my own thoughts with less interruption."*

The mind of the individual, who gives this interesting account, gradually recovered its regular action. He then recollected the receipt which he had begun to write; and in regard to which he remembered that he had laboured under some strange inability. On examining the receipt, he found, to his great astonishment, that, instead of the words *fifty dollars, being one half year's rate*, which he ought to have written, the words were, *fifty dollars through the salvation of Bra.* He adds further, that he could not recollect any perception or business which he had to transact, that could, by means of an obscure influence, have produced this phenomenon. This we acknowledge to be a striking instance ; but we do not doubt, from the observations we have been able to make on the operations of the human mind, that there have, from time to time, been many others

* The German Psychological Magazine, as quoted in Macnish's Philosophy of Sleep, ch. xvi.

like it. Cases where the concentrative element, the power of attention, the ability to fasten the mind upon its appropriate object, has suddenly and strikingly failed, although, perhaps, not permanently.

§ 93. *Additional illustration of this disordered Action.*

There is rather a striking instance of the failure of the Concentrative or Attentive power, mentioned by Dr. George Combe, which came within his personal knowledge. He relates, that the gentleman who was the subject of it experienced a feeling, as if the power of concentrating his mind were about to leave him. This naturally caused some anxiety; and he accordingly used vigorous efforts to preserve it. "He directed his attention to an object, frequently a spire at the end of a long street, and resolutely maintained it immovably fixed there for a considerable length of time, excluding all other ideas from his mind. The consequence was, that, in his then weak state, a diseased fixity of mind ensued, in which feelings and ideas stood, as it were, bound up and immovable; and, thereafter, a state in which every impression and emotion was floating and fickle like images in water."*

§ 94. *Of the course to be taken to restore the power of Attention.*

It would be desirable, if possible, to suggest some remedies of this state of mind, particularly as it exists in its less marked but more frequent forms.

* Combe's Phrenology, Boston ed., p. 137.

I.—And the first thing to be done is to secure a healthy and vigorous state of the body, especially of the nervous system. If the bodily system be diseased, especially if there be a weak, tremulous, and uneasy state of the nerves, there will probably be, in connexion with this state of things, an uncertain and dissatisfied state of the mind. Deficient in energy, and yielding to the slightest cause of despondency, it will find itself incapable of directing itself, " with a single eye," to the proper object of its contemplations. Not because there is naturally and necessarily any defect in itself, but because its efforts, even when put forth with no small degree of energy, are borne down by the appendant burden of a weak and inefficient body.

II.—In other cases, the state of mind in question has been brought about by a wrong course of mental training. The individual has never been subjected to anything like severity of discipline ; but in study, as in everything else, has pursued his own pleasure, promptly leaving every inquiry which involved a laborious effort, and seeking some object of thought or action that was less repugnant. Such a course is ultimately fatal to that energy of mind which is requisite to a high degree of attention, and can be remedied only by a different course. The mind must be restored to energy by a course the opposite of that which has reduced it to its present lassitude, viz., by labour, which always has been, and always will be, the necessary condition of menal as well as of physical ability.

III.—There are cases where the inordinately inattentive state of mind has been caused, not by any weakness of the physical system, nor by a defect in the process of mental training, but is probably owing to something in the constitution of the mind itself. If there may be a constitutional weakness of the memory or of the reasoning power, may there not also be a constitutional weakness of the power of attention, or of those elements, whatever they may be, which constitute the power of attention? Whenever this is the case, it may be difficult wholly to eradicate the evil; but it may undoubtedly be diminished by a suitable course of mental training. Perhaps the ground of the imbecility of attention may be found in the weakness of the desires, per haps in the feebleness of the will, or in some othe. condition of the mind incidental to the exercise of attention. If this be the case, a course should be taken appropriate to such a state of things. Efforts should be made (such as will naturally suggest themselves) to increase the desires; in other words, to excite an interest in the subjects brought before the mind, to impart energy to the action of the will, and to discipline the mind in whatever other respects may be necessary.

CHAPTER X.

ON DREAMING.

§ 95. *General statement in regard to Dreams.*

ONE of the modifications of Disordered Mental Action (not permanent, it is true, but occasional and temporary disordered action) exists in the form of Dreams. We sometimes say of a man, who is under partial mental hallucination, that he is a dreamer ; or, that he has no more correctness of perception and understanding than if he were dreaming. Hence it is obviously proper to give some attention to these states of mind. Furthermore as dreams are found, for the most part, to be particularly and very closely connected with external perceptions and conceptions, there seems to be a propriety in considering them in this place, viz., under the general head of the External Intellect.

In undertaking to give the reader some account of dreams, it will not be necessary, in the first instance, to be particular in our statements. It will, perhaps, approach sufficiently near to a correct gen eral description to say, that they are our mental states and operations while we are asleep. But the particular views, which are to be taken in the ex amination of this subject, will not fail to throw light on this general statement.—We proceed, therefore,

to give some explanation of them in their more
common or ordinary appearance. And, in doing
this, shall find it convenient (as we have already
done in some cases, in giving an account of the regular or normal mental processes) to repeat essentially the statements which are to be found in the
recently published Elements of Mental Philosophy;
a work, where we have made it an especial object,
although probably with very imperfect success, to
give what we consider the correct view of the mind's
regular and ordinary action.

§ 96. *Connexion of dreams with our waking*
thoughts.

In giving an explanation of dreams, our attention
is first arrested by the circumstance that they have
an intimate relationship with our waking thoughts.
The great body of our waking experiences appear
in the form of trains of associations ; and these
trains of associated ideas, in greater or less continuity, and with greater or less variation, continue
when we are asleep.—Accordingly, Franklin has
somewhere made the remark, that the bearings and
results of political events, which had caused him
much trouble while awake, were not unfrequently
unfolded to him in dreaming.—Mr. Coleridge relates, that, as he was once reading in the Pilgrimage
of Purchas an account of the palace and garden of
the Khan Kubla, he fell into a sleep, and in that
situation composed an entire poem of not less than
two hundred lines ; some of which he afterward

committed to writing.   The poem is entitled **Kubla Khan**, and begins as follows:

" In Xanadu did Kubla Khan
      A stately pleasure-dome decree;
      Where Alph, the sacred river, ran
      Through caverns measureless to man
            Down to a sunless sea."

It is evident, from such statements as these, which are confirmed by the experience of almost every person, that our dreams are fashioned from the materials of the thoughts and feelings which we have while awake ; in other words, they will, in a great degree, be merely the repetition of our customary and prevailing associations.

§ 97. *Dreams are often caused by our sensations.*

But while we are to look for the materials of our dreams in thoughts which had previously existed, we further find that they are not beyond the influence of those slight bodily sensations of which we are susceptible even in hours of sleep.   These sensations, slight as they are, are the means of introducing one set of associations rather than another.— Dugald Stewart relates an incident, which may be considered an evidence of this, that a person with whom he was acquainted had occasion, in consequence of an indisposition, to apply a bottle of hot water to his feet when he went to bed ; and the consequence was, that he dreamed he was making a journey to the top of Mount Ætna, and that he found the heat of the ground almost insupportable.

A cause of dreams closely allied to the above, is

the variety of sensations which we experience from
the stomach, viscera, &c.   Persons, for instance,
who have been for a long time deprived of food, or
have received it only in small quantities, hardly
enough to preserve life, will be likely to have dreams
in some way or other directly relating to their condition.   Baron Trenck relates, that, being almost
dead with hunger when confined in his dungeon,
his dreams every night presented to him the well-
filled and luxurious tables of Berlin, from which, as
they were presented before him, he imagined he was
about to relieve his hunger.

The state of health also has considerable influence, not only in producing dreams, but in giving
them a particular character.   The remark has been
made by medical men, that acute diseases, particularly fevers, are often preceded and indicated by
disagreeable and oppressive dreams.

§ 98. *Explanation of the incoherency of dreams.*

There is frequently much of wildness, inconsistency, and contradiction in our dreams.   The mind
passes very rapidly from one object to another;
strange and singular incidents occur.   If our dreams
be truly the repetition of our waking thoughts, it
may well be inquired, How this wildness and inconsistency happen?

The explanation of this peculiarity resolves itself
into two parts.—The FIRST ground or cause of it is,
that our dreams are not subjected, like our waking
thoughts, to the control and regulation of surrounding objects.   While we are awake, our trains of

thought are kept uniform and coherent by the influence of such objects, which continually remind us of our situation, character, and duties, and which keep in check any tendency to revery. But in sleep the senses are closed; the soul is, accordingly, in a great measure excluded from the material world, and is thus deprived of the salutary regulating influence from that source.

In the SECOND place, when we are asleep, our associated trains of thought are no longer under the control of the WILL. We do not mean to say that the operations of the will are suspended at such times, and that volitions have no existence; but only that their influence in a great degree ceases.

A person, while he is awake, has his thoughts under such government, and is able, by the direct and indirect influence of volitions, so to regulate them, as generally to bring them in the end to some conclusion, which he foresees and wishes to arrive at. But in dreaming, as all directing and governing influence, both internal and external, is at an end, our thoughts and feelings seem to be driven forward, much like a ship at sea without a rudder, wherever it may happen.

§ 99. *Apparent reality of dreams.* (1st cause.)

When objects are presented to us in dreams, we look upon them as real; and events, and combinations and series of events, appear the same. We feel the same interest, and resort to the same expedients as in the perplexities and enjoyments of real life. When persons are introduced as forming a part in the transactions of our dreams, we see them clearly in their living attitudes and stature ; we converse with them, and hear them speak, and behold them move, as if actually present.

One reason of this greater vividness of our dreaming conceptions, and of our firm belief in their reality, seems to be this. The subjects upon which our thoughts are then employed, occupy the mind *exclusively*. We can form a clearer conception of an object with our eyes shut than we can with them open, as any one will be convinced on making the experiment ; and the liveliness of the conception will increase in proportion as we can suspend the exercise of the other senses. In sound sleep, not only the sight, but the other senses also, may be said to be closed ; and the attention is not continually diverted by the multitude of objects which arrest the hearing and touch when we are awake.—It is, therefore, a most natural supposition, that our conceptions must at such times be extremely vivid and distinct.

Furthermore, it will be recollected, that very vivid conceptions are often attended with a momentary belief in the actuality of the things conceived of, even when we are awake. But as conceptions exist in the mind when we are asleep in a much higher degree distinct and vivid, what was in the former case a momentary, becomes in the latter a permanent belief. Hence everything has the appearance of reality ; and the mere thoughts of the mind are virtually transformed into persons, and varieties of situation, and events, which are regarded by us in precisely the same light as the persons, and situations, and events of our every day's experience.

§ 100. *Apparent reality of dreams.* (2d *cause.*)

A second circumstance, which goes to account for the fact that our dreaming conceptions have the appearance of reality, is, that they are not susceptible of being controlled, either directly or indirectly, by mere volition.—We are so formed as almost invariably to associate reality with whatever objects of perception continue to produce in us the same effects. A hard or soft body, or any substance of a particular colour, or taste, or smell, is always, when presented to our senses, followed by certain states of mind essentially the same ; and we yield the most ready and firm belief in the existence of such objects. In a word, we are disposed, from our very constitution, to believe in the existence of objects of perception, the perceptions of which do not depend on the WILL, but which we find to be followed by certain states of the mind, whether we choose it or not.—But it is to be recollected that our dreaming thoughts are, for the most part, mere conceptions ; our senses being closed and shut up, and external objects not being presented to them. This is true. But if we conclude in favour of the real existence of objects of perception, because they produce in us sensations independently of our volitions, it is but natural to suppose that we shall believe in the reality of our conceptions also, whenever they are in like manner beyond our voluntary control. They are both merely states of the mind ; and if belief always attends our perceptions, wherever we find them to be independent of our choice, there is no reason why conceptions, which are ideas of absent objects of perception, should not be attended with a like belief under the same circumstances.—And essentially the same circumstances exist in dreaming ; that is, a train of conceptions arise in the mind, and we are not conscious at such times of being able to exercise any direction or control whatever over them. They exist, whether we will it or not ; and we regard them as real.

§ 101. *Of our estimate of time in dreaming.*

Our estimate of time in dreaming differs from that when awake. Events, which would take whole days or a longer time in the performance, are dreamed in a few moments. So wonderful is this compression of a multitude of transactions into the very shortest period, that, when we are accidentally awakened by the jarring of a door which is opened into the room where we are sleeping, we sometimes dream of depredations by thieves, or destruction by fire, in the very instant of our awakening.—" A friend of mine" (says Dr. Abercrombie) " dreamed that he crossed the Atlantic and spent a fortnight in America. In embarking on his return, he fell into the sea ; and, having awoke with the fright, discovered that he had not been asleep above ten minutes."

This striking circumstance in the history of our dreams is generally explained by supposing that our thoughts, as they successively occupy the mind, are more rapid than while we are awake. But their rapidity may at other times be very great; so much so, that, in a few moments, crowds of ideas pass through the mind, which it would take a long time to utter, and a far longer time would it take to perform all the transactions which they concern. This explanation, therefore, is not satisfactory, for our thoughts are oftentimes equally rapid in our waking moments.

The true reason, we apprehend, is to be found in those preceding sections, which took under examination the apparent reality of dreams. Our conceptions in dreaming are considered by us real; every thought is an action; every idea is an event; and successive states of mind are successive actions and successive events. He who in his sleep has the conception of all the particulars of a distant military expedition, or of a circumnavigation of the globe, seems to himself to have actually experienced all the various and multiplied fortunes of the one and the other. Hence what appears to be the real time in dreams, but is only the apparent time, will not be that which is sufficient for the mere thought, but that which is necessary for the successive actions.

§ 102. *Dreams sometimes lay the foundation of a permanently disordered state of mind.*

It is sufficiently evident that Dreams, as we have already had occasion to intimate, must be considered as disordered, and not as sane or sound states of mind. They do not, however, necessarily imply insanity of mind in the ordinary sense of the term. As soon as the powers of the body are restored, and the state of sleep terminates, the mental action, which was subject during the period of dreaming to a temporary disorder, ceases to exhibit those irregularities which just before characterized it.   Dreams, nevertheless, in consequence of the feelings of horror which they sometimes occasion, have, in a few instances, been the cause of a permanently disordered mental state.   In themselves they involve nothing more than a temporary disorder ; but in their results they may, by possibility at least, lay the foundation of a permanent one.

Mr. Macnish, in his recent Work on the Philosophy of Sleep, relates the case of a woman in the West Highlands of Scotland, who became deranged in consequence of a terrific dream.   He states, that in her derangement she escaped to the mountains, and lived and herded with the wild deer for seven years.   She became so swift of foot, that the shepherds of those regions, and others by whom she was occasionally seen, could never arrest her.   At the end of her seven year's wanderings a severe storm drove the herds of deer and the woman with them into the valleys, where she was surrounded and caught.   She was conveyed to her husband, by whom she was kindly received, and in the course of three months regained her reason.

§ 103. *Mental disorder sometimes developes itself in connexion with dreams.*

Sometimes persons, under the influence of dreams, perform actions indicative of an unsound state of mind, although the unsoundness of mind may never have been suspected before. It is the dream which first brings to light the hidden trait of insanity. Of this the following facts are an instance.

Some years since, an individual resident in Gardiner, in the State of Maine, dreamed that he was instructed by the Supreme Being to burn a neighbouring church, and also to kill a certain woman of his acquaintance. His mind was powerfully affected. And, not doubting that he had the highest possible authority, he succeeded in burning the place of worship, and exhibited every disposition to execute, as soon as possible, the remaining part of his terrific commission. Before he could effect his purpose, however, he was seized and prevented.—Nevertheless, he remained firm in his intention to perform, at the first favourable opportunity, what he considered to be the will of God. As there was now no doubt of his insanity, he was imprisoned for life, not merely as a punishment for what he had already done, but as the only sure means of preventing the atrocities which he still intended to perpetrate. To his dying day he clung to the belief, that he did right in destroying the building, and much lamented that he was not permitted to perform all that had been prescribed to him.—As has been intimated, this man was essentially insane previous to this time. That is to say, he had the elements of Insanity in him, although they were first developed and put in operation by the dream.

Pinel mentions a case very similar to the foregoing. The individual was an old monk, whose excessive religious feelings had assumed the form o

enthusiasm.   In this state of mind, he dreamed one
night that he saw the Virgin, and that she gave him
an express order to put to death a person of his acquaintance, whom he suspected of infidelity. "This
projected homicide" (says Pinel) "would, no doubt,
have been executed, had not the maniac, in consequence of betraying his purpose, been timely and
effectually secured."

§ 104. *Case of destruction of life arising from a dream.*

In Hoffbauer's Treatise on Legal Medicine is a
case narrated, which may properly be introduced
here. It is the case of Bernard Schidmaizig. This
individual, under the influence of some terrific dream,
as is supposed, awoke suddenly at midnight, and
beheld, at the moment of awaking, what he conceived to be a frightful phantom standing near him. The
object before him was his wife, who was probably
passing across the room at the time.   In this state
of mind, half dreaming and half awake, he mingled
his own disturbed conceptions with the reality before
him, and still continued to see, as he thought, some
phantasmagorial appearance.   He cried out, "Who
goes there?" but received no answer.   In the
greatest affright he seized a hatchet, which he generally kept near him, sprung from his bed, and
assaulted the imaginary spectre. The blow felled
his wife to the ground, and she died the next day.

This case, it will readily be perceived, is an important one in a legal point of view.   Although the
result was horrible in the extreme, the man could

not well be considered as guilty of a crime. It is
true he was not insane, and no valid excuse of his
conduct could be found in insanity. Nor was he,
strictly speaking, asleep ; but there was such a combination of the sleeping and waking states, such a
mingling of what was actually perceived with what
was dreamed, combined too with extreme affright,
that the same reasons which would nullify the crime
of an insane person would seem to apply here, and
be sufficient to extract the moral guilt from this.
The man evidently was not himself. He laboured
under a delusion, which, though different from insanity, practically amounted to it.*

CHAPTER XI.

SOMNAMBULISM.

§ 105. *General view of Somnambulism.*

WITH the subject of dreaming, that of Somnambulism is naturally and very intimately connected.
And if the term Dreaming, in some important sense,
indicates a perplexed and irregular mental action,
Somnambulism does not less so. Hence the propriety of giving some account of it in a treatise
which proposes to give the outlines, if nothing more,
of disordered mental action.

* Hoffbauer's Médecine Légale, Des Maladies Mentales du
Sommeil (French ed., by Chambeyron).

In attempting to give a definition, we are not certain of being perfectly safe. Perhaps we shall come near enough to the fact in the case, in saying, that somnambulists are persons who are capable of walking and of other voluntary actions while asleep. Of such persons many instances are on record; and of some a particular account is given. The instance in the following section, which in some respects is a somewhat striking one, will help to illustrate the nature of the subject now before us.

§ 106. *Singular instance of Somnambulism.*

A farmer in one of the counties of Massachusetts, according to the account of the matter which was published at the time, had employed himself, for some weeks in winter, thrashing his grain. One night, as he was about closing his labours, he ascended a ladder to the top of the great beams in the barn, where the rye which he was thrashing was deposited, to ascertain what number of bundles remained unthrashed, which he determined to finish the next day. The ensuing night, about two o'clock, he was heard by one of the family to arise and go out. He repaired to his barn, being sound asleep and unconscious of what he was doing, set open his barn doors, ascended the great beams of the barn where his rye was deposited, threw down a flooring and commenced thrashing it. When he had completed it, he raked off the straw, and shoved the rye to one side of the floor, and again ascended the ladder with the straw, and deposited it on some rails that lay across the great beams. He then threw down another flooring of rye, which he thrashed and finished as before. Thus he continued his labours until he had thrashed five floorings, and on returning from throwing down the sixth and last, in passing over part of the haymow, he fell off, where the hay had been cut down about six feet, on to the lower part of it, which awoke him. He at first imagined himself in his neighbour's barn; but, after groping about in the dark a long time, ascertained that he was in his own, and at length found the ladder, on which he descended to the floor, closed his barn doors which he found open, and returned to his house. On coming to the light, he found himself in such a profuse perspiration that his clothes were literally wet through. The next morning, on going to his barn, he found that he had thrashed, during the night, five bushels of rye, had raked the straw off in good order, and deposited it on the great beams, and carefully shoved the grain to one side of the floor, without the least consciousness of what he was doing until he fell from the hay.

§ 107. *Of the senses falling to sleep in succession.*

Before attempting to offer anything in explanation of cases of somnambulism, we wish to delay a moment for the purpose of stating very briefly the manner in which the senses are supposed successively to fall asleep. What sleep is, mentally considered and independently of the body, it might be difficult to say. But we know this, at least, that in a state of sleep the mind, as a general thing, ceases to retain its customary power over the muscular movements of

P

the system ; and also that all the senses are at such times locked up, as it were, and no longer perform their usual offices. And furthermore, the effect upon the senses takes place in such a way, that it seems to be proper to speak of them as separately or individually going to sleep and awaking from sleep. The additional fact is, that they appear to fall asleep at different times and in succession.

This last fact is one of considerable importance in its practical applications. But we do not undertake here to enter into particulars and proofs. Reference must be had for the details and the confirmatory reasonings and facts to Cullen, and particularly to Cabanis,* a distinguished French writer on subjects of this nature. We give merely the conclusions at which they arrive.

The sight, as we gather from the writers who have been named, ceases, in consequence of the protection of the eyelids, to receive impressions first, while all the other senses preserve their sensibility entire ; and may, therefore, be said to be first in falling asleep. The sense of taste, according to the above writers, is the next which loses its susceptibility of impressions, and then the sense of smelling. The hearing is the next in order, and last of all comes the sense of touch.—Furthermore, the senses are thought to sleep with different degrees of profoundness. The senses of taste and smelling awake the last ; the sight with more difficulty than the hearing, and the touch the easiest of all. Sometimes a very considerable noise does not awake a

* Rapports du Physique et du Moral de L'Homme, Mem. x.

person ; but, if the soles of his feet are tickled in the slightest degree, he starts up immediately.

§ 108. *Similar views applicable to the muscles.*

Similar remarks are made by the writers already referred to on the muscles. Those which move the arms and legs cease to act, when sleep is approaching, sooner than those which sustain the head : and the latter before those which support the back. —And here it is proper to notice an exception to the general statement made in the preceding section, that the mind in sleep ceases to retain its power over the muscles. Some persons can sleep standing, or walking, or riding on horseback ; with such we cannot well avoid the supposition, that the voluntary power over the muscles is in some way retained and exercised in sleep.—These statements are particularly important in connexion with the facts of somnambulism ; only admit that the susceptibility of the senses, and the power of the muscles may remain, even in part, while we are asleep, and we can account for them. We know that this is not the case in a vast majority of instances ; but that it does sometimes happen is a point which seems at last to be sufficiently well established.

§ 109 *Of the connexion of Somnambulism with dreaming.*

Keeping in mind the views that have been given in the preceding sections, we proceed to remark, as has already been intimated, that a number of things may be satisfactorily said in explanation of somnam-

bulism.   The somnambulist, in the first place, is in
all cases dreaming, and we may suppose, in general,
that the dream is one which greatly interests him.
After he has awaked, the action he has passed
through appears, in his recollection of it, to be merely a dream, and not a reality.   " A young nobleman
(says Dr. Abercrombie), " living in the citadel of
Breslau, was observed by his brother, who occupied
the same room, to rise in his sleep, wrap himself in
a cloak, and escape by a window to the roof of the
building.   He there tore in pieces a magpie's nest,
wrapped the young birds in his cloak, returned to his
apartment, and went to bed.   In the morning he
mentioned the circumstances as having occurred in
a dream, and could not be persuaded that there had
been anything more than a dream, till he was shown
the magpies in his cloak."   And this is noticed to
be commonly the fact.   What has been done has
the appearance of being a dream.   And there is no
doubt that the mind of the somnambulist is in that
particular state which we denominate dreaming.

    II.—In the second place, those volitions, which
are a part of his dreams, retain their power over the
muscles, which is not the fact in the sleep and the
dreaming of the great body of people.—Consequently, whatever the somnambulist dreams, is not
only real in the mind, as in the case of all other
dreams, but his ability to exercise his muscles enables him to give it a reality in action.   Whether he
dream of writing a letter, of visiting a neighbour's
house, of cutting and piling wood, of thrashing his
grain, or ploughing his fields (acts which have a/

various times been ascribed to the somnambulist), his muscles are faithful to his vivid mental concep tions, which we may suppose in all cases closely connected with his customary labours and experiences, and frequently enable him to complete what he has undertaken, even when his senses are at the same time closed up.

But the inquiry arises here, how it happens, while in most cases both senses and muscles lose their power, in these, on the contrary, the muscles are active, while the senses alone are asleep ?—In reference to this inquiry, it must be acknowledged, that it is involved at present in some uncertainty, although there is much reason to anticipate that it may hereafter receive light from further investigations and knowledge of the nervous system and functions. There is a set of nerves, which are understood to be parti ularly connected with respiration, and which appear to have nothing to do with sensation and with muscular action. There is another set, which are known to possess a direct and important connexion with sensation and the muscles. These last are separable into distinct filaments, having separate functions ; some being connected with sensation merely, and others with volition and muscular action. In sensation, the impression made by some external body exists at first in the external part of the organ of sense, and is propagated along one class of filaments to the brain. In volition and voluntary muscular movement, the origin of action, as far as the body is concerned, seems to be the reverse, commencing in the brain, and being propagated along other and ap-

propriate nervous filaments to the different parts of
the system.

Hence it sometimes happens, that, in diseases of
the nervous system, the power of sensation is, in a
great measure, lost, while that of motion fully remains; or, on the contrary, the power of motion
is lost, while that of sensation remains. These
views help to throw light on the subject of somnambulism. Causes, at present unknown to us,
may operate, through their appropriate nervous filaments, to keep the muscles awake, without disturbing the repose and inactivity of the senses. A
man may be asleep as to all the powers of external perception, and yet be awake in respect to the
capabilities of muscular motion. And, aided by the
trains of association, which make a part of his
dreams, may be able to walk about and to do many
things without the aid of the sight and hearing.

§ 110. *Further illustrations of somnambulism.*

III.—Further, we are not to forget here some remarks in the preceding chapter to this effect, viz
that the sleep of the senses is sometimes an imperfect or partial one; and that at such times the
senses are susceptible of slight external influences.
Both in somnambulism and in ordinary cases of
dreaming, the senses are not always entirely locked
up; many observations clearly show, that it is possible for the mind to be accessible through them, and
that a new direction may be given in this way to a
person's dreams without awaking him. Hence
somnambulists may sometimes have very slight vis-

ual perceptions; they may, in some slight measure, be guided by sensations of touch; all the senses may be affected in a small degree by their appropriate objects, or this may be the case with some and not with others, without effectually disturbing their sleep.—These facts will be found to help in explaining any peculiar circumstances, which may be thought not to come within the reach of the general explanation which has been given.

§ 111. *Reference to the case of Jane Rider.*

IV.—But this is not all. There are some cases which are not reached by the statements hitherto made. There are not only slight exceptions to the general fact, that somnambulists, like persons in ordinary sleep, are insensible to external impressions, but occasionally some of a marked and extraordinary character. There are a few cases (the recent instance of Jane Rider in this country is one) where persons, in the condition of somnambulism, have not only possessed slight visual power, but perceptions of sight increased much above the common degree. In the extraordinary narrative of Jane Rider, the author informs us, that he took two large wads of cotton, and placed them directly on the closed eyelids, and then bound them on with a black silk handkerchief. "The cotton filled the cavity under the eyebrows, and reached down to the middle of the cheek; and various experiments were tried to ascertain whether she could see. In one of them a watch enclosed in a case was handed to her, and she was requested to tell what o'clock it was by it; upon which, after examining both sides of the watch, she opened the case, and then answered the question. She also read, without hesitation, the name of a gentleman, written in characters so fine that no one else could distinguish it at the usual distance from the eye. In another paroxysm, the lights were removed from her room, and the windows so secured that no object was discernible, and two books were presented to her, when she immediately told the titles of both, though one of them was a book which she had never before seen. In other experiments, while the room was so darkened that it was impossible, with the ordinary powers of vision, to distinguish the colours of the carpet, and her eyes were also bandaged, she pointed out the different colours in the hearth-rug, took up and read several cards laying on the table, threaded a needle, and performed several other things, which could not have been done without the aid of vision."*—Of extraordinary cases of this kind, it would seem that no satisfactory explanation (at least no explanation which is unattended with difficulties) has as yet been given.

* As quoted in Dr. Oliver's Physiology, chap. xxx.

IMPERFECT AND DISORDERED

MENTAL ACTION

DIVISION FIRST.

DISORDERED ACTION OF THE INTELLECT.

PART II.

DERANGEMENT OF THE INTERNAL INTELLECT.

DISORDERED ACTION

INTERNAL INTELLECT

CHAPTER I.

DISORDERED SUGGESTION.

§ 112. *Of the Internal in distinction from the Ex-ternal Intellect.*

It was remarked, in one of the Introductory Chapters to this Work, that the Mind may be con-sidered under the three general heads of the Intel-lect, the Sensibilities, and the Will. The Intellect, so far as it is brought into action, in consequence of being immediately in contact with the External World, is designated by the epithet External. We find it convenient to call it the External Intellect. But, so far as the Intellect has an internal action, that is to say, an action carried on without any di-rect or very close connexion with the external world, it is a matter of convenience, besides involving a great philosophical truth, to designate it as the In-ternal Intellect. In support of this great distinction in the Intellectual action, it is not necessary to say anything further here, than to make the general remark, that it is a distinction fully recognised, and sustained, at greater or less length, by many of the most distinguished mental philosophers. On this matter, therefore, it is not necessary to delay. We are to regard it, in this discussion at least, as a well ascertained and clearly established point of departure.

§ 113. *Original suggestion to be regarded as a distinct power of the mind.*

Some of the cases of thought and knowledge (as we have had occasion to remark in the Elements of Mental Philosophy), which the mind becomes possessed of in itself, without the direct aid of the Senses, are to be ascribed to Suggestion. This word, in its application to the mind, is used merely to express a simple but important fact, viz., that the mind, by its own activity and vigour, by the originative impulse of its own spontaneity, gives rise to certain thoughts. We have already had occasion, in the chapter on the Outlines of Mental Philosophy, to refer to some remarks of Dr. Reid, who speaks, in his Inquiry into the Human Mind, of certain notions (for instance, those of EXISTENCE, MIND, PERSON, &c.), as the "judgments of nature, judgments not got by comparing ideas, and perceiving agreements and disagreements, but immediately inspired by our constitution."

Pursuing this train of thought, he ascribes those notions, which cannot be attributed directly to the senses on the one hand, nor to the reasoning power on the other, to an internal or mental Suggestion, as follows : "I beg leave" (he expressly says) " to make use of the word Suggestion, because I know not one more proper, to express a power of the mind, which seems entirely to have escaped the notice of philosophers, and to which we owe many of our simple notions."

Mr. Stewart also, in his Philosophical Essays and in other parts of his valuable Works, appears very clearly to take similar ground. Referring to certain mental phenomena, particularly such as would naturally come under the general head of Internal Origin, he speaks of them, not as the objects of consciousness, but as merely attendant upon those objects, and as SUGGESTED by them.

Suggestion, therefore (or, as we should prefer to designate it, Original Suggestion, thus distinguishing it from Relative Suggestion or Judgment), is to be regarded as a distinct source of ideas. And certainly no conceptions of the human mind are more fundamental and important than those, the origin of which is to be assigned here. Such as the ideas of EXISTENCE, PERSONAL IDENTITY, UNITY, PLURALITY, NUMBER, SUCCESSION, DURATION, TIME, POWER, SPACE, and the like.—What remains to be done in this chapter, is to show that it is possible for insanity, in a greater or less degree, to attach to the mental action, in connexion with the origin of some of these fundamental conceptions.

§ 114. *Insanity in connexion with the conviction of personal identity.*

Among other important conceptions, the origin of which may be traced to Original Suggestion, or which, in other words, are originated by an ultimate and spontaneous movement of the mind, is that of our Personal Identity. This is not only one of the earliest, but one of the strongest convictions which men have ; and is essential, in the highest sense of that term, to soundness of mind. But this great link of thought, which makes a man one with himself in all the varieties of his past and present existence, is sometimes broken. In such cases the portion of past existence is let loose from the present ; and the individual, who is subject to this form of mental malady, confounds himself with other persons and other beings, and constantly reasons and acts upon this false view.

Dr. Rush mentions a case to which this statement will apply. " There is now" (he says) " a madman in the Pennsylvania Hospital, who believes that he was once a calf, and who mentions the name of the butcher that killed him, and the stall in the Philadelphia market on which his flesh was sold, previously to his animating his present body." He likewise mentions the case of one of the princes of Bourbon, who believed himself transformed into a plant ; and with such sincerity, that he often went and stood in his garden, and insisted upon being watered in common with the plants around him.[*]

[*] Diseases of the Mind, p. 80.

It is stated, on the authority of Pinel, that a celebrated watchmaker of Paris became insane during
the French Revolution. This man believed that he
and some others had been beheaded, but that the
heads were subsequently ordered to be restored to
the original wners. Some mistake, however, as
the insane person conceived, was committed in the
process of restoration, in consequence of which he
had unfortunately been furnished with the head of
one of his companions instead of his own. He was
admitted into the Hospital Bicetre, " where he was
continually complaining of his misfortune, and la-
menting the fine teeth and wholesome breath he had
exchanged for those of very different qualities."*

Such instances show that the fundamental perception, which we commonly denominate the feeling
or consciousness of Personal Identity, and in virtue
of which we confidently speak of ourselves as the
same being, amid all the changes incident to our existence, may be disordered; and that, too, to such
an extent as to cause, as it were, a dislocation of
our continuity, and to separate our personality into
remote and unrelated fragments. I am aware that
this aspect of Insanity, considered as holding a separate and distinctive place, is not prominent in the
writers on that subject. Dr. Rush, however, expressly states, that, in certain marked cases which
he describes, the conviction of Personal Identity
may for a time be destroyed. And, in confirmation
of his remark, he refers to Shakspeare, where the

* Treatise on Insanity, p. 69.

poet represents King Lear as uttering the following words :

> " I am mainly ignorant
> What place this is ; and all the skill I have
> Remembers not these garments, nor I know not
> Where I did sleep last night."

Dr. Combe also explicitly says, " Patients are sometimes insane in the feeling of Personal Identity." " Such individuals" (he adds) " lose all consciousness of their past and proper personality, and imagine themselves different persons altogether; while, with the exception of this erroneous impression, they feel and think correctly."

§ 115. *Disordered mental action, in connexion with the idea of space.*

The idea of Space, which we next propose for consideration, is revealed to us in the Internal intellect, and by a suggestive rather than a deductive act.   The idea or conception of space is one of the clearest which the mind has.   It seems indispensable that it should be so, inasmuch as it furnishes the basis for all our ideas of the position or place of things.   Nevertheless, this important and elementary conception may be disordered ; and this disorder may extend to everything that is incidental to, or involved in it, viz., to the position or place of things. There is at such times an expansion, an amplification of the great reality developed in the idea of space, which is not only strange and unprecedented in itself, but which has the effect to enlarge and exaggerate everything which is subordinate to it, in the sense of having a place or locality.

The Leper of Aost, an interesting little work of Count le Maistre, appears to me to contain some allusions to this peculiar state of mind.—" I yield" (says the leper, whose mind had become affected and disordered by the intensity of disease) "to extraordinary impressions, which I feel in these unhappy moments. Sometimes it is as if an irresistible power were dragging me to a *fathomless abyss.* Sometimes I see nothing but bleak forms ; when I endeavour to examine them, they cross each other with the rapidity of lightning, *increase in approaching, and soon are like mountains, which crush me under their weight.* At other times I see dark clouds arise from the earth around me ; they come over me *like an inundation, which increases, advances, and threatens to ingulf me.*"

It is well known that the mind is powerfully and very injuriously affected by the use of opium. De Quincey's Confessions of an Opium Eater, containing very interesting and striking statements, drawn from the author's own unhappy experience, may be considered an authentic document on this subject. This publication throws some light upon the inquiry now directly before us. When he was awake, his mind was powerfully affected. But still more so in his dreams. Everything seemed expanded immeasurably. In one place, giving an account of his dreams, he says, " My imagination was infinite." Again he says, more directly to our present purpose, 'I seemed to descend into chasms and sunless abysses, *depths below depths,* from which it seemed hopeless that I could ever reascend. Nor did I, by

Q

waking, feel that I *had* reascended. Buildings, landscapes, &c., were exhibited in proportions so vast as the bodily eye is not fitted to receive. *Space swelled, and was amplified to an unutterable infinity.*"

These statements seem to show the possibility that the mind may be injuriously affected in this respect, as well as in others.

As the idea of space is, in the order of nature, antecedent to that of place, and may be considered as the foundation or basis of it, it is possible we may find, in what has now been said, a reason, in part at least, that insane persons frequently misapprehend the position or place of things, and are at a loss where they are.

§ 116. *Disordered mental action in connexion with Time.*

The idea of DURATION (or Time, as we commonly express it) is not given us, whatever may be true of the *measurements* of time, by means of the outward senses. It is correctly regarded as a communication from the internal intellect, in the exercise of its power of original suggestion. The existence of this important mental conception depends (not the thing itself, but merely the conception or idea of it) upon the previous fact of a succession in our mental operations, of which we are conscious. If the succession be disordered, the notion of time will be disordered. If, for instance, in a case of insanity, which is sometimes the fact, the mind be fixed upon one thought; if it suffer a sort of paralysis in respect to every other movement, and revolve continually in the monotonous circle of a single conception, the power of original suggestion, acting upon such a basis, must, of necessity, give but an imperfect idea of the actual duration.

Essentially this view appears to be taken by Dr. Gall. "It appears" (says this laborious and valuable collector of mental facts) "that there is no idea of time with those insane persons who remain days and weeks fixed in the same place. A madman at Vienna had but one fixed idea, namely, that it was always the 17th of October. It often happens in mental alienation, as in other grievous diseases, that the idea of time is completely destroyed. When these patients recover, they begin to count the time from the moment when they regained the distinct perception of their existence. After twenty-seven years of seclusion and mania, a lady experienced a revolution favourable to her moral state. Her delirium and madness continued during this space of time to the extent of tearing her clothes, of remaining naked, &c. At the moment of the cessation of her delirium, she appeared to come out as from a profound dream, and asked after two young children which she had previous to her alienation, and could not conceive that they had been married several years previous."*

Other similar cases might be introduced. Dr. Rush mentions the case of a clergyman, which furnishes an illustration of the doctrine which has been laid down. The person referred to was insane four years and a half. The peculiarity or type of

* Gall's Works, Boston ed., vol. v., p. 95.

his insanity was DESPAIR, resulting from the belief.
that he had lost his Maker's favour, and was necessarily and inevitably exposed to everlasting misery.
He kept his hands constantly in motion, and constantly repeated his conviction of his lost condition.
The single thought of his present and prospective
misery, without any alleviation, seems to have occupied his mind.   After his recovery, he asserted, in
reference to the period of his insanity (what, indeed,
the principles of the philosophy of the mind would
naturally lead us to expect), "that he lost all sense of
years, months, weeks, days, and nights, and even of
morning and evening ; that, in this respect, time was
to him no more."*

Dr. Haslam relates the case of a man who was
attacked with insanity at the period of the year when
people were planting their corn.   Having recovered
at the period when the corn was ripe and was being
gathered, he seriously asserted that he had seen the
corn planted only three or four days before, and considered it a very uncommon and remarkable circumstance that it should have become ripe so soon.
The simple fact was, that his insanity was of such a
nature as directly or indirectly to reach and perplex
the mental process, by which we have a knowledge
of time and of its measurements.   Time, as a sub
ject of distinct conception, had been virtually annihilated to him, almost as much so as if he had been,
during the whole period, in sound sleep or deprived
of life.†

* Diseases of the Mind, 2d ed., p. 95.
† Burrows's Commentaries, p. 677.

§ 117. *Further illustrations of disordered Time.*

Under this head we may properly introduce an interesting and instructive statement, which is to be found in the first volume of the American Journal of Science. The statement is given in a letter to the editor, Professor Silliman, in the following terms :

" Some years ago, a farmer of fair character, who resided in an interior town in New-England, sold his farm, with an intention of purchasing another in a different town. His mind was naturally of a melancholy cast. Shortly after the sale of his farm, he was induced to believe that he had sold it for less than its value. This persuasion brought on dissatisfaction, and eventually a considerable degree of melancholy. In this situation, one of his neighbours engaged him to enclose a lot of land with a post and rail fence, which he was to commence making the next day. At the time appointed he went into the field, and began, with a beetle and wedges, to split the timber out of which the posts and rails were to be prepared. On finishing his day's work, he put his beetle and wedges into a hollow tree, and went home. Two of his sons had been at work through the day in a distant part of the same field. On his return, he directed them to get up early the next morning, to assist him in making the fence. In the course of the evening he became delirious, and continued in this situation several years ; when his mental powers were suddenly restored. The first question which he asked after the return of his reason, was, whether his sons had brought in the

beetle and wedges.   He appeared to be wholly un
conscious of the time that had elapsed from the
commencement of his delirium.   His sons, apprehensive that any explanations might induce a return
of his disease, simply replied that they had been unable to find them.   He immediately arose from his
bed, went into the field where he had been at work
a number of years before, and found the wedges
and the rings of the beetle where he had left them,
the beetle itself having mouldered away.   During
his delirium, his mind had not been occupied with
those subjects with which it was conversant in
health."

The question so promptly put by the individual
who is the subject of this narrative, in regard to the
beetle and wedges, seems to indicate clearly that his
mental disorder extended to that form of mental action which is involved in the origination of our ideas
of TIME.   There was, subjectively or relatively to
the mind, a virtual extinction of time.   It could not
well be otherwise.   The mind, in its actual position,
was incapable of revealing a distinct and well-reg-
ulated conception of it.   The philosophy in this
case, and the facts which are narrated, evidently correspond to each other.

§ 118. *Varieties or peculiarities in disordered ideas
of Time.*

We may add here, and in connexion with what
has been said, that disordered time assumes very
different phases in different persons.   Sometimes
it is annihilated, lost beyond recovery, as in some of

the instances which have been mentioned. Sometimes it stops short in its movement ; or, if it moves
at all, returns at brief intervals upon its own steps,
and continually revolves around the same point ; as
in the case of Dr. Gall's madman of Vienna, who
believed it was always the 17th of October. But in
other cases, it appears to take a new pair of wings,
and fly with astonishing rapidity, so that the madman
seems to live years, perhaps centuries, in an hour.
This last view receives some confirmation in the
statements of persons who have been on the point of
drowning, but have been rescued from that situation.
These persons inform us, that the operations of their
minds were exceedingly quickened. Their families, their friends, their past life, with its thousand minute incidents, presented themselves before the mind
with the greatest rapidity ; in appearance almost simultaneously. The consequence was, that time was
greatly expanded ; and a few moments became of
almost interminable length. The author of the Confessions of an Opium Eater, who has already been
quoted, refers to this state of mind, particularly as
it developed itself in his dreams. After saying that
space was amplified to an unutterable infinity, he
adds : " This, however, did not disturb me so much
as the *vast expansion of time*. I sometimes seemed
to have lived seventy or a hundred years in one
night. Nay, sometimes had feelings representative
of a millennium passed in that time." In another
place he speaks of himself as " being buried for a
thousand years in stone coffins, with mummies and

sphinxes, in narrow chambers, in the heart of eternal pyramids."

We propose to go no further under this head, viz., of Original Suggestion, although there are other important ideas which, in their origin, may be attributed to this source.   Indeed, it is not necessary, nor even proper, to say everything under every subordinate division which might be said.   The powers of the mind are in their exercise so implicated with each other, and disorder in one part so frequently extends to another part, that such a course would be likely.to be attended with too many needless repetitions.

CHAPTER II.

DISORDERED CONSCIOUSNESS.

§ 119. *Of the meaning of the term Consciousness.*

WE proceed now to the second great source of internal knowledge, viz., Consciousness.—The term Consciousness, as we had occasion to remark in one of the Introductory chapters, is appropriated to express the way or method in which we obtain the knowledge of those objects which belong to the mind itself, and which do not, and cannot exist, in dependently of some mind.   Imagination and rea soning, as was also remarked in the chapter just re ferred to, are terms expressive of real objects of thought ; but evidently, the objects for which they stand cannot be supposed to exist, independently of some mind which imagines and reasons. Hence every instance of Consciousness may be regarded as embracing in itself three distinct notions at least, viz., the idea of Self or of personal existence ; besides this, the idea or notion of some quality, state, or operation of the mind; and also the relative perception of possession, appropriation, or belonging to, which announces or substantiates the mental quality, whatever it is, as an attribute of the person or self.

It may be added further, in connexion with this topic, that Consciousness, properly speaking, relates exclusively to the present time, and takes no cognizance of the past. We cannot be said, in strictness of speech, to be conscious of the feelings which we had yesterday, but merely of the *recollection* of them. But we may be conscious of any mental acts or feelings which exist now.

§ 120. *Two forms of disordered Consciousness.*

It will be particularly understood, from what has been said, that the great fact of Consciousness always implies something in the first person ; an EGO ; in plain English, a SELF or I. The terms SELF MYSELF, I, and the like, are expressions for the simple fact of our personal existence, which is one of our earliest conceptions, and is made known by what we have denominated Original Suggestion. Consciousness, in distinction from this, expresses the fact, that we naturally and necessarily recognise all

R

the acts or operations of the mental part, of the SELF or I, as belonging to such mental SELF or I; in other words, as belonging to our own minds.— Consequently, in a sound state of Consciousness, the EGO or I is one, and one only; and all mental acts and operations are promptly and invariably referred to this great centre of personality. And, on the other hand, there is an insanity of mind (specifically an insanity of Consciousness) when the EGO becomes divided; in other words, when a man has a different self at different times; and also in all cases when Consciousness is unable to connect an individual's mental acts or operations invariably with one and the same personal centre.

In accordance with these views, there are two forms, at least, of an unsound state of Consciousness; FIRST, Suspended Consciousness, which is the more common form, and, SECOND, Divided or Intermittent Consciousness.

§ 121. *Illustrations of suspended Consciousness.*

Various instances are recorded of what may be called SUSPENDED CONSCIOUSNESS.—The case already mentioned in the preceding chapter, of the man who placed his beetle and wedges in a hollow tree, and became maniacal the night after, is an instance in point. It is, of course, unnecessary that the statement should be repeated. There is another instance found in the same Work, the American Journal of Science, vol. i., p. 432. The statement is given in the following terms:

"Mrs. S., an intelligent lady, belonging to a respectable family in the State of New-York, scme years ago undertook a piece of fine needlework. She devoted her time to it almost constantly for a number of days. Before she had completed it she became suddenly delirious. In this state, without experiencing any material abatement of her disease, she continued for about seven years, when her reason was suddenly restored. One of the first questions which she asked after her reason returned, related to her needlework. It is a remarkable fact, that during the long continuance of her delirium, she said nothing, so far as was recollected, about her needlework, nor concerning any such subjects as usually occupied her attention when in health."

The case of an English clergyman, the Rev. Simon Browne, seems properly to be mentioned here. This gentleman entertained the idea that " he had fallen under the sensible displeasure of God, who had caused his rational soul gradually to perish, and left him only an animal life in common with the brutes."* He was a man of exemplary life, and of no small ability and learning. His insanity was limited to the single conviction that, although he possessed a vital principle or sort of animal life, the perceptive and reasoning part or mind was totally extinct. Accordingly, as every case of consciousness implies not only a recognition of the mental acts, but a reference of those acts to the mind as their subject, it would seem that, in his case, consciousness was disordered and suspended.

This case, as well as the preceding one in this

* Conolly, p. 412.

section, might also have been introduced under the head of Suggestion, since the facts stated evidently involve a disordered state of the suggestive power as well as of consciousness.

§ 122. *Illustrations of divided or intermittent Consciousness.*

There are other cases of disordered consciousness, somewhat different from those which have been mentioned, which may be designated as cases ot DIVIDED or INTERMITTENT CONSCIOUSNESS. That is to say, the mind, at two different periods of time, is found to be in two different states. In one state its action is marked by certain peculiarities; it has thoughts, reasonings, feelings, remembrances peculiar to itself at that particular time. In the other state it is the subject of thoughts, reasonings, and feelings wholly different; the point of transition from one state to a subsequent one is distinct; and in the actually existing state, whatever it is, there is a forgetfulness of the other. "I once attended" (says Dr. Rush) "the daughter of a British officer, who had been educated in the habits of gay life, who was married to a Methodist minister. In her paroxysms of madness she . resumed her gay habits, spoke French, and ridiculed the tenets and practices of the sect to which she belonged. In the intervals of her fits she renounced her gay habits, became zealously devoted to the religious principles and ceremonies of the Methodists, and forgot everything she did and said during the period of her insanity."*

* Rush's Diseases of the Mind, p. 165.

The writer in the American Journal of Science, already repeatedly referred to, narrates a case which may properly be introduced here.   The case is a marked and interesting one, as follows :

" A lady in New-England, of a respectable family, was for a considerable period subject to paroxysms of delirium.   These paroxysms came on instantaneously, and, after continuing an indefinite time, went off as suddenly, leaving her mind perfectly rational.   It often happened that, when she was engaged in rational and interesting conversation, she would stop short in the midst of it, become in a moment entirely delirious, and commence a conversation on some other subject, not having the remotest connexion with the previous one, nor would she advert to that during her delirium.   When she became rational again, she would pursue the same conversation in which she had been engaged during the lucid interval, beginning where she had left off. To such a degree was this carried, that she would complete an unfinished story or sentence, or even an unfinished word.   When her next delirious paroxysm came on, she would continue the conversation which she had been pursuing in her preceding paroxysm ; so that she appeared as a person might be supposed to do who had two souls, each occasionally dormant and occasionally active, and utterly ignorant of what the other was doing."

There is a particularly interesting case of divided or intermittent consciousness to be found in the Medical Repository, in a communication from Dr. Mitchell, of the City of New-York, to the Rev. Dr Nott.

" When I was employed" (says the writer of
this communication), " early in December, 1815,
with several other gentlemen, in doing the duty
of a visiter to the United States' Military Academy at West Point, a very extraordinary case of
Double- Consciousness in a woman was related
to me by one of the professors. Major Elicott,
who so worthily occupies the mathematical chair
in that seminary, vouched for the correctness of
the following narrative, the subject of which is related to him by blood, and an inhabitant of one of
the western counties of Pennsylvania. Miss R.
possessed, naturally, a very good constitution, and
arrived at adult age without having it impaired by
disease. She possessed an excellent capacity, and
enjoyed fair opportunities to acquire knowledge.
Besides the domestic arts and social attainments,
she had improved her mind by reading and conversation, and was well versed in penmanship. Her
memory was capacious, and stored with a copious
stock of ideas. Unexpectedly, and without any
forewarning, she fell into a profound sleep, which
continued several hours beyond the ordinary term.
On waking, she was discovered to have lost every
trait of acquired knowledge. Her memory was
tabula rasa; all vestiges, both of words and things,
were obliterated and gone. It was found necessary
for her to learn everything again. She even acquired, by new efforts, the art of spelling, reading, writing, and calculating, and gradually became acquainted with the persons and objects around, like a being
for the first time brought into the world. In these

exercises she made considerable proficiency. But, after a few months, another fit of somnolency invaded her. On rousing from it, she found herself restored to the state she was in before the first paroxysm, but was wholly ignorant of every event and occurrence that had befallen her afterward. The former condition of her existence she now calls the Old State, and the latter the New State; and she is as unconscious of her double character as two distinct persons are of their respective natures. For example, in her old state, she possesses all her original knowledge; in her new state, only what she acquired since. If a gentleman or lady be introduced to her in the old state, and *vice versa* (and so of all other matters), to know them satisfactorily she must learn them in both states. In the old state she possesses fine powers of penmanship, while in the new she writes a poor, awkward hand, having not had time or means to become expert. During four years and upward, she has undergone periodical transitions from one of these states to the other. The alterations are always consequent upon a long and sound sleep. Both the lady and her family are now capable of conducting the affair without embarrassment. By simply knowing whether she is in the old or new state, they regulate the intercourse, and govern themselves accordingly."

It would not be difficult, probably, to multiply cases similar to those which have been mentioned. They are of great interest in themselves, and they seem clearly to establish the existence of that peculiar form of mental disorder in connexion with which

they are introduced.   It is unnecessary, after what
has already been said, and especially in connexion
with what remains to be said, to intimate how erroneous was that ancient doctrine of insanity, which
resolved it, in all cases and under all its aspects, into
one type or form.

CHAPTER III.

DISORDERED ACTION OF RELATIVE SUGGESTION OR JUDGMENT.

§ 123. *Relative Suggestion or Judgment a distinct Power.*

AMONG other powers or susceptibilities of the
human mind is that by which we perceive or feel
the relation of objects to each other in certain respects.   The office of this power is not merely to
perceive objects in themselves, which may be done
by means of the senses, or by original suggestion, or
in some other way, but precisely what has been said,
viz., to perceive and to make known to us their relations.   Hence the name, which is properly given
to it, that of RELATIVE SUGGESTION ; although, as
we have already stated in a previous chapter, it is
frequently expressed by the less definite term JUDG-
MENT.   We shall employ the two terms, in what
we have to say at present, as synonymous with each
other.

The power of relative suggestion, or the judgment, if we choose so to term it, is very properly regarded in systems of Mental Philosophy as a connatural and ultimate principle of the mind ; in other words, a principle so thoroughly elementary, that it cannot be resolved into any other.   The human intellect is so made, so constituted, that, when it perceives different objects together, or has immediately successive conceptions of any absent objects of perception, their mutual relations (we do not mean to say all, but some of them at least) are immediately felt by it.

§ 124. *Of the views which have sometimes been taken of this power.*

We are aware, however, that the view which has now been presented, and which is the prevalent one at the present time, has not always been taken.   It has sometimes been made a question whether man really possesses the power under consideration, regarded as a distinct and original power.   Some of the earlier French philosophers seem to have espoused the negative of this question.   It was the doctrine of Helvetius, and of the French philosophic school generally, which was predominant in his day, that all mental acts may be resolved into Sensation. "All the operations of the mind" (he expressly says) "are reduced to mere sensations.   Why then admit in man a faculty of *judging* distinct from the faculty of sensation."*   He then goes on with a

* Helvetius on Man, Hooper's translation, sec. ii. chs. iii., iv., and v.

train of reasoning, to show that the comparing or
judging power and sensation are essentially one.

This, as seems to be generally conceded at the
present time, is an erroneous view of the human
mind ; a doctrine equally at variance with our personal consciousness, and with the facts gathered from
the observation of others.   Nothing can be more
obvious than the fact, notwithstanding the assertions
of these writers, that men possess not only the powers of sensation and of external perception, but of
judgment, in the positive and full sense of that term ;
that is, of perceiving the relations of agreement and
disagreement, and other relations existing in the objects which they perceive.   But this is not all.   It
is not enough to say that the power of Relative
Suggestion or Judgment has an existence merely.
It is necessary to add, that it is a leading power of
the mind ; a characteristic and exceedingly important
element ; one which not only furnishes an explanation, to a considerable extent, of man's intellectual
ability, but of those diversities of mental efficiency
by which one man is distinguished from another.

§ 125. *Weak or disordered Judgment arising from*
natural obtuseness of Mind.

Without delaying longer upon the subject of the
existence and of the nature of this power, we shall
proceed at once to consider it in connexion with the
general inquiry of imperfect and disordered mental
action.   And our first general remark is, that an
imperfect, defective, or disordered judgment may
exist in various forms.   I.—In the first place we

discover in some persons, owing to the original constitution of the mind, or to accidental injuries, or occasionally, perhaps, to some other causes, an obtuseness or want of quickness in relative perceptions. The external perceptive faculties of these persons may be sufficiently acute and active ; they may exhibit a quick reception of everything which is addressed to the outward senses ; but, when they are required to judge of one thing as compared with another, and to indicate in what they agree and in what they differ, and thus to call into exercise the discriminating power in distinction from mere perception, they discover at once a degree of mental inferiority, which would not have been suspected by merely looking at another form of mental action. This trait of mind is happily described by Dr. Conolly in the following terms.—" Defect of the Comparing power" [by which he means the judgment, as every act of judging involves comparison] " is observable in the pursuits and progress of many men in all professions. The industry of such men is great, but often ill-directed : they do not distinguish trifles from things of importance, and are generally occupied about matters of little worth. In my own profession, we see such minds engaged in the prosecution of minute observations ; all the larger features of pathology, all general principles of practice, escape them ; but a symptom not heeded or not valued by others, or any deviation from common anatomical arrangement, or a line in the face, or a pimple on the hand, or a streak on the tongue, or a pretended specific, fills them with the anticipated delight of a dis-

covery.   They do not compare one symptom with
another ; they pronounce diseases to exist which
are really not present ; they do not contrast the reputation of a new medicine with that of other medicines, once brought forward in the same way, and
then abandoned ; they do not compare effects with
causes, but suppose they have cured diseases which
were only imaginary, with specifics of which the
virtue is equally imaginary ; and thus, but in a state
of continual satisfaction, they grow old without experience.   These errors and many others, to which
something analogous may doubtless be found in every department of study, arise from defective powers
of comparing one thing with another."

§ 126. *Disordered Judgment as connected with incapacity of Attention.*

II.—In other cases the defect in the exercises of
the power of Judgment does not seem to be owing
so much to any obtuseness in the power itself, as to
an inability of fixing the attention, and a consequent
rapid transition from one object to another.   There
are some men who have a quick perception, who
bestow more or less notice on almost everything
which comes in their way, but do not appear to be
capable of a fixedness or continuity of thought.   They
are like the winds, always in motion, but always
veering from one point of the compass to another.

This state of things may be owing to two causes
in particular ; FIRST, a want of voluntary energy ;
SECOND, a disordered action of the principle of association.—Where there is a want of voluntary power,

it will be found difficult, in a multitude of cases, to keep the mind long enough fixed upon the object of inquiry to estimate it properly in all its bearings. I am aware that some writers adopt the opinion, that the Will has no direct power over trains of thought, either in originating them, or in directing and regulating them when they are already called into existence. But this opinion, so far at' least as it relates to the regulation of trains of thought already present to the mind, is undoubtedly an erroneous one. The power of the Will is unquestionably great in this respect; but it is no less true, that it is much greater in some persons than in others. In some it is very deficient; and the consequence is an incapacity of continuity of thought, and a rapid transition from one thing to another, which is necessarily very unfavourable to accurate judgment.

But that trait of mind which we are now considering is more frequently owing to a disordered action, or, at least, a peculiarity in the principle of Association. The peculiarity of mind which we now have in view is known in common parlance under the designation of "light-headedness." And we often speak of the persons who exhibit it as "flighty" or "hairbrained," in consequence of their thoughts flying rapidly from one thing to another. But as it will be necessary to recur to this subject under another head, we will not dwell upon it here.—All we have to add is, that whether this unfixedness and evanescence of perception be owing to a weakness of the Will or to a too rapid action of the Associating principle, it is in either case inconsistent, to a

great degree, with entire soundness of Judgment.
And one, at least, of the forms of disordered Judgment is to be explained by keeping these facts in
view.

§ 127. *Of disordered Judgment in connexion with facility of Belief.*

III.—Another form of weak or imperfect Judgment seems to be closely connected with a disordered state of the susceptibility of Belief. There
are some persons whom, in consequence of the facility with which they receive the statements made
to them, we are accustomed to designate as CREDU-
LOUS persons. And it will hardly be denied, that
we generally connect the idea of weakness of Judgment with the existence, whenever it is ascertained
to be a permanent mental trait, of Credulity.

Credulous persons (pursuing the subject a little
more into particulars) take statements too much
upon trust. It is a characteristic trait, that they receive without hesitation the most exaggerated accounts. Their belief, instead of being graduated to
the degrees of presumption, probability, and certainty, in some degree of accordance with the evidence,
assumes the highest form at once, and receives everything that is proposed to it as a thing unquestionable.

Now let us consider a moment the bearing of this
state of things on the Judgment. It is evidently not
so much the office of the Judgment, in its original
and appropriate exercise, to ascertain facts, as to
ascertain the relations existing among them, and to

decide upon their character, as compared one with another. Furthermore, it is not the less clear that facts, as they come under the cognizance of the Judgment, exist in the mind in the shape of beliefs, either presumptive, probable, or certain. And if the position of the belief be wrong, it does not easily appear how the decision of the Judgment, which is founded upon such belief, can be right.

We have here, therefore, another class of persons who exhibit a defective or disordered Judgment; the defect arising not so much from anything in the judging power itself, as from its connexion with the disordered action of another susceptibility.

It seems to be this form of disordered judgment, more than any other, which is found in that busy, amusing, and sometimes beneficial class of men who are known as Projectors. These persons are not only characterized by adopting some new idea, or forming some untried plan, or prosecuting some novel invention, which a man of very sound judgment may sometimes do; but the difficulty is, that the thing, whatever it is, at once assumes a disproportionate place in the estimation of the mind. It not only controls the belief inordinately, but may be said to occupy the whole heart; either banishing for a time all other objects of contemplation, or making them entirely subordinate. And there is this further difficulty, that the strong passion which these persons exhibit, whether it exists in the shape of love, or of faith, or in some other form, is less permanent than strong. It is very desultory; excitable and powerful while it lasts. but suddenly changing its object; and, both in its location and its transitions, in its excessive adhesions at one time and its sudden disruptions at another, is the subject of abundant ridicule to those sober and discriminating minds, that have less facility of belief as well as less energy of emotion.

§ 128. *Of disordered Judgment in connexion with obstinacy of Belief.*

IV.—Another form of disordered Judgment is owing to the fact of its being connected with extreme obstinacy of Belief, and is nearly the opposite of that which has just been mentioned. The persons to whom we now refer attach themselves to a particular object or to a particular aspect of an object; they seize upon a particular opinion, or, perhaps, the minute fragment of an opinion; and they hold it with a tenacity which neither life nor death can separate. All appeals to their feelings, to their sympathies, to their common humanity, would be out of place, and abundantly ridiculous. " Leviathan is not so tamed." But this is not all. With imperturbable coolness, they turn the scaly hide of their obstinacy to the fiery darts of truth, and shake them off unharmed. No statements of facts, no suggestions of venerable wisdom, no deductions of reasoning, and, least of all, the persuasions even of Athenian eloquence, have the effect to disturb, even for a moment, the invincibility of their adhesion. They give themselves up to their object, "for better or worse;" not temporarily, but, as it were, through all time.

This is, perhaps, a strong statement; but it shows what we mean. It would be absurd to say that this state of things does not imply a disordered action of the mind. But undoubtedly there are varieties here as elsewhere.

§ 129. *Of mere unsoundness in distinction from insanity of Judgment.*

We have thus given some general and imperfect idea of the more common forms of defective or disordered Judgment; but we do not wish the reader to understand, that the matter, as we have now stated it, comes up to the true idea of INSANITY of the Judgment. The cases which have been stated are such as occur very frequently; and, though they disqualify the persons to whom they attach for very many things, these persons may still, in many respects, be very valuable men. Their judgment is perplexed in its action, and enfeebled, but not extinct. It may even be found, in some individuals, to possess a high degree of strength, when exercised upon any or all matters which do not come within the reach of the intellectual malady.

Insanity of the Judgment, in distinction from mere ordinary defect or disorder, implies something more. It implies an entire disqualification of correct views, either upon all subjects or upon some particular subjects. Not necessarily upon all, because we sometimes find the insanity directing itself to a particular thing, and not extending beyond it. In illustration of what has now been said, take the case of the Projector, the man of new schemes. His de-

S

votedness to the particular object before him is, in
many cases, essentially harmless and amusing rather
than otherwise.   His time is occupied ; he is abundantly happy in prosecuting to its anticipated results
the "grand experiment ;" and when the experiment
fails ; when the bubble, which had so long delighted
him, bursts, he has the satisfaction of knowing, whatever may be true of himself, that he has contributed
to the happiness of others, by exciting to activity the
pleasant sentiment of the ridiculous.   Such cases
as these are the more frequent and common cases ;
and they are indicative, beyond all question, of real
unsoundness of mind ; but common parlance would
not, as a general thing, speak of these persons as
"mad people," as "crazy people."   They certainly
are not to be regarded as suitable candidates for
banishment from society, for guardianship, and for
hospitals.   With all their faults, they are often found
to have their associates and friends, and are often
deeply loved in their families.

Nevertheless, it must be acknowledged that they
approximate, if they are not already on the very borders of that frightful condition of mind, which insanity, in the more common acceptation of the term, is
understood to indicate.   They stand, dizzy-headed,
on the brink of the precipice.   Sometimes the malady increases.   They engage in plans which every-
body else knows to be not only doubtful, but even
hopeless.   They are unable to do anything else ;
they exaggerate the importance of their object ; they
dissipate their property, ruin their health, and distress their families.   These people are called crazy,

and they *are* so. They are unable to see the precise and full relations of things. They omit to take into account a multitude of circumstances, which are necessary to such precision and comprehensiveness of relative perception. In a single word, the inexpressibly important trait of sound judgment is not merely .weakened or perplexed (which is the fact in all cases of disordered judgment), but is annihilated. Insanity, in the strict sense of the term, has supervened ; and there is an evident necessity of the substitution of the guidance of friends and of the law for their own personal and self-responsible control.

CHAPTER IV.

DISORDERED ACTION OF THE PRINCIPLE OF ASSOCIATION.

§ 130. *General remarks on the nature of Association.*

THE laws of the mind, the great principles which regulate its action, as well as its mere perceptions or states, may be disordered ; for instance, the laws of Association. The term Association expresses the general fact, that there is a regular consecution of the mental states. This succession of mental states, however, as is well ascertained, is not an accidental and irregular one, but has its laws. The leading laws of Association, modified by some subordinate ones, are Resemblance, Contrast, Contiguity in time and place, and Cause and Effect. Such is the specific and just operation of these laws in their application to the thoughts and feelings, that a just and coherent action, in other words, a movement regularly successive, and reducible to fixed principles, will characterize the operations of the mind in a perfectly sane state. When the mind is disordered in the associating principle, the mental action will be very different; characterized by wildness, exceedingly rapid transitions, and, in general, by great incoherency. Perhaps an instance of this form of insanity, taken from real life, will best illustrate what we mean to say. The following extract was taken down from the remarks of an insane young man of a good education, who was formerly detained as a lunatic in the Pennsylvania Hospital.

"No man can serve two masters. I am King Philip of Macedonia, lawful son of Mary, Queen of Scots, born in Philadelphia. I have been happy enough ever since I have seen General Washington with a silk handkerchief in High-street. Money commands sublunary things, and makes the mare go; it will buy salt mackerel, made of tenpenny nails. Enjoyment is the happiness of virtue. Yesterday cannot be recalled. I can only walk in the nighttime, when I can eat pudding enough. I shall be eight years old to-morrow. They say R. W. is in partnership with J. W I believe they are about as good as people in common; not better, only on certain occasions, when, for instance, a man wants to buy chincopins, and to import salt to feed pigs.

Tanned leather was imported first by lawyers. Mo·
rality with virtue is like vice not corrected. L. B.
came into your house and stole a coffeepot in the
twenty-fourth year of his majesty's reign. Plum-
pudding and Irish potatoes make a very good dinner.
Nothing in man is comprehensible to it. Born in
Philadelphia. Our forefathers were better to us
than our children, because they were chosen for
their honesty, truth, virtue, and innocence. The
Queen's broad R. originated from a British forty-
two pounder, which makes too large a report for
me. I have no more to say. I am thankful I am
no worse this season, and that I am sound in mind
and memory, and could steer a ship to sea, but am
afraid of the thiller. ****** ******, son of Mary,
Queen of Scots. Born in Philadelphia. Born in
Philadelphia. King of Macedonia."*

This extract will serve to explain what we have
said in respect to a want of coherency and regularity
of mental action, where the associating principle is
disordered. In all cases of perfectly sound mental
action, there is a chain, a connecting link, binding
one part of the train of thought to another; generally easily discoverable, but less obvious in some
cases than others. But in the extract which has
been given, and in all similar cases of disordered
mind, it is very different. Nearly each successive
thought has the appearance of being entirely independent of what went before.

* Rush's Diseases of the Mind.

§ 131. *Of sluggish and ineffective Association.*

Imperfect and disordered association exists in a number of varieties, and assumes various aspects. There are some cases where the Associating principle appears to be more sluggish and ineffective in its action than would naturally be expected in a perfectly symmetrical mind. The action of the mind is amazingly slow; it seems to labour under a sort of paralytic torpidity; so much so, that it creeps on with great difficulty from one topic to another. This is sometimes noticed in conversation. We are conversing, for instance, with such a person; as a natural result of the effort of conversation, we become in some degree excited; our minds, in consequence of greater associating activity, take a position far ahead; and we look back with a degree of impatience for the corresponding movements of our sluggish interlocutor. After a while we discover in his uplifted eye the gleams of nascent intelligence, and a thought, perhaps a very just and appropriate one, emerges from the depths of mental inactivity, which we imagine, judging from our own different mental structure, ought to have .been on its journey long before.

The facetious author of Knickerbocker's History of New-York, in exaggerating some peculiarities of national character, has given an uncommonly favourable view of this mental defect, viz., *the ideas are so large they cannot be turned over.* He is speaking of the venerable Wouter Van Twiller. "He was a man shut up within himself like an oyster, and of such a profoundly reflective turn, that he scarcely ever spoke, except in monosyllables, yet did he never make up his mind on any doubtful point. This was clearly accounted for by his adherents, who affirmed, that he always conceived every object on so comprehensive a scale, that he had not room in his head to turn it over and examine both sides of it, so that he always remained in doubt, merely in consequence of the astonishing magnitude of his ideas."

It is here, in the view which has now been given, we find one element of that great phasis of human nature, mental dulness or stupidity. We do not mean Idiocy, but merely dulness, a want of a quick and penetrating apprehension of things. We say that we find here *one* element of this, because the elements, or, rather, the sources of dulness, are many, and are implicated in various parts of the mental structure. A man may be accounted a dull or stupid person in consequence of a naturally dull or blunted power of external perception, or in consequence of a weakness in the power of relative suggestion, or in consequence of a great defect in the imaginative power, as well from the circumstance of great weakness and tardiness in the action of the associating principle.

§ 132. *Of mental defect in consequence of too quick and rapid Association.*

A more striking associative defect than that which we have just been commenting on, is one of a directly opposite kind, viz., too great rapidity of association. We not unfrequently find persons whose thoughts fly from one subject to another with great rapidity ; not by choice or an act of the will, but in spite of it. A rapid transference of the mind by a voluntary act (a trait which is recorded of some distinguished men, such as Julius Cæsar and Napoleon Bonaparte), is clearly an evidence of mental power ; a like rapidity of transition, which is not voluntary, is not less clearly an evidence of mental weakness. Persons of this description exhibit what may be called an *incontinence* of thought ; there is no conservative power of restraint ; the floodgates of the mind are thrown open, and it rushes onward, not to some fixed and available consummation, but in every possible direction, and bearing every strange thing in its current.

It is worthy of remark, that the trait of mind under consideration is commonly attended with great volubility of tongue, and also with almost constant motion of the body. It is well known that the mental action, as a general thing, has its external signs. And in this case there is an agitation and movement of the outward members, and a rapidity of utterance corresponding to the unfixed and rapid movement within. We have already had occasion to refer to the relation existing between this form of disordered association and a defective or disordered judgment. As the subject of this form of derangement is incapable of checking and regulating the train of his ideas, so as to make them distinct objects of comparison and reflection, it is a matter of course, that he constantly forms incorrect judgments of things.

§ 133. *Instances illustrative of the preceding section.*

Almost every one will recollect instances within the circle of his own acquaintance, which illustrate the mental traits that have now been described. And not a few cases have been made matters of record by medical and other writers. An English clergyman who visited Lavater, the distinguished physiognomist, has given an account of that singular character, which seems to me accurately to illustrate one of the less marked forms of the mental disorder now before us.—" I was detained" (says he) " the whole morning by the strange, wild, eccentric Lavater, in various conversations. When once he is set a going, there is no such thing as stopping him till he runs himself out of breath. He starts from subject to subject, flies from book to book, from picture to picture ; measures your nose, your eye, your mouth, with a pair of compasses ; pours forth a torrent of physiognomy upon you ; drags you, for a proof of his dogma, to a dozen of closets, and unfolds ten thousand drawings ; but will not let you open your lips to propose a difficulty ; and crams a solution down your throat before you have uttered half a syllable of your objection.

‘ He is as meager as the picture of famine ; his nose and chin almost meet. I read him in my turn, and found little difficulty in discovering, amid great genius, unaffected piety, unbounded benevolence, and moderate learning, much caprice and unsteadiness, a mind at once aspiring by nature and

grovelling through necessity ; an endless turn to
speculation and project ; in a word, a clever, flighty,
good-natured, necessitous man."*

Dr. Conolly also happily illustrates the subject,
although the case seems to have been less marked
and decisive than the one just mentioned, in his reference to a man who was unable to tell a story
continuously from beginning to end.—" He would
begin with the best intentions, and proceed a little
way tolerably well ; but the chairs and tables, and
all the objects around him, a hat hung upon a peg,
or an ornament in the chimney-piece, would become
interwoven with his narrative, and lead him from
subject to subject with irresistible rapidity."

§ 134. *Remarks on Fickleness of Character.*

Some cases of what are called FICKLENESS OF
CHARACTER may be explained in connexion with the
mental traits which have now been described.—The
opposite of fickleness of character is permanency ;
that is to say, a continuity and fixedness of plan and
pursuit, unless there are sound reasons for a change.
The fickle man is pleased with new objects ; they
assume an undue place in his estimation, as compared with other objects which have previously interested him ; and he is found frequently changing
from one thing to another.

This trait of mind, it is true, may sometimes be
owing to other causes than that which we are particularly considering in this connexion.   It is sometimes, for instance, found connected with great

* As quoted by Dr. Rush in his Diseases of the Mind.

quickness of sensibility. A person susceptible of very vivid emotions is more likely to be affected by present objects than another; and, in consequence of this, may attach an undue. value to them, which may lead to an uncertain and vacillating course of conduct.

Fickleness of character, a trait which is obviously very prejudicial to any person, may also, and, perhaps, more frequently, find its basis in a variable and incontinent action of the associating principle. It will not be necessary to delay, after the illustrations which have already been given, and the remarks already made in various places, in order to show how this may be the case.

§ 135. *Of temporary excitement of the Associating Principle.*

Persons of minds that, in their ordinary action, are apparently, in all respects, sound and symmetrical, are at times subject to singular excitements of the associating principle. The cause of this peculiar mental malady is commonly to be sought for in a disordered condition of the physical system. The late Professor Fisher, of New-Haven, has left a statement illustrative of this inordinate mental affection. Like that of Nicolai, it is the more valuable in coming from a scientific man, as the narration is, in consequence, placed above any suspicion of mistake. It was in his case, however, not a permanent, but merely a *temporary* state of the mind, arising unquestionably, as is generally the fact in this form of disorder, from some physical derangement.—" To whatever subject" (he says) "I happened to direct my thoughts, my mind was crowded with ideas upon it. I seemed to myself able to wield the most diffi cult subjects with perfect ease, and to have an entire command over my own train of thought. I found myself wonderfully inventive; scarce a subject presented itself in which I did not seem to myself to perceive, as it were by intuition, important improvements. I slept but a part of the night, my mind being intensely occupied with planning, inventing, &c. All the writing that I did was done in the utmost hurry. Ideas crowded upon me five times as fast as I could put down even hints of them, and my sole object was to have some memorial by which they might be recalled. I was employed the whole time in the most intense meditation; and, at the same time, thinking never seemed to be attended with so little effort. I did not experience the least confu sion or fatigue of mind. My thoughts flowed with a rapidity that was prodigious; and the faculties of association, memory, &c., were wonderfully raised. I could read different languages into English, and English into Hebrew, with a fluency which I was never before or since master of. During the whole time, though I was in a low state of health, I never felt the least pain or fatigue of body."

§ 136. *Additional instance of this view of the subject.*

A striking instance of quickened association recently occurred under my immediate notice. A student had, by special efforts, wrought himself into considerable mental excitement on religious subjects; and this unusual rapidity and power of mental action soon transferred itself to scientific subjects.   In this state of things he was led to direct his attention (a very unfortunate direction of the mind under such circumstances) to the difficult subjects of Fore-knowledge, Free Agency, and Time.   In the course of a day or two, he was very much absorbed in the latter subject in particular.   It was now that conceptions, strange and unheard of before, came into his mind.   Thinking was no task to him.   His thoughts flowed with very great rapidity.   Among other things, he made a grand discovery, or what he considered to be such, viz., not only that *God is truth*, but the converse of the proposition also, which is a very different thing, viz., that *truth is God.* His grand discovery he supposed to be the commencement of the long-expected millennium; and, as such, it was an era never to be forgotten; and his imagination was full of the glorious events about to follow.   For a week he slept almost none, and ate but very little; and his nervous system was evidently very much disordered.   Finally, he reduced everything, mind and matter, infinite worlds and countless intelligences, and all forms of knowledge, to this simple equation, *to wit*, $1+1=2$.

The young gentleman read his lucubrations to myself and another person, who I suppose is capable of understanding any ordinary flights of intellect; but, humbling as it was, we were obliged to confess our inability to understand the nature of his wonderful discoveries.   However, he consoled himself with

the saying of Scripture, that not many wise men
after the flesh are called ; and continued to pursue
the subject of his inquiries in his own way.   In his
own language, " his whole soul was absorbed and
drawn forth with an intensity utterly inconceivable
by any one who never experienced the like.   Ideas
were rushing into his mind in torrents.   He was
exceedingly inventive.   He could not write one idea
in ten.   He could have dictated to ten amanuenses.
His powers of memory and association were quickened in a wonderful degree.   He could make all
he ever knew converge, like rays from the burning-
glass, to one tremendous focus.   He had the whole
Bible at his tongue's end.   Every muscle of his soul
was in exercise, but he felt no fatigue."   He began
to write a book, which he thought would be another
inspired volume ; and he accordingly divided it into
chapters and verses.   Finally, his mind was carried
forward with such rapidity, and into such before unknown conceptions, that he began to doubt his identity.   Sometimes he thought that Christ had reappeared on earth in his own person, and at other
times he questioned whether Paul or Adam had not
thus appeared.   But, however he might doubt of
this point, he was certain of one thing, that true religion was to be propagated by his instrumentality
through the world.   He read, in particular, the
prophet Daniel and the Revelation, and every syllable was as plain as the multiplication table.   He
searched in these books for some prediction concerning himself ; and, though not successful, discovered, as he thought, all the mysteries of Masonry and

of the Romish church. The Bible was a new book to him. He fastened his eyes on its pages with maddening intensity.

In this state of mind he had determined upon leaving college, with the intention of communicating his discoveries to the world. But being at last persuaded by some friends that this was improper, and that his mind was somewhat out of order, he was finally induced to take some medicine, leave books, mingle in society, and divert the mind in every possible way. In this way a check was given to the mental disease; the mind gradually recovered a healthy tone, and all his wonderful discoveries vanished like a dream.

CHAPTER V.

DISORDERED ACTION OF THE MEMORY.

§ 137. *General nature of the Memory.*

THE examination of the Memory, considered as the subject of imperfections and irregularities of action, naturally follows that of Association. In its general nature, we cannot but suppose that the memory, a power so constant in its action and so important in its results, is well understood; certainly so much so as to require but few words to be said upon that point.

On another occasion, and having other objects in view, we proposed to define the Memory as that power or susceptibility of the mind by which those conceptions are originated which are modified by a perception of the relation of past time. Accordingly, we are to regard it as a complex rather than a simple principle; implying, when called into exercise, 1. A conception of the object; 2. A perception of the relation of priority in time. That is to say, we not only have a conception of the remembered object, but this conception is attended with the conviction, that it underwent the examination of our senses, or was in some way perceived by us at some former period.

The intellectual principle which we designate as the memory, whatever views may be taken of its general nature, is subject to various disorders. The other parts of the intellect, such as the powers of perception, association, imagination, and reasoning, may be sound and regular in their movement, at least so far as they are able to act independent of the memory; while the action of the latter power is either essentially obliterated, or is the subject of strange and unaccountable deviations.

§ 138. *Cases involving a general prostration of the Memory.*

One class of cases, where we perceive a disorganization of the memory, are those in which there is a general prostration of power; in other words, a defect or prostration of power, not limited, as is sometimes the case, to particular objects, but

extending to all.   Such cases sometimes occur.
Individuals are found from time to time, in whom
the power of memory seems to be entirely gone ;
plucked up, as it were, and erased from the mind ;
giving scarcely the least sign of vivification.

This form of defective memory is sometimes natural or congenital.   Persons may come into the
world almost entirely destitute of the power of memory, just as some other persons come into the world
destitute, in an equal degree, of the abstractive and
ratiocinative powers.   We do not propose, however,
to remark upon these cases here.   A general prostration of memory (saying nothing here of those cases where it is natural or congenital) may be caused
in various ways ; perhaps, we may add, in very
many ways ; some of which we shall proceed to point
out, without attempting, however, a complete enu-
meration.

1.—And, in the FIRST place, it may be caused by
the indulgence of deep and long-continued sorrow.
—This source of injury to the memory is somewhat
frequent.   A person, for instance,. finds himself the
subject of various and great disappointments.   Grief,
seated deeply at the heart, continually preys upon
him ; and one of the early and very common results, as already intimated, is a weakness, and ultimately an entire prostration of the memory.   How
this happens, although there can be no question as
to the fact, it may not be entirely easy to see.   But
the explanation may, in part, perhaps, be this.   The
mind is so entirely occupied with the particular subject of its sorrow, whatever it is, that it feels no in

T

terest in anything else, and gives no attention ; and
the natural consequence of this state of things is,
to a greater or less extent, a defect of memory.
It is a great law of the memory, that it must and
will fail where there is a want of attention, or, what
is nearly the same thing, a want of interest.

2.—We not unfrequently see, in the second place,
an almost entire prostration of the memory caused
by the advances and influences of extreme old age.
The explanation in this case seems to be this.   In
the great mass of mankind there is but little developement of the Internal Intellect ; the mind almost
exclusively operates in connexion with what is presented to the cognizance of the outward senses :
so that their knowledge, whatever may be its amount,
deals chiefly with the outward and visible, and rests
substantially upon a basis of materiality.   Accordingly, when their outward senses fail ; when the eye,
and the ear, and the taste no longer furnish their wont
ed materials for the mental action, it is no wonder
that their minds, so far as they have ever been called into exercise, should sink back into a state of utter sluggishness and decrepitude, and that the memory should suffer at the same time with the other
mental powers.

3.—The memory sometimes fails, furthermore,
and fails utterly, in connexion with some violent
disease.   Such is the close connexion between the
physical and mental system, particularly between the
brain and the mind, that an affection of the former,
as we have already had occasion to remark, is very
likely to be attended with an affection of the latter.

Accordingly, it is sometimes the case, that a violent fever, a sudden and violent blow on the head, and other causes of physical injury and disorder, are followed by an entire loss of the power of recollection.

§ 139. *Of loss of memory in relation to particular subjects.*

It is one peculiarity of disordered memory, that it sometimes exists exclusively in relation to particular subjects. A certain portion or section of the memory seems to be lost, while in all its applications beyond these particular limits, whatever they may be, it remains unimpaired.

It does not appear that any explanation of these cases has been given, or is likely to be given, which will be generally satisfactory. They undoubtedly involve the general fact of a connexion between the mind and the body, particularly between the mind and the brain; but do not seem to admit of a definite and specific explanation, which will not be found to be attended with some formidable objections. Accordingly, in this state of things, we shall feel at liberty merely to give some facts or instances, without attempting to go further.

Dr. Beattie mentions the case of a person who, in consequence of a violent blow on the head, lost his knowledge of the Greek language, but did not appear to have lost anything else. It is related of a certain Spanish author (Good's Study of Medicine, vol. iv.), that, being attacked by an acute fever, he forgot all the languages he ever knew, and had no recollection even of his own writings. It does not appear, from anything that is said in connexion with this statement, that this person's memory was equally impaired on other subjects. Dr. Good also mentions the case of a certain Welshman, who left his native land in his youth, forgot his native dialect, and used the English language for thirty years. This man was attacked by the brain fever, and, in consequence of it, suddenly recovered the knowledge of the Welsh language, which he had forgotten, and lost the knowledge of the English, with which he had been so long familiar.—Other facts of a similar nature might be introduced if it were necessary.

§ 140. *Impaired memory in connexion with names.*

There have been persons whose impairment of memory was limited exclusively, or nearly so, to proper names. This fact is noticed by Mr. Combe, who makes the remark, that " numerous cases are on record of the power of using words having been impaired by disease, when the ability to articulate, and the powers of perception and judgment remained entire." And, in confirmation of this general statement, he introduces from the Phrenological Journal the case of a Mr. Hood. It is stated, in respect to this person, that he suddenly forgot the *name* of every object in nature. " His recollection of *things* seemed to be unimpaired ; but the *names*, by which men and things are known, were entirely obliterated from his mind ; or, rather, he had lost the faculty by which they are called up at the control of the will. He was by no means inattentive, however, to what was going on, and he recognised friends and acquaintances perhaps as quickly as on any former occasion; but their names, or even his own, or his wife's name, or the names of any of his domestics, appeared to have no place in his recollection."*

The father of the late Dr. Watson, bishop of Landaff, was unable, in consequence, as was supposed, of an apoplectic attack, to recollect the name of his eldest son. He was obliged to designate him, which he had very frequent occasion to do, in connexion with his pursuits or his place of residence; calling him, for instance, the "lad at college," instead of repeating his name. "And yet he was able to repeat, without a blunder, hundreds of lines out of classic authors."

A case, coming under this general head, occurred a few years since in the city of Washington. A respectable and intelligent lady residing there experienced a slight attack of apoplexy. It is stated that, up to the time of this attack, she possessed rather uncommon powers of conversation; was fluent, and had a ready command of five languages. The apoplectic attack, although it left her general power of language untouched, destroyed entirely her ability, with a single exception, of recalling proper names. And this power, it seems, she has never, as yet, recovered. She still converses fluently, so far as proper names are not concerned. But, whenever a name of this kind occurs, she is arrested in her conversation, and cannot proceed till the name is sug-

* Combe's Phrenology, 3d Am. ed., p. 430.

gested. Whenever this is done, she instantly recognises the person or thing for which the name stands, as the one appropriate to her train of thought and conversation, and is thus enabled to go on.

In connexion with these facts, it will not be surprising when we state that persons sometimes forget their own names. A case of this kind is related in the Psychological Magazine. Some years since, a German gentleman, who held a high rank in political life, had occasion to call at another person's house on some business. The servant of the house, being unacquainted with him, asked him his name. But he was unable to answer; he had entirely forgotten it; and was under the disagreeable and rather ridiculous necessity of asking a friend who was with him what his own name was.[*]

§ 141. *Of loss of memory during particular periods of time.*

Another striking modification of disordered memory is that which exists for a particular period of time.—Dr. Beattie relates the case of a clergyman who was attacked with apoplexy; and, on recovering, was found to have lost the recollection of exactly four years. Dr. Abercrombie also relates, that he once attended a lady in a protracted illness, whose impairment of memory assumed this form. She lost the recollection of a period of about ten or twelve years, but spoke with perfect consistency of things as they stood before that time.—Facts of this

[*] For some of the above and other similar statements, « ᵠ Good's Medicine, vol. iv., p. 189.

kind cannot fail to convince us, that no inconsiderable degree of mystery, in some respects at least,
still rests upon the operations and laws of the human mind. It is true that various explanations of
the facts which have been given in this section
may be attempted; but they will all be found, on
examination, to involve more or less of merely hy-
pothetical views. What further developements the
well-disciplined inquiries of science will be able to
make in future time, we are, of course, unable to say.
Certainly we have no reason for saying that, in the
existing state of mental knowledge, we know all
which possibly can be known; although it is undoubtedly the case, that at present we know only in
part.

§ 142. *Of other modifications of disordered*
Memory.

The imperfect and disordered action of the memory appears in a variety of forms, too numerous to
render it practicable, in the narrow limits to which
the present work is restricted, fully to describe them.
We shall leave the subject, therefore, with briefly referring to one other modification of disorder, somewhat different from any which has hitherto been
mentioned. It consists in putting one name for
another, but always employing the words which are
used in the same sense. An individual who was
the subject of this form of mental disorder, is mentioned by Dr. Abercrombie; and some accompanying explanations are given in the following terms.—
" He uniformly called his snuff-box a hogshead, and

the association which led to this appeared to be obvious. In the early part of his life he had been in
Virginia, and connected with the trade in tobacco:
so that the transition from snuff to tobacco, and from
tobacco to a hogshead, seemed to be natural. Another gentleman affected in this manner, when he
wanted coals put upon his fire, always called for paper, and when he wanted paper called for coals;
and these words he always used in the same manner. In other cases, the patient seems to invent
names, using words which to a stranger are quite
unintelligible; but he always uses them in the same
sense, and his immediate attendants come to understand what he means by them."*

CHAPTER VI.

IMPERFECT AND DISORDERED ACTION OF THE REA-
SONING POWER.

§ 143. *Of the nature of the Reasoning Power.*

It will be noticed, so far as we have gone in the
examination of the subject of the imperfections and
disorders of mental action, that we have considered
the powers of the mind separately. Probably every
power of the mind, but particularly those of the intellect in distinction from the sensibilities, may be-

* Abercrombie's Intellectual Powers, Harpers' ed., p. 130.

come more or less disordered.   It is not safe to restrict the doctrine of insanity, much less of mental
disorder, in the more general sense of the terms. by
arbitrary and narrow definitions.   The statements
which have already been given seem sufficiently to
show the correctness of the general doctrine laid
down at the commencement of the work, that the
true limits of disordered mental action are coexten-
sive with the opposite, viz., with a just, orderly,
sound, or sane state of the mind.   Having successively considered sensation, external perception, the
conceptive power, original suggestion, consciousness, relative suggestion or judgment, association,
and memory, we propose, as coming next in order
in the arrangement which we have adopted, to examine the subject before us, in its connexion with the
reasoning power.

Of the nature of the reasoning power, inasmuch
as the present work takes for granted some general
knowledge of the mind's ordinary or regular action,
it is unnecessary to speak except very briefly.
When the power in question is in exercise, we term
such exercise of it REASONING.   Accordingly, reasoning may be defined the mental process or operation whereby we deduce conclusions from two or
more propositions premised.   A train of reasoning
may be regarded, therefore, as a *whole*, and, as such,
it is made up of separate and subordinate parts
which are usually denominated PROPOSITIONS.

The reasoning power, great as it is in its nature
and its results, has its specific position, and also its
specific duties or office ; and in both points of view

is clearly enough distinguished from all other intellectual powers. It is, perhaps, more likely to be confounded with the power of Relative Suggestion or the Judgment than any other. Nevertheless, there is a distinction between them. Without Relative Suggestion, which is to be regarded as a distinct source of knowledge, there would be no perception of relations in their simplest possible forms. And, unassisted by reasoning, which, as compared with the power just named, takes a higher stand and operates in a wider field, we could have no knowledge of the relations of those things, which cannot be compared without the aid of intermediate propositions.

This great and ennobling faculty, which avails itself of the intimations and appliances of nearly all the other powers, may be subject to imperfection and disorder in various ways and degrees, as we shall now proceed to explain.

§ 144. *Of failure of Reasoning from the want of ideas.*

There can be no reasoning, in the first place, where there are no ideas previously laid up in the mind. Such is the nature of the reasoning power, that it must have its DATA, its materials on which to act. Reasoning deals with propositions, and propositions involve ideas. He, therefore, who is content to be without ideas, must not complain to find himself no reasoner.

It is here we find one ground of the failure of the reasoning power in idiocy. The idiot is almost wholly destitute of ideas ; so that, if he happens to possess those powers of comparison and combination which are implied in reasoning, still he has no materials on which to employ them.   In such persons, therefore, the reasoning power, even if it has an existence, is not only not exercised in fact, but it is impossible that it should be ; and, consequently, it is virtually extinct.   Even a few ideas, although they undoubtedly have their value, will not be enough to furnish a ratiocinative basis.   The reasoning which is raised on such a basis will generally be found unsymmetrical, built up in some parts and not in others, weak in one place and strong in another, and presenting, on the whole, either an imperfect or a distorted view of the subject. Hence we have, with the failure of ideas, either no reasoning or false reasoning, either no action or perverted action.

§ 145. *Of mere weakness or imbecility of the Reasoning power.*

In the second place, we are led to remark, that there is in some persons a natural weakness or imbecility of the reasoning power, in itself considered.   The difficulty does not consist, as in the case just now mentioned, in the want of ideas ; of these they perhaps have multitudes : but it consists rather in their want of a power to perceive and to estimate consecutively their relations.   They may, perhaps, be able to perceive and understand separate relations ; for instance, the relation existing between two objects or two simple propositions ; but they are not able, by connecting object with object, and proposition with proposition, to deduce remote and ultimate relations. The mind does not expand itself sufficiently so as to embrace the whole subject; or it has not energy enough so as to advance safely and firmly from step to step ; or, if these be not the proper expressions, we still have the general and undeniable fact that it comes short, utterly and absolutely, of the consecutive process which is involved in every mental effort deserving the name of ratiocination.

Mr. Locke seems to have had this class of persons in mind, where he remarks in the following terms : " There are some men of one, some but of two syllogisms, and no more ; and others that can advance but one step farther. These cannot always discern that side on which the strongest proofs lie ; cannot constantly follow that which in itself is the more probable opinion."—These persons are not insane in the ordinary sense of that term, but they are accountable only so far as they have ability. They have, intellectually, but a feeble light ; and, such as it is, they are often obliged to borrow, from the lamp of their neighbours, the oil that feeds their own.

§ 146. *Of disordered Reasoning in relation to particular subjects.*

One of the forms of disordered reasoning, and one, too, of very frequent occurrence, is characterized by the circumstance that the disordered or abnormal tendency has relation to particular subjects, and is limited to them. Beyond this limit, whether more or less restricted, the operation of this power appears to be entirely unobstructed. It might, perhaps, be suggested here, that the disordered action does not exist so much in the reasoning power, in itself considered, as in that antecedent state of mind, whatever it is, which furnishes the premises upon which the ratiocinative process is based. That is to say, the reasoning process goes well in itself, but is upon a wrong track. It arrives at an erroneous issue, because it started from a wrong point.

A man, for instance, believes that he is made of glass. He reasons correctly, in deducing the conclusion from premises of this kind, that he must move slowly and cautiously. Another person believes that he is a plant; an idea which is said to have taken possession of one of the Bourbon princes. He reasons correctly when he goes into the garden and insists on being watered in common with the plants around him. Another, again, believes that he is a king; and he reasons correctly in requiring for himself the homage suited to a king, and in expressing dissatisfaction on account of its being withheld.

In all such cases, it is very true that the fundamental error is in the premises. Nevertheless, when we consider that reasoning must necessarily have its preliminaries or basis, and that the true idea of reasoning, at least in the higher sense of the term, embraces premises as well as conclusion, we shall not hesitate to speak of such reasoning as has been mentioned, although erroneous in the incipient rath-

er than the deductive stage, as on the whole wrong
perverted, or insane.

§ 147. *Instance of the foregoing form of perverted Reasoning.*

We have an instance of the form of mental disorder just described, namely, that which is limited
to a particular subject or class of subjects, in the
character of Don Quixote. Cervantes, it will be
recollected, represents the hero of his Work as having his naturally good understanding perverted by
the perusal of certain foolish, romantic stories, false-
ly purporting to be a true record of knights and
deeds of chivalry. These books, containing the
history of dwarfs, giants, necromancers, and other
preternatural extravagance, were zealously perused,
until the head of Don Quixote was effectually turned by them. Although he was thus brought into a
state of real mental derangement, it was limited to
the extravagances which have been mentioned. We
are expressly informed, that in all his conversations
and replies, he gave evident proofs of a most excellent understanding, and never " lost the stirrups"
except on the subject of chivalry. On this subject
he " was crazed."—Accordingly, when the barber
and curate visited him on a certain occasion, the
conversation happened to turn on what are termed
reasons of state, and on modes of administration ;
and Don Quixote spoke so well on every topic as
to convince them that he was quite sound, and had
recovered the right exercise of his judgment. But
something being unadvisedly said about the Turkish

war, the knight at once remarked, with much so-
lemnity and seriousness, that his majesty had nothing to do but to issue a proclamation, command-
ing all the knights-errant in Spain to assemble at his
court on a certain day ; *and, although not more than
half a dozen should come, among these one would be
found who would alone be sufficient to overthrow the
whole Turkish power.*

When the subject of conversation turned upon
war, which had so near a connexion with shields,
and lances, and all the associations of chivalry, it
came within the range of his malady, and led to the
absurd remark, which showed at once the unsoundness of his mind, notwithstanding the sobriety and
good sense which he had just before exhibited.

§ 148. *Of disordered Reasoning arising from a disordered state of the other powers of the Mind.*

All the powers of the mind have a connexion,
more or less close, with each other.   Hence their
action may be said, in reference to this connexion,
to be a conditional one.   Consequently, if the condition fails, the action fails.   As an illustration, the
exercise of the reasoning power implies, as the necessary condition of its own existence, the antecedent exercise of memory, of relative suggestion, of
the external and internal perceptive powers, and also
of the susceptibility of belief.   It is obvious that
disorder cannot attach to any one of these without
indirectly affecting any power which, although it
may be distinct, is, nevertheless, in some sense built
upon them.   'Hence the reasoning power is often

disordered, in consequence of derangement in some one of these powers, or in some other part of the mind, with which its action is particularly connected.

We make here this general remark, as one which it may be important to keep in mind, without deeming it necessary to dwell upon it.

§ 149. *Of readiness of Reasoning in the partially insane.*

Those, who have been personally acquainted with the intellectual condition of the partially insane, have sometimes observed in them great quickness of thought in some little emergencies, and an unusual degree of cunning. When, for instance, an attempt has been made to seize and confine them, they steadily and promptly mark the motions of their pursuers ; they rapidly decipher their intentions from their countenance, and cause them no small degree of perplexity. In particular, it has been observed in some instances that they discover more fluency of expression and rapidity of deduction than others of a perfectly sound mind, or than themselves could have exhibited before their derangement. This singular fact is to be briefly explained.

The unusual quickness of deduction and of expression, which has sometimes been noticed in partially insane persons, may be referred to two causes; first, an uncommon excitation of the attention and of all the intellectual powers ; and, secondly, a removal of those checks which attend the sober and the rational in their reasonings.

Some of the checks which retard the process of

reasoning in the case of men whose powers are in a good state, are these.   I.—There is a distrust of phraseology, a fear of mistakes, from the ambiguity and vagueness of language.—The object of a rational man is supposed to be to arrive at truth, and not merely to gain a victory.   He therefore feels anxious not only to employ terms which appear to himself proper, but which shall be rightly understood by his opponent.   But the irrational man, as might be expected, does not find himself embarrassed with considerations of this nature.   II.—A second obstruction to facility and promptness in argumentation, in the case of the sober-minded and rational, is this : they fear that they may not be in possession of all those premises on which the solution will be found in the event to depend.—Many disputes are carried on without previously forming an acquaintance with those facts, which are necessarily and prominently involved.   While disputants of sound minds have any suspicion on this point, and know not but it will be labour lost, they of course feel their interest in the dispute very much diminished. III.—The third circumstance to which reference was had, is this : the influence of certain feelings of propriety and of good sense, which ordinarily govern men in the full exercise of their powers.

The disputant feels himself under obligations to profess a deference for his opponent ; it is due to the customary forms of society.   He is sometimes restrained and embarrassed by what he considers due to those who are present to hear the argument. He is particularly careful to say nothing foolish, ab-

surd, or uncharitable.—All these things weigh nothing with the insane person.   He is not troubled
about exactness of expression or the observance of
ceremonies, but strangely rushes, as it were, upon
the main points of the controversy, regardless of all
minor considerations.*

CHAPTER VII

DISORDERED ACTION OF THE IMAGINATION.

§ 150. *General remarks on the nature of Imagi-*
nation.

WE proceed now to a consideration of the defective and disordered exercises of the Imagination.
The mental process which is involved in any exercise of the Imagination, is a complex rather than a
simple operation.   Such a process implies, in particular, the exercise of the power of Association, in
furnishing those conceptions which are combined together ; also the exercise of the power of Relative
Suggestion, by means of which the combination is
effected.   Hence we may properly propose as a definition of Imagination, that it is a complex exercise
of the mind, by means of which various conceptions
are combined together so as to form new wholes.
The conceptions may very properly be regarded as

* See Stewart's Philosophy of the Human Mind, vol. ii., ch. iii.

the materials from which the new creations are made; but it is not until the existence of those acts which are implied in every process of the Imagination, such as Association and Relative Suggestion, that they are selected, detained before the mind, and ultimately united in various beautiful combinations.

A dry definition will give but little idea of the fruitful and vast results which flow out of the exercise of this power. Sometimes it is chiefly descriptive, catching the images of things as they exist in nature, subjecting them to the finest analysis, and recombining them in forms of exquisite beauty. So that nature herself, coming from the hands of the infinite and perfect Artist, finds herself rivalled in the productions which man's imagination gives rise to. Sometimes it assumes the suggestive and creative aspect, as in Spenser and Milton, giving existence to things and beings which have no parallel in earthly shapes; creating new worlds, peopling them with new inhabitants; adorning and rendering them happy with arts, and sights, and harmonies unknown before.

§ 151. *Great Imagination does not necessarily imply a disordered or insane action of the Mind.*

Without delaying further upon the general nature of Imagination, we now proceed to some remarks more closely connected with the subject properly before us. And, in doing this, it may be proper to allude to an opinion somewhat prevalent, that great power of imagination implies a tendency to disordered mental action. In regard to this opinion, it may be remarked, that this is not necessarily the case, although there is some foundation for this view. It is undoubtedly true, that there are some men of fertile and vigorous imaginations, whose minds are not well balanced; who discover a lack of judgment; and who would not be wisely trusted in many things where sound judgment is necessary. Perhaps there are *many* such cases. And it is certain there are some, perhaps many, exceptions, especially in men of the very highest forms of imagination.

If we may judge from their writings, which is almost the only means of judging we have, Homer and Shakspeare, who, by common consent, are placed at the head of poets, could not have been deficient in those qualities of mind which constitute the man of sound judgment. The admirable poems of Virgil discover no such deficiency in him. On the contrary, it may be said without hyperbole, that almost every line discovers, not only those powers of language and that exquisite sensibility which are requisite to the higher forms of poetry, but also a judgment sound and well disciplined in the very highest degree. Dante and Milton, without mentioning other names, men who were emphatically kindred geniuses in the powers of the imagination, were also men of such practical tact, men of such discrimination and general capabilities for business, that they were considered suitable persons to hold high stations, and to exercise important influence in the political movements of their times.

Great imagination, therefore, does not necessarily imply a tendency to disordered mental action, provided there is a suitable division of power ; in other words, a corresponding energy in the other faculties. The imagination, in order to be great in the highest sense of the term, must draw nourishment from the other powers. Unquestionably, if the poet is of imagination *all* compact, in the sense of excluding a due mixture of the other capabilities, he may properly be located, where Shakspeare has placed him, in the same category with the lunatic. But such a man, although he may be a poet, is not to be confounded with a *great* poet, any more than Phaeton is to be confounded with Apollo. He holds the reins of the horses of the sun, but he has not the strength to guide them.

§ 152. *Of cases of marked deficiency of Imagination.*

There may, however, notwithstanding what has been said, be unsoundness of mind arising from excess of imagination. And is not the reverse equally true ? Are we to speak of that as a sound mind where imagination has no place ? Can there well be a greater mental defect than this ? Certain it is, there are some persons in whom the power of imagination appears to be almost totally extinct. They are matter-of-fact men, in the literal sense of the terms. They seem to have no possible conception of anything beyond the limit and boundary of what actually is. In vain would Sir Philip Sidney, in his beautiful Defence of Poetry, attempt to convince them that the imagination hath profit. They at once apply to all the delightful creations of this wonderful faculty Ezekiel's reed ; they measure the walls, and the porches, and the threshold, and the chambers, that they may thereby estimate the utilities, not that they may get a clearer perception of the beautiful. Wonderful to them is the idea, that there may be truth and beauty, standing imperishable and beaming with radiance, and yet without the substantial and literal realization of anything which profiteth the body. What would such men make of Paradise Lost? Would not even the flute of Burns, sounding in its simplicity from his native Ayr, prove a mystery? Awakening no emotion of the heart, giving birth to no conception above this "diurnal sphere."

At the same time, it must be acknowledged, that this faculty is more frequently dormant than absent; that it wants cultivation, not existence. In almost all minds, not excepting the peasant who humbly labours among the sods of the earth, there are some feeble twinklings of this inner light. In many cases where neither of the powers exists in a remarkable degree, the power of imagination is more vigorous and active than that of reflection. Often uncultured men catch by the outward eye a glance of the charms of nature, and imagination awakens at the happy moment, and adds to the beauty of her tints.

§ 153. *Disorder of the Imagination as connected with Association and excited Conceptions.*

As imagination, considered as a whole, implies the exercise of various subordinate powers, we may sometimes more fully understand the nature of the disorders to which it is found to be subject by a reference to those powers. If, for instance, the power of association be in any degree disordered, the effects of this disorder will be more or less felt in the imagination. The results of the imagination will in that case be discontinuous, bizarre, and incoherent. If the susceptibility, by which we form conceptions of absent objects, be disordered, the results of the imagination will probably be characterized by a too vivid and unnatural aspect of things. Both features seem to be combined in the following case, which Dr. Gall has extracted from Fodéré's Memoir of M. Savary: "A carpenter forty-seven years old, with every appearance of good health, was assailed by a crowd of strange and incoherent ideas. He often imagined himself fluttering in the air, or traversing smiling fields, apartments, old chateaus, woods, and gardens, which he had seen in his infancy. Sometimes he seemed to be walking in public courts, places, and other spots that were known to him. While at work, the moment he was going to strike his axe at a given place, an idea would pass through his head, make him lose sight of his object, and he would strike somewhere else. He once rose at midnight to go to Versailles, and found himself there without being sensible of having made this journey. —None of these hallucinations prevent the patient from reasoning correctly. He is astonished, and laughs at himself for all these fantastic visions, but still is unable to withdraw himself from their influence."

§ 154. *Disorder of the Imagination as connected with the Sensibilities.*

When the imaginative power exists in the same mind in connexion with strong sensibilities, it is sometimes the case that its operation is stimulated to an excessive and morbid degree. It is well known that men of marked imaginative genius, combined with deep sensibility, often become mentally disordered. Not that we are authorized, as a general thing, to include these among the more striking forms of insanity. Certain it is, that they generally attract but little notice. But such are the extravagant dreams in which these persons indulge ; such are the wrong views of the character and actions of men which their busy and melancholy imaginations are apt to form, that they cannot be reckoned persons of truly sound minds. These instances, which are not rare, it is difficult fully to describe ; but their most distinguishing traits will be recognised in the following sketch from Madame de Stael's Reflections on the Character and Writings of Rousseau.

After remarking that he discovered no sudden emotions, but that his feelings grew upon reflection, and that he became impassioned in consequence of his own meditations, she adds as follows : "Sometimes he would part with you with all his former affection ; but, if an expression had escaped you which might bear an unfavourable construction, he would recollect it, examine it, exaggerate it, perhaps dwell upon it for a month, and conclude by a total breach

with you.   Hence it was that there was scarce a
possibility of undeceiving him ; for the light which
broke in upon him at once was not sufficient to ef-
face the wrong impressions which had taken place
so gradually in his mind.   It was extremely difficult, too, to continue long on an intimate footing
with him.   A word, a gesture, furnished him with
matter of profound meditation ; he connected the
most trifling circumstances like so many mathematical propositions, and conceived his conclusions to
be supported by the evidence of demonstration.

" I believe (she farther remarks) that imagination
was the strongest of his faculties, and that it had
almost absorbed all the rest.   He dreamed rather
than existed, and the events of his life might be said
more properly to have passed in his mind than without him : a mode of being, one should have thought,
that ought to have secured him from distrust, as it
prevented him from observation ; but the truth was,
it did not hinder him from attempting to observe ; it
only rendered his observations erroneous.   That his
soul was tender, no one can doubt after having read
his works ; but his imagination sometimes interposed
between his reason and his affections, and destroyed
their influence : he appeared sometimes void of sensibility, but it was because he did not perceive objects such as they were.   Had he seen them with
our eyes, his heart would have been more affected
than ours."

§ 155. *Other illustrations of the same subject.*

There is some ground for supposing that state-
X

ments, similar to those which have now been made, will apply, in a considerable degree, to the case of Dean Swift. Frequent attempts have been made to analyze the character of Swift, but, in general, with doubtful success. That he was, however, a person of imagination in a high, though not in the highest, sense of the term, cannot well be doubted. Of this his writings, and his prose more than his poetry, are a proof. Moreover, notwithstanding the asperity and repulsiveness which his character sometimes assumed, he was, in the elements of his nature, a man of generous and vivid sensibilities. It is true they were not obtruded upon the public eye, but were assiduously nourished in solitude; and, gaining strength from this solitary nurture, they had the effect to give an impulse to his imagination, by means of which the facts of friendship and enmity, of life and manners, were presented before him in a distorted and exaggerated aspect.

He had, in particular, a keen perception, arising in part from this exciting tendency of the imagination, of the follies and vices of men; but he does not appear to have understood so well the nature and extent of the sanative principle which the Christian religion furnishes: consequently, the world presented to him a morbid appearance, "dark, with no entrance of light." Disgusted with what he saw around him, he retired into the recesses of his own bosom. No star of hope, however it should have been otherwise, arose there. The image of evil continually presented itself before him, which the imaginative power, never relaxing from its solitary labours, expanded to gigantic dimensions. He brooded over it in silence and sorrow, and died in a madhouse.

Such are the results (and the history of literary men gives too many sad instances of them) when this power is permitted to operate without the checks of a sound judgment. This is the process by which generous minds, dwelling too intently upon the evils which all flesh is heir to, are often converted into misanthropists. They mingle the cup of poison with their own hands, and drink it.

§ 156. *Of inordinate Imagination, the opposite of Misanthropical.*

It is to be noticed, further, that the operation of the imagination is sometimes just the reverse of what has been mentioned, particularly in those persons in whom the element of hope is naturally strong. The souls of such persons have no harmony with thoughts of evil. If the inflictions of present sorrows cannot be avoided, they flatter themselves with coming good, and build airy castles for the future. They are like the cottage maiden whom some English poet celebrates.

> " Nor, while she turns the giddy wheel around,
>   Revolves the sad vicissitudes of things."

Pleased with the present and happy in the future, they kindle the torch of the imagination at the fires of a rejoicing heart. It is not with them, " Who shall show us any good ?" but who shall show us anything that is not good ? Infinite are the creations which their busy invention forms, some to be realized to-morrow, some to be realized the next year ; some located in their native land, and, as it were, on the very tomb of their fathers, and others shining in some distant and conjectural El Dorado of the East or West. Their imagination is all upon one track, onward to the regions of light. They see no darkness in the clouds ; they hear no rumbling of the tempest.

How different this state of mind from that which has just now been described. But, unfortunately, it is equally at variance with the true state of things. Such a man is a marvel to his neighbours, who, although they are not misanthropes, do not see all things bright ; but brightness and darkness mingled together, with a full proportion of the latter. They wonder he is so happy, and yet they call him a fool. They shake their heads in their wisdom, and mournfully predict that he will end his days in a madhouse. And so it is. But the distinctive trait of his malady does not leave him even there. His mind is in ruins ; but it is shrouded in a rainbow. He rattles his chains with joy, and makes the walls of his prison echo with his songs.

CHAPTER VIII.

NATURE AND CAUSES OF IDIOCY.

§ 157. *Idiocy generally implies a defective action
of the whole Mind.*

WE propose to close this part of the general subject with some remarks upon Idiocy. A topic
which naturally has a place in a work that professes
to treat of defective or imperfect, as well as of disordered mental action. In the matter of arrangement, it is of but little consequence whether we introduce this subject here or in some other place.
Idiocy does not imply merely an imperfect action of
the External Intellect, or of the Internal Intellect, or
of the Natural and Moral Sensibilities, but of the
whole. Generally speaking, it may be considered
as covering the whole mental area; presenting a
scene of desolateness and vacuity throughout. It
has, therefore, no specific place in the minor divisions into which the treatise naturally resolves itself.
Nevertheless, as the basis of this unfortunate state of
mind may, with a good degree of probability, be
generally located in the intellect, we have conclu-
ded to introduce the following remarks in reference
to it in the present connexion, rather than in the
subsequent part of the work, which has particular relation to the Sensibilities. Such is the nature of the

subject that it will not require an extended discussion.

§ 158. *Of the degree of Intellectual Power possessed in Idiocy.*

It will be proper, in the first place, in entering
upon this subject, to notice some of the marks or
characteristics which are commonly found to attach
to a state of idiocy.   And here the first remark is,
that persons in this condition will always be found
to have but few ideas of any kind whatever.   This
small number of ideas they are able, except in some
extreme cases, to compare together, so far as to distinguish those in which there are any striking differ-
ences.   Such, however, is the general weakness,
and, at times, the total incapacity of the power of
relative suggestion, that the class of General Abstract ideas, which are of such a nature as always
to imply the exercise of that power, are not only
fewer in idiots than those of any other class, but are
ill-defined and indistinct.   The few ideas which they
actually possess, they are sometimes, but not always,
able to combine together, and to form from them
some simple propositions.   They have, however,
the power of deducing inferences from the comparison of a number of consecutive propositions, that is,
by reasoning only in a very small degree.   Their
great feebleness of reasoning power is to be attributed partly to the fewness of the ideas and propositions which they possess ; partly to the dulness of
their susceptibility of perceiving relations, the exercise of which is always implied in the comparison of

propositions ; and partly, in some cases, to a great weakness of memory. We say in *some cases*, because idiots have occasionally been found, who, while they have been deficient in every other mental power, have still been remarkable for memory. There is one characteristic of idiocy which very seldom fails ; and that is, an inability to give attention. We never, for instance, find an idiot who can steadily attend to a long argument, and estimate the point and weight of its conclusion ; even if it be of such a simple nature that he can understand the separate ideas and propositions involved in it.

§ 159. *Of the natural and moral Sensibilities in Idiocy.*

Such is the intellectual power, or, rather, want of intellectual power, which characterizes the condition of this unfortunate class of persons. If we pass from the Intellect into the region of the Sensibilities, we shall find them estranged, in an almost equal degree, from the common measure of human emotion and passion. In general, they take but a little interest in the loves and hatreds, the joys and the sorrows of others, even of their near friends. They show no disposition to engage in the pursuits which fire the hearts and prompt the efforts of all around them, but appear to be lost, if one may use the expression, in the abyss of their own fatuity. Their want of emotion, as well as the defect of thought, is indicated by a vacant gaze, and a general absence of meaning and expression in the countenance.

If we pass from the natural to the moral sensibilities, we find it no better. Whatever injury the idiot may do, he is not, in general, regarded as accountable for it. In a multitude of cases, he is not capable of distinguishing right from wrong; and, consequently, is not considered a proper subject of moral blame or approbation from others. Nor can it well be otherwise. Our moral nature is so constituted, that it necessarily acts in view of facts, knowledge, the deductions of reasoning. We cannot feel a thing to be right or wrong, unless we know something of the nature of the thing and of its relations. If a man has no knowledge, from the nature of the case, he will have no conscience; or, rather, there will be no developement, no exercise of the conscience. If a man of a sound mind sets fire to an inhabited house, he does wrong, and is justly punishable, because he fully understands the consequences of such an act; but the idiot, who does the same thing, is not treated as a wrong-doer and as punishable, simply because to estimate the consequences in such a case is beyond his capacity. The idiot, therefore, possesses, as a general thing, no conscience, because he has no adequate basis for conscience to rest upon; in other words, no adequate powers of perception and reasoning.—This is a description of common cases of idiocy; but there are gradations in this, as well as in all other mental weaknesses and disorders.

§ 160. *Of certain marked or peculiar aspects of Idiocy.*

There is one peculiarity of idiocy which it seems

proper to notice here.   It is sometimes the case that there is something left ; some form of mental power, which exists as an exception to the general character of the mind.   Some persons, for instance, who are justly considered as idiots, nevertheless show con siderable power in matching rhymes.   This power alone seems to be left to them ; and, by means of it, they are enabled to furnish some degree of amuse-ment to themselves and others.   Others, again, will exhibit some degree of mechanical genius ; enough, in the general prostration of their powers, to attract the notice of strangers, while it gives employment to themselves ; but it is always exercised on a small scale, and is remarkable only from the fact of its ex isting in connexion with idiocy.

There have also been instances of idiots, as we have already had occasion to intimate, who have shown considerable power of memory.   They ac-curately repeat what they have seen and heard, al-though they cannot apply to their knowledge, which generally consists of a mere series of external and unimportant facts, the ordinary powers of judgment. Some are said to be interested with diversities of colours, and to show a talent for the copying of paintings.   Sometimes they appear to understand the nature of musical sounds ; and continually re-peat some simple and melancholy air.   These things relieve, although they do not essentially alter, the character of their fatuity.   There is just enough left imperfectly and sadly to indicate what the mind might have been if a mysterious Providence had oth-wise ordained.

§ 161. *Of the origin and causes of Idiocy.*

Idiotism is sometimes congenital or natural ; that is, the causes of it exist from the commencement of life.   In many of these cases, there is a greater or less bodily malformation ; the scull is of a size less than common, and there is a disproportion between the face and the head, the former being larger in proportion than the latter.   The bones of the head are asserted by Dr. Rush to be preternaturally thick ; and the consequence of this is a diminution of the internal capacity of the cranium.—" What appears most striking" (says Pinel, in giving an account of an idiot in the asylum BICETRE) " is the extremely disproportionate extent of the face compared with the diminutive size of the cranium.   No traits of animation are visible in his physiognomy.   Every line indicates the most absolute stupidity.   Between the height of the head and that of the whole stature, there is a very great disproportion.   The cranium is greatly depressed, both at the crown and at the temples.   His looks are heavy, and his mouth wide open.   The whole extent of his knowledge is con- fined to three or four confused ideas, and that of his speech to as many inarticulate sounds."*

From this instance, which is one of the lowest forms of idiocy, and from others where there was a similar conformation of the head, Pinel seems to be inclined to the opinion that a malconformation of the head in particular is the cause of idiotism when it exists from infancy.

* Pinel's Treatise on Insanity (Davis's Translation), sect. iii.

The absence or weakness of intellectual power, which is termed idiocy, is often found to exist from other causes. Men of great mental ability have sometimes sunk into the state of idiotism, in consequence of too great and long-continued application of the mind, a tasking of its powers beyond their greatest strength.   Sometimes, on the contrary, the same results seem to have followed from too little application, especially when combined with a disrelish for social intercourse, which might have checked, and probably have prevented, an entire prostration.   It is obviously one of the great laws of the mind, that the progress or advancement of its powers is connected with a suitable degree of exercise.   If, therefore, a person withdraws into inane and idle solitude ; if he pertinaciously withholds himself from the communion and conflicts of society, and thus loses the opportunity both of acquiring a fund of new ideas and of renovating his former stores of knowledge, he will be likely to find his mind collapsing into a state of weakness and ignorance, approaching, in the end, the condition of idiocy.

§ 162. *Idiocy to be ascribed sometimes to the effects of Age.*

Idiocy appears, in some cases, to be induced by mere old age.   The senses at that period of life become dull ; the ideas received from them are less lively than formerly ; the memory fails, and with it the power of reasoning ; and there is sometimes combined with these unfavourable circumstances a want of interest in persons and events a coldness and sluggishness of feeling, which perhaps cannot be considered altogether surprising at that period of life, but which is obviously unpropitious to the preservation of mental energy. In referring to old age, however, in this connexion, it is proper to modify this general statement by one or two remarks. When idiocy is superinduced by the influences of old age, this result is found for the most part to take place in those persons only in whom the External intellect alone has been cultivated. They have been so situated, being deprived in early life of instruction, and always deprived of the use of books, that their minds have been exercised exclusively in connexion with the senses. They know but very little more than what has been directly addressed to the touch, sight, and taste. The inward fountains of thought, original suggestion, consciousness, judgment, reasoning, are in a great degree sealed up. Consequently, when in extreme old age the outward senses are unable to perform their office, it is unavoidable, that the mind should sink back into a state of feebleness, exhibiting all the ordinary characteristics of idiocy.

Further; this state of the mind may be caused by various diseases, such as violent fevers, which at times suddenly disturb the mental powers, produce a temporary delirium, and then leave the faculties of the mind in a permanently torpid and inefficient condition. It may originate also in the abuse of ardent spirits, from great grief, from violent blows on the head, from sudden and great terror, &c. The idiocy, which is natural, and exists from infancy, has sometimes been distinguished from that which is brought on by the above-mentioned and other causes in after life ; but the mental condition being in both cases essentially the same, they may properly be considered together in one view.

§ 163. *Illustrations of the causes of Idiocy.*

Great and sudden terror was mentioned as one of the causes of idiocy. Very great and sudden excitements of any of the passions may produce the same effect. We know of no illustrations of this statement more striking than the following, from the interesting work of Pinel on Insanity.—" The feelings of individuals, endowed with acute sensibility, may experience so violent a shock, that all the functions of the mind are in danger of being suspended in their exercises or totally abolished. Sudden joy and excessive fear are equally capable of producing this inexplicable phenomenon. An engineer proposed to the committee of public safety, in the second year of the [French] republic, a project for a new invented cannon, of which the effects would be tremendous. A day was fixed for the experiment at Meudon ; and Robespierre wrote to the inventor so flattering a letter, that, upon perusing it, he was transfixed motionless to the spot. He was shortly afterward sent to Bicetre in a state of complete idiotism.

" About the same time, two young conscripts, who had recently joined the army, were called into action. In the heat of the engagement one of them was killed by a musket-ball at the side of his brother. The surviver, petrified with horror, was struck motionless at the sight. Some days afterward he was sent, in a state of complete idiotism, to his father's house. His arrival produced a similar impression upon a third son of the same family. The news of the death of one of the brothers, and the derangement of the other, threw this third victim into such a state of consternation and stupor as might have defied the powers of ancient or modern poetry to give an adequate representation of it. My sympathetic feelings have been frequently arrested by the sad wreck of humanity, presented in the appearance of these degraded beings; but it was a scene truly heart-rending to see the wretched father come to weep over these miserable remains of his once enviable family."

§ 164. *Of restoration from a state of Idiocy.*

Idiocy, so far as we have been able to learn, is considered incurable; at least a restoration from it is more difficult and less probable than from the more common forms of defective mental action. This is especially true when it is natural and congenital; which is understood, as a general thing, to imply an imperfect or deformed structure of the cerebral organ. And, when it is otherwise, it cannot be denied that the encouragement to effort is small. One thing, however, ought to be done. The idiot should be instructed to the extent of his capacity, whether more or less. Who knows but a faithful training within the narrow limits of his mental capability may arouse some dormant energy, may disentangle and adjust some disordered intellectual action, may open to his astonished apprehension some new fountain of thought, and thus produce a complete internal revolution.   Such a result, as facts might be adduced to show, is not altogether hopeless ; although undoutedly the preparatory efforts are such as to require a high degree of faith and patience.

§ 165. Of the beneficial results connected with Idiocy.

And here it might be inquired with some propriety, what end Providence could have had in view in permitting the existence of these unfortunate beings, except it be to try the faith and patience, to quicken the sensibilities, and to discipline the virtues of those by whom they are surrounded.   If there were no vice and no suffering in the world, how could any of us know that we possess a nature which would turn with horror from crime, or would melt with pity at misfortune ?

There is an interesting poem of Wordsworth, entitled the Cumberland Beggar.   The whole business of the poor old man is to go from cottage to cottage, on his daily errands of want.   In the decrepitude of age, he advances so slow that " the cottage curs, ere he have passed the door, will turn away weary of barking at him."   But Wordsworth contends, in the spirit of a philosopher as well as of a poet, that the old man, though wholly dependant upon others, is not without some benefit to mankind.   He not only serves to remind the villagers, as he wanders in his poverty among them, of the past offices of kindness which they have shown him, and again to **awaken,** as he presents anew his decrepit form, the spirit of benevolence ; but he helps to quicken in their hearts the recollection of their own comparatively favoured situation, and to keep more vividly alive the decaying sentiments of religious gratitude.   This is the important office which Providence assigns him ; and who will say that the IDIOT, a being still more degraded, still more capable of appealing to our sympathies, does less !   He stands a perpetual monitor, appointed in the wisdom of an inscrutable Superintendence, to teach us that man, in his natural elements, is what he is, not by his own volition, but by the gift of God ; and to remind us individually of what we have more than others, and of what we are bound in pity and in duty to do for those who have less.

> " And while in that vast solitude, to which
>   The tide of things has led him, he appears
>   To breathe and live but for himself alone,
>   Unblamed, uninjured, let him bear about
>   The good, which the benignant law of Heaven
>   Has hung around him ; and, while life is his,
>   Still let him prompt the unletter'd villagers
>   To tender offices and pensive thoughts."

IMPERFECT AND DISORDERED

MENTAL ACTION.

DIVISION SECOND.

DISORDERED ACTION OF THE SENSIBILITIES.

Y

DERANGEMENT

OF THE

SENSIBILITIES.

CHAPTER I.

DISORDERED ACTION OF THE APPETITES.

§ 166. *Classification and method of inquiry.*

WE now enter upon a distinct and very important department of the mental nature, viz., the Sensibilities.—The Sensibilities, like the Intellect, are susceptible of some subordinate divisions; the most important of which is the leading and most general one of the Natural and the Moral Sensibilities. Of these two we propose to consider, first, the Natural Sensibilities. Of the elementary or simple feelings, which come under this general head, the leading division is into Emotions and Desires. As we advance from the Intellect to the Natural or Pathematic Sensibilities, we find ourselves in the region of the natural Emotions. These are followed by Desires.

The Desires, for the most part in combination

with Emotions, assume a number of distinct and important modifications or forms, viz., the Appetites, Propensities, and Affections. We propose, under this general head of the Natural Sensibilities, to prosecute the subject of alienated or depraved mental action, in connexion with these principles in particular.—It is true that the emotions and desires, in their simple or elementary state, are susceptible of an inordinate or depraved action; but they do not appear to furnish, in that form, a sufficient basis for a prolonged, definite, and scientific discussion. It is in their combination with each other; it is in the shape of appetitive, propensive, and affective principles, which, in general, are the result of such combination, that they stand out prominently to the eye, and give a definite aspect to the character. We shall begin, therefore, with the Appetites, which will be followed in the order in which they have been named by remarks on the Propensities, and, finally, by a consideration of the Affections, including under that term the two leading divisions of the Benevolent and Malevolent Affections.

§ 167. *Of the distinction between mere disorder and Insanity of the Sensibilities.*

It may be proper to keep in mind here, that a distinction may be drawn satisfactorily between mere disorder or irregularity of the sensibilities, and insanity of the sensibilities. Insanity indicates not merely disorder, but disorder existing in a high degree. When, for instance, the disordered or irregular state of mind, which at first existed only in a slight degree, continually increases, so as at last to pass a certain boundary, which is more easily conceived of than described, it becomes Insanity or Alienation. That is to say, the merely irregular action becomes an insane or aliented action, when it becomes so great, so pervading, and so deeply rooted in the mind that the individual has no power of restoration in himself. So that it would seem to follow, in view of this remark, that there may be a disordered state of the mind which is insanity; and, under other circumstances, a disordered state of the mind which is not insanity, or, rather, which is less than insanity. But, in either case, this condition of mind is not to be regarded, nor is it, in point of fact, a sound mental state. Although we may not be able to say, specifically, in a given case, that the disorder has reached the point of insanity, yet it is certain that the mind in this disordered state, whether the disorder be greater or less, is presented to our view in a new and important aspect.

§ 168. *Of the disordered and alienated action of the Appetites.*

In accordance with the plan of discussion proposed in the first section of this chapter, we proceed to remark, in the first place, that there may be a disordered and alienated action of the Appetites.— It is well known, that the appetites grow stronger and stronger by repeated indulgence. While the process of increased appetitive tendency is going on, there still remains, in the majority of cases, enough of remonstrance in the conscience, and of restrictive and aggressive energy in the will, to ward off that state of thraldom which is rapidly approaching. But in some melancholy cases it is otherwise ; the line of demarcation, which separates the possibility and the impossibility of a restoration, is passed ; and from that time onward there is nothing but interminable sinking. Such cases as these may undoubtedly be regarded as coming within the limits of some of the multiplied forms of mental alienation.

The most frequent instances of mental alienation, originating in a disordered and excessive energy of the appetites, are to be found in that numerous class of persons who habitually indulge in the use of intoxicating drugs, particularly ardent spirits. When the person who indulges in the use of intoxicating liquors has so increased the energy of this pernicious appetite as really to bring himself within the limits of mental alienation, there is no hope of a return by means of any effort which he himself is capable of making. He may have a clear perception of the misery of his situation ; the desire of esteem may still arouse within him the recollection of what he once was and of what he still ought to be ; the conscience may still speak out in remonstrance, though probably with a diminished voice ; the will may continue to put forth some ineffectual struggles ; but it is found to be all in vain. If left to himself, and not put under that constraint which is proper to persons in actual insanity, it may be regarded as a matter of moral certainty that he will plunge deeper and deeper in the degrading vice of which he is the subject, so long as the remaining powers of life shall support him in the process.

§ 169. *Facts illustrative of the preceding statements.*

The individuals who are in this situation seem themselves to have a consciousness of their danger. They see clearly that in their own strength there is no hope. Some years since there was a pamphlet published in England, entitled the Confessions of a Drunkard. The statements made in it are asserted, on good authority, to be authentic. And what does the writer say ? " Of my condition there is no hope that it should ever change ; the waters have gone over me ; but out of the black depths, could I be heard, I would cry out to all those who have but set a foot in the perilous flood. Could the youth, to whom the flavour of his first wine is delicious as the opening scenes of life, or the entering upon some newly-discovered paradise, look into my desolation, and be made to understand what a dreary thing it is when a man shall feel himself going down a precipice with open eyes and a passive will ; to see his destruction, and have no power to stop it, and yet to feel it all the way emanating from himself ; to perceive all goodness emptied out of him, and yet not be able to forget a time when it was otherwise ; to bear about the piteous spectacle of his own self ruins : could he see my fevered eye, feverish with the last night's drinking, and feverishly looking for this night's repetition of the folly ; could he feel the body of the death out of which I cry hourly, with feebler and feebler outcry, to be delivered, it were enough to make him dash the sparkling beverage to the earth in all the pride of its mantling temptation."*

In repeated instances persons, whose desire for intoxicating articles has become inordinately strong, have gone to keepers of penitentiaries and other prisons, and earnestly entreated for admission, on the ground that nothing short of strict seclusion within their massy walls would secure them against the ruinous indulgence of their appetite.—" The use of strong drink" (says Dr. Rush, Diseases of the Mind, chap. x.) "is at first the effect of free agency. From habit it takes place from necessity. That this is the case, I infer from persons who are inordinately devoted to the use of ardent spirits being irreclaimable, by all the considerations which domestic obligations, friendship, reputation, property, and sometimes even by those which religion and the love of life can suggest to them. An instance of insensibility to the last, in an habitual drunkard, occurred some years ago in Philadelphia. When strongly urged by one of his friends to leave off drinking, he said, ' Were a keg of rum in one corner of a room, and were a cannon constantly discharging balls between me and it, I could not refrain from passing before that cannon, in order to get at the rum.' "

§ 170. *Further notices on the disorder of the Appetites.*

Before leaving this subject we wish to recur

* London Quarterly Review, vol. xvii. p. 120.

moment to some remarks of Mr. Stewart in regard to the Appetites. He says they may be distinguished by the three following things : (1.) They take their rise from the body, and are common to men with the brutes. (2.) They are not constant, but occasional. (3.) They are accompanied with an uneasy sensation, which is strong or weak, in proportion to the strength or weakness of the Appetite.

He then goes on to state that our Appetites are three in number, viz., HUNGER, THIRST, AND THE APPETITE OF SEX.—What has been said will sufficiently illustrate, in consequence of the close analogy between them, the disordered action of the first two, although the statements given had particular relation to the irregularities of the Appetite of thirst.

The Appetite of Sex, also, is susceptible of an unrestrained and inordinate action, not only indicating insanity in the specific principle or Appetite itself, but resulting in a disorganization and insanity of other parts of the mind. On this subject, as this Treatise is designed for general reading, we do not propose to dwell. It will be enough to say, that very melancholy instances of the operations and effects of this disordered Appetite are found in many writers on Insanity, to which we hope the reader will excuse us for referring him.—(See, among other Works, Rush on the Diseases of the Mind, ch. xviii.)

Z

CHAPTER II.

DISORDERED ACTION OF THE PROPENSITIES.

(I.) PROPENSITY OF SELF-PRESERVATION.

§ 171. *General remarks on the Propensities.*

As we proceed in the examination of the Natural or Pathematic Sensibilities, we meet with certain modifications or forms of Desire which, as they are different from the Appetites, require a distinct consideration. These distinct principles, which are known as the propensive principles or Propensities, differ from the Appetites, FIRST, in the circumstance that they are much less dependant for their existence and exercise upon the condition of the body ; and, SECONDLY, because, in that comparative estimation which is naturally attached to the different active principles of our nature, they confessedly hold a higher rank. At the same time they evidently, in the graduation of our regard, fall below the Affections, besides being distinguished from them in other respects. And hence they may be regarded as holding a sort of intermediate place between the Appetites on the one hand, and the Affections on the other.

Among the leading or more important of the Propensities may be enumerated the principle of Self-preservation, or the desire of continued existence; Curiosity, or the desire of knowledge; Sociality, or the desire of society; Self-love, or the desire of happiness; the desire of Esteem; Imitativeness, or the propensity to imitate; and some others. All these, it will be noticed, are modifications of Desire; and yet there is reason to believe that a pleasant emotion, in view of the object towards which the desire is directed, is the preparatory condition or basis of the existence of the desire. And not only this, it is possible at least that the emotion may continue subsequently (as is the fact in the Affections) to exist in connexion with the desires; constituting, in this manner, the ground of their continuance, as well as the ground or condition of their origin. But these are points which may properly and safely be left to mental philosophers.

What we have to say here is, that the various Propensities which have been mentioned (and whatever others may properly come under the denomination of Propensities) are susceptible of irregularity, from the lowest degree of disorder to the higher form of Insanity.

§ 172. *Disordered action of the principle of Self-preservation.*

In the prosecution of this part of our subject, we begin, as it is one which would naturally present itself first for our consideration, with the propensive principle of Self-preservation, or what may be designated, in other terms, as the natural desire of a continuance of existence. This principle, like the

others of the same class, although not generally in
so marked a degree, will sometimes manifest itself
under such circumstances, and in such a manner, as
obviously to show that its action is not a natural,
regular, or healthy action.   Persons under the influence of the disordered action of the principle
which is connected with the preservation of life
multiply, as they would be naturally disposed to do,
images of danger and terror which have no existence, nor likeness of existence, except in their own
disordered minds.   They not only see perils which
are invisible to others, but are led to take a multitude of precautions which, in the estimation of those
around them, are altogether unnecessary, and even
ridiculous.

Pinel, under the head of Melancholy, mentions
a case which may be considered as illustrating this
subject : " A distinguished military officer" (he says),
" after fifty years of active service in the cavalry, was
attacked with disease.   It commenced by his experiencing vivid emotions from the slightest causes ;
if, for example, he heard any disease spoken of, he
immediately believed himself to be attacked by it ;
if any one was mentioned as deranged in intellect,
he imagined himself insane, and retired into his
chamber full of melancholy thoughts and inquietude.
Everything became for him a subject of fear and
alarm.   If he entered into a house, he was afraid
that the floor would fall and precipitate him amid
its ruins.   He could not pass a bridge without terror, unless impelled by the sentiment of honour for
the purpose of fighting."*

* Pinal, as quoted in Combe's Phrenology, Boston ed., p 241

§ 173. *Other disordered forms of the Self-preserv-*
ative principle.

The Propensity of Self-preservation, or desire of
the continuance of existence, is generally, and, as
we suppose, very correctly, considered an original or
implanted principle of the human mind. As such
it unquestionably has its distinctive nature, adapted
to the precise object for which it was implanted.
We must suppose, therefore, that it has a regular or
normal action, as well as an irregular or abnormal
one. And it is deviation from the regular action
which constitutes irregularity of action. This irregularity, therefore, may show itself either in the
form of excess of action, or of defect of action, or,
what amounts to nearly the same thing, by too great
energy or too great weakness of action. The instance which has been given from Pinel shows a
disorder or irregularity of the action of this principle
in excess. There are other cases, which seem not
less clearly to show, that the form or shape of the
disorder may sometimes be that of inordinate weakness or defect. We shall proceed here to introduce
one or two cases of this kind.

We find the following statement in the Commentaries on Insanity of Dr. Burrows (p. 440) : " Har-
riet Cooper, of Haden Hill, Rowley Regis, aged ten
years and two months, upon being reproved for a
trifling indiscretion, went up stairs, after exhibiting
symptoms of grief by crying and sobbing, and hung
herself in a pair of cotton braces from the rail of a
tent-bed A girl named Green, eleven years old,

drowned herself in the New River, from the fear of correction for a trivial fault."

" A French journal" (says Dr. Ray, in his valuable Treatise on Medical Jurisprudence, p. 375) " has lately reported the case of a boy twelve years old, who hung himself by fastening his handkerchief to a nail in the wall, and passing a loop of it around his neck, for no other reason than because he had been shut up in his room, and allowed only dry bread, as a punishment for breaking his father's watch. The same journal gives another case of a suicide committed by a boy eleven years old, for being reproved by his father; and several more of a similar description are also recorded."*

The records of such cases, melancholy as they are, might undoubtedly be very much multiplied. We have ourselves known a lad, about fourteen years old, on the occasion, as was supposed, of some trifling disquietude or offence similar to those which have just been mentioned, go out of the shop where he worked, and, in the light and pleasantness of a summer's day, put an end to his life by hanging himself from a tree in a neighbouring garden.

§ 174. *Explanation of the above-mentioned cases.*

Attempts have been made to trace the origin of all such cases exclusively to some form of disease existing in the physical system ; to a disease, for instance, of the thoracic or abdominal viscera, or somewhere else ; but, so far as we have been able to perceive, not with entire satisfaction. In many

* Medico-Chirurgical Review, No. 8, vol. xxvii., p. 212.

cases, undoubtedly, the cause of mental disorder is to be sought in the previously disordered condition of the body, particularly the nervous system; but it does not appear that this is always the fact. Not unfrequently, in cases of suicide, there is no perceptible change, no morbid developement in the body, which can furnish an explanation of that peculiar, and, for the most part, insane state of mind which leads to self-destruction. This is acknowledged, if we may rely upon the statements of Dr. Burrows in the case, by a number of distinguished physicians. "The same" (says Burrows, Comm., p. 416) "is observed in all cases of Insanity where the patient dies from any accident soon after he has become insane. The maniacal action [by which he means the disorder existing mentally] has not had time to take deep root, and no visible change in the intellectual organ [the brain] is therefore detected. This is additional testimony, which leads to the natural inference, that, when morbid changes are discovered in the brain, *they are generally the consequences, and not the causes of mental derangement.*"

What view, then, shall be taken of the cases which have just now been mentioned, and others like them? If physical disease, so far as we can judge, will not account for all of them, what further can be said? The simple fact seems to be, that frequently, in the instance of such persons, the principle of self-preservation, which in almost all cases binds men so strongly to the present life, either does not exist at all, or exists in very much diminished strength. If a man may be born destitute, in a great

degree, of some of the appetites or affections, or destitute of all powers of reasoning, as in the case of
idiots, why may he not also come into the world with
the propensity of self-preservation inordinately weak,
so much so as scarcely to have any influence over
his actions?

§ 175. *Further remarks on this subject.*

This view is confirmed not only by the consideration that, in many cases of suicide, medical philosophers themselves being the judges, there is no pre-
tence at all of there being any disease or lesion of the
physical organs; but also by the fact, although this
circumstance might not of itself alone be a decisive
one, that the tendency to suicide appears frequently
to be hereditary.—" I have had several members of
one family under my care" (says Dr. Burrows),
" where this propensity declared itself through three
generations.   In the first, the grandfather hung himself; he left four sons.   One hung himself; another cut his throat; and a third drowned himself
in a most extraordinary manner, after being some
months insane; the fourth died a natural death,
which, from his eccentricity and unequal mind, was
scarcely to be expected.   Two of these sons had
large families.   One child of the third son died insane; two others drowned themselves; another is
now insane, and has made the most determinate attempts on his life.—Several of the progeny of this
family, being the fourth generation, who are now arrived at puberty, bear strong marks of the same
fatal propensity."

Mental traits and peculiarities are propagated (such is the great law of Providence) with nearly as much certainty, in other words, with nearly as definite reference to the principles of propagative succession, as those of the body. If the parents exhibit a mental defect or disorder, the children will be very likely to do the same. If the parents are suicides, and if the suicidal tendency, as is frequently the fact, has its basis in undue weakness or estrangement of the self-preservative principle, we should not be surprised to find the same tendency developing itself in some of their descendants.

The supposition, then, which we make, in reference to such cases of suicide as have been detailed, and many others like them, is, that the Propensity of Self-preservation is, naturally and by the inheritance of birth, disordered by *defect ;* in other words, inordinately weak, so much so as to fail in fulfilling the ordinary purposes of life. Consequently, when some disappointment arises, when some slight punishment is inflicted, when some current of public opinion sets against the individual, the dissatisfaction and melancholy which naturally follow are frequently found to be too great for the opposing and conservative principle of self-preservation, which, in their case, is unfortunately almost destitute of power. The strong chain which ordinarily binds men to the present scene, is, in their case, so exceedingly weak, that, one after another, they escape out of life on the very slightest occasions, and leave those behind them to weep and wonder at the strangeness of the event. It is like what we sometimes witness in a time of storms and inundations, when those things which are but weakly moored in their position are swept away, and only those which are strongly fastened remain.

CHAPTER III.

DISORDERED ACTION OF THE PROPENSITIES.

(II.) PROPENSITY TO ACQUIRE OR ACQUISITIVENESS.

§ 176. *The propensity to acquire an original or implanted one.*

So far as we have been able to observe, it seems to be at last very generally conceded by writers on the Human Mind, however much they may differ on other points, that there is implanted within us an original disposition or propensity to acquire. Nor could we reasonably expect that it should be otherwise. It is difficult to conceive of a being, sustaining in the moral world the high rank which man does, and yet constituted on the principle of an entire exclusion of the Possessory desire. How can a rational being, in the undisturbed exercise of his powers, do otherwise than desire his own existence and happiness; and, consequently, those things, whatever they may be, which are essential to his existence and happiness. Accordingly, an inspired apostle directs the Corinthians not only to " covet tc prophesy," but, in general terms, "to covet earnestly the best gifts." 1 Cor., xii., 31 ; xiv., 39.

On this topic, however, we need not delay. We take it for granted (and do not suppose, after the inquiries that have been made on the subject, that it will be considered a matter of dispute) that the principle in question is a connatural or implanted one. Like all the other propensive principles (and the same view will apply to the appetites and the affections), the Acquisitive or Possessory principle has a twofold action, viz., INSTINCTIVE and VOLUNTARY. And in both of these forms, as we shall now proceed to show, it is susceptible of an abnormal or disordered movement.

§ 177. *Instances of the first kind or form of disordered action of the Possessory Principle.*

The instances of disordered action of the principle of Acquisitiveness, which naturally present themselves to our notice first, are what may be termed Congenital or Constitutional ; and are evidently the irregular or disordered manifestations of the Instinctive, rather than of the Voluntary modification of this propensity. In the case of the persons to whom we now have reference, the disposition to get possession of whatever can be regarded as property, whether of greater or less value, shows itself, not only in great strength, but at a very early period of life. And at no period of life does it appear to be a matter over which they have a full voluntary control.

There are a considerable number of cases of this kind to be found in the writings of Gall and Spurzheim ; and there are some notices of similar cases in a few other writers.—Foderè (*Medicine Legale*, t. i., p. 237) relates the case of a female servant in his own family, " who could not help stealing secretly from himself and others articles even of trifling value ; though she was intelligent, modest, and religious, and was all the while conscious of and admitted the turpitude of her actions.   He placed her in an hospital, considering her insane, and, after apparent restoration and a long trial, he again took her into his services.   Gradually, in spite of herself, the instinct again mastered her ; and in the midst of an incessant struggle between her vicious propensity on the one hand and a conscientious horror of her condition on the other, she was suddenly attacked with mania, and died in one of its paroxysms."*

Dr. Rush, in his Medical Inquiries, mentions a woman who was entirely exemplary in her conduct, except in one particular.   " She could not refrain from *stealing*.   What made this vice the more remarkable was, that she was in easy circumstances, and not addicted to extravagance in anything.   Such was the propensity to this vice, that, when she could lay her hands on nothing more valuable, she would often, at the table of a friend, fill her pockets secretly with bread.   She both confessed and lamented her crime."

* This case is given as it is found in Dr. Ray's Medical Jurisprudence, p. 190.

§ 178. *Instances illustrative of the subject from Dr. Gall.*

Some of the facts which are given by Dr. Gall are as follows.—" Victor Amadeus I., king of Sardinia, was in the constant habit of stealing trifles. Saurin, pastor of Geneva, though possessing the strongest principles of reason and religion, frequently yielded to the propensity to steal. Another individual was, from early youth, a victim to this inclination. He entered the military service, on purpose that he might be restrained by the severity of the discipline ; but, having continued his practices, he was on the point of being condemned to be hanged. Ever seeking to combat his ruling passion, he studied theology and became a Capuchin. But this propensity followed him even to the cloister. Here, however, as he found only trifles to tempt him, he indulged himself in his strange fancy with less scruple. He seized scissors, candlesticks, snuffers, cups, goblets, and conveyed them to his cell. An agent of the government at Vienna had the singular mania for stealing nothing but kitchen utensils. He hired two rooms as a place of deposite ; he did not sell, and made no use of them. The wife of the famous physician Gaubius had such a propensity to pilfer, that, when she made a purchase, she always sought to take something. The Countess M., at Wessel, and P., at Frankfort, had also this propensity. Madame de W. had been educated with peculiar care. Her wit and talents secured her a distinguished place in society. But neither her education

nor her fortune saved her from the most decided propensity to theft. Lavater speaks of a physician,
who never left the room of his patient without rob-
bing them of something, and who never thought of
the matter afterward. In the evening his wife used
to examine his pockets; she there found keys, scissors, thimbles, knives, spoons, buckles, cases, and
sent them to their respective owners."*

§ 179. *Second form of the alienated action of the
Possessory principle.*

There is another, a second form of the irregular
and alienated action of the Acquisitive Propensity,
which differs from the first-mentioned modification
in the important circumstance of its depending more
upon the Will of the person himself than upon any
constitutional or connatural trait. Cases of this
kind, therefore, are voluntary; that is to say, are
brought about by a course of action, the responsibility of which rests upon the individual himself.

Nor is there anything inconsistent with reason,
any philosophical anomaly in this view. It is well
known that all the principles of the mind rapidly increase in energy and facility of movement by mere
repetition. Not only this; but the process may be
carried so far as to give altogether an undue degree
of strength to some one principle as compared with
another. In other words, a right or healthy action
of the mind may in this way be gradually converted
into an inordinate, uncontrollable, or unhealthy action. Such as we see it not unfrequently in game-

* Gall's Works, vol. iv., Am. ed., p. 132.

sters, mercantile men, and in other classes of persons, whose minds are continually exercised upon the sole object of increasing their possessions.

Among the class of confirmed misers we shall be likely, from time to time, to find instances and illustrations of this view of the subject. There are individuals in this denomination of persons, who have so increased the energy of the Possessory principle (Acquisitiveness, as it is sometimes conveniently termed) by a long, voluntary course of repetition, that its action is obviously no longer under the control of the Will, but has passed over, not merely into the region of temporary disorder, but of positive and permanent insanity. Such, probably, must have been the situation of a certain individual mentioned by Valerius Maximus, who took advantage of a famine to sell a mouse for two hundred pence, and then famished himself with the money in his pocket.—It is difficult to tell, however, although a person may unquestionably become insane in his avarice, whether this is actually the case in any given instance, or whether, notwithstanding its intensity, it falls in some degree short of actual alienation.

§ 180. *Reference to the singular case of Sir Harvey Elwes.*

The reader will be able, probably, by consulting the resources of his own recollection, to understand the applications of this subject. Nevertheless, we take the liberty to delay a moment upon the well-known and somewhat singular case of Sir Harvey Elwes, of Stoke, in the county of Suffolk, England.

Sir Harvey Elwes inherited from a miserly mother, and an uncle of the same parsimonious disposition, the large property of £350,000. This singular individual, as is sometimes the case with misers, is said to have punctually discharged his obligations towards others, and in some instances even to have conducted with liberality ; but, in whatever concerned himself, his parsimony, notwithstanding his great riches, was extreme and unalterable. When travelling he accustomed himself to great abstinence, that he might lessen the charges of his maintenance ; and for the same reason he supported his horse with the few blades of grass which he could gather by the sides of hedges and in the open commons. Like his predecessor, Sir Harvey, from whom he seems to have derived his title, and who was hardly less miserly than his nephew, he wore the clothes of those who had gone before him ; and when his best coat was beyond the ability of any further service, he refused to replace it at his own expense, but accepted one from a neighbour. He was so saving of fuel, that he took advantage of the industry of the crows in pulling down their nests ; and if any friend accidentally living with him were absent, he would carefully put out his fire and walk to a neighbour's house, in order that the same chimney might give out warmth to both. Although he never committed any of his transactions to writing, he could not have been ignorant of his immense wealth ; but this did not prevent his being exceedingly apprehensive that he should at last die with want. " Sometimes hiding his gold in small parcels in different parts o

his house, he would anxiously visit the spot to ascertain whether each remained as he had left it :
arising from bed, he would hasten to his bureau to
examine if its contents were in safety. In later life,
no other sentiment occupied his mind : at midnight
he has been heard as if struggling with assailants,
and crying out in agitation, 'I will keep my money,
I will ; nobody shall rob me of my property !' though
no one was near to disturb him in its possession.
At length this remarkable person died in the year
1789, aged nearly eighty, and worth nearly a mill-
ion." *

§ 181. *Reference to the case of Jeremiah Hallet.*

The case of Jeremiah Hallet, who recently died
at Yarmouth, in Massachusetts, at the age of sixty-
four, is very similar in a number of respects to the
foregoing. If the statements which were circulated
at the time of his death in the public newspapers are
correct (and we see no reason to doubt them), he
was certainly a very eccentric character.—It is related of him that his mind was constantly engrossed
by two subjects, viz., getting money, and the mathematics. The first was the business, the other the
amusement of his life. He was a miser in every
sense of the word ; living alone for the last ten years
of his life, and denying himself all the luxuries, and
many of what are regarded the necessaries of life.
He lived upon the coarsest fare ; and would sit in his
room in cool weather without a fire, when his wood

* Origin and Progress of the Passions (Anonymous), vol. i.,
p. 310.

A A

was rotting in piles ; and a shingle served him for the double purpose of a fireshovel and bellows. It is a confirmatory evidence of the disordered state of his mind, that he committed suicide, probably for some reason connected with the excited and insane position of the acquisitive principle. After his death, on examining his rooms, it was found that the whole value of his furniture and bedding would not exceed three dollars, and every room was covered with filth and dirt.

And yet this man was profoundly skilled in the science of numbers, and could boast of greater proficiency in the higher branches of mathematics than any man in the part of the country in which he lived.

CHAPTER IV.

DISORDERED ACTION OF THE PROPENSITIES.

(III.) AMBITION, OR THE DESIRE OF POWER.

§ 182. *The desire of Power an original or implant ed principle.*

ANOTHER of the Original Propensities, if we may reason from the facts which are almost constantly presented to our notice, is the Desire of Power.—It is true, that power is not a thing which is directly addressed to or cognizable by the outward senses.

We do not see Power as we see any extended object; nor do we touch it ; nor is it, properly speaking, an object of the taste or of the smell.   But, as it is itself an attribute of mind rather than of matter, so it is revealed to us as an object of perception and knowledge, by the Internal rather than the External Intellect.   Nevertheless, although it is not a thing which is cognizable by the outward senses, it is as much a reality, as much an object of emotion and desire, as if that were the case. This being the case, we may with entire propriety speak of the Desire of Power ; for, wherever there is a thing, a reality, an object, that object may, in possibility at least, be desired ; but, on the other hand, where there is no object before the mind, it is not possible for desire to exist.

In connexion with these explanatory remarks we repeat, what has already been stated, that the desire of power is natural to the human mind ; in other words, it is an original or implanted principle.   Such is the doctrine of Dugald Stewart ; and it is a view of the subject which at the present time is very generally assented to.

§ 183. *This propension, like others, susceptible of derangement.*

We will not stop to enter into proofs of the view which has now been presented, for that is not our appropriate business at present ; but taking it for granted that such an original principle exists in the human mind, we proceed to say that this important propensity, like the other propensive principles, is

susceptible of a disordered and insane action.—
And why should it not be so? Men place Power
before them in its various forms of authority, honour, high office, titled dignity, and the like, as a
specific and brilliant object of contemplation and
pursuit. This great object, whatever the particular
shape in which it presents itself, they behold constantly with an excited heart and a constrained eye,
till the corresponding Desire, strengthened by constant repetition, becomes the predominant feeling.
If the desire increases beyond a certain point, as it
is very likely to do under such circumstances, the
excess of its action cannot fail to interfere with the
appropriate action of other parts of the mind; and
the result is in all cases a state of disorder, often
existing in the specific form of insanity.

The leading characteristic of a sane and well-or-
dered mind, as is well understood, is a harmony of
all its parts. But such harmony does not exist, and
no approximation to harmony, when any one principle becomes so strong, so overbearingly dominant,
as to suppress and trample on all the rest. The principle under consideration may, by a gradual increase
and exercise, become so powerful (and who can say
that this was not the fact even in the case of such
men as Julius Cæsar, Napoleon, and others of that
class?) as to bring the Will itself, which is the great
regulating principle of the mind, into subjection.
And such complete subjection, too, that persons in
this situation can no more be accounted persons of
truly free and sane minds than the drunkard can,
mentioned by Dr. Rush, whose appetite was such,

that cannon balls discharged between him and his liquor could not prevent his rushing after it.

§ 184. *Results of a disappointed love of Power.*

And this is not all ; nor the only point of view in which the subject is to be contemplated. If the aspiring and ambitious tendency, when it has increased in strength to a high degree, is suddenly and greatly disappointed, as it is very likely to be, the reaction upon the whole mind may be such as to cause disorder in all its functions, and leave it a wide mass of ruins.

The history of those who are confined in Insane Hospitals furnishes a strong presumption that such results are not unfrequent. Although the mind is deranged, the predominant feeling which led to the derangement seems still to remain. One individual challenges for himself the honours of a chancellor, another of a king ; one is a member of Parliament, another is the lord-mayor of London ; one, under the name of the Duke of Wellington or Bonaparte, claims to be the commander of mighty armies another announces himself with the tone and attitude of a prophet of the Most High. Pinel informs us that there were at one time no less than three maniacs in one of the French Insane Hospitals, each of whom assumed to be Louis XIV. On one occasion these individuals were found disputing with each other, with a great degree of energy, their respective rights to the throne. The dispute was terminated by the sagacity of the superintendent, who, approaching one of them, gave him, with a se-

rious look, to understand that he ought not to dispute on the subject with the others, since they were
obviously mad. "Is it not well known" (said the
superintendent) "that you alone ought to be acknowledged as Louis XIV.?" The insane person,
flattered with this homage, cast upon his companions a look of the most marked disdain, and immediately retired.

§ 185. *Additional illustrations of this subject.*

Dr. Gall has given an account of an individual,
in whom undoubtedly the passions of self-esteem
and pride were somewhat marked, but who seems
equally well, and perhaps in a higher degree, to furnish an illustration of the inordinate exercise of the
principle before us. He speaks of this individual
as a person who, in childhood, could never get familiar with his companions, nor in adult age with
his equals. During a long-continued illness, resulting from a blow on his head, he exhibited his
predominant traits in a still higher degree; so much
so, that if he could not be considered insane in the
ordinary sense of the term, he certainly could not
be considered a person of a perfectly sound mind.
Among other things indicative of his peculiar state
of mind, it is remarked of him, that " he treated his
superiors like subordinates, and wrote them letters
in a laconic imperative style, ordering them to yield
this or that favour or distinction." *

Mr. Locke also, in his Letters on Toleration,
gives some notice of an individual of an ambitious

* Gall's Works, Boston ed., vol. iv , p. 178.

temperament, whose mind was so long and earnestly fixed on some high object that he became insane.

§ 186. *Of this form of Insanity in connexion with particular periods of society.*

During the tremendous events of the first French Revolution, and for some subsequent years, when, in consequence of the great disorganization of civil and political principles and precedents, the way was open to the indulgence and the attainment of splendid hopes, the desire of Power (the ambitious principle, as we may, perhaps, conveniently term it) was called into frequent and energetic exercise : so much so as to authorize the assertion, by well-informed persons, that the cases of insanity occurring during that period took their character in a very marked degree from this state of things. Superior to various other influences which sometimes disorder the human mind, they nevertheless went mad with Ambition. Accordingly, if a person entered the lunatic establishments of that country during the period in question, he found, in the language of Dr. Conolly, a great proportion of the male patients believing "themselves to be persons of great importance, mayors, prefects, directors of France, generals, marshals, kings, or emperors, possessing vast territories, or extensive influence, or wealth which nothing can exhaust."

Some, it seems, took a higher bound than this, and, like Alexander, who, in the intoxication of success, claimed to be descended from Jupiter Ammon, were not satisfied with anything short of the ac-

knowledgment of their divine lineage.   One of the
patients confined at Charenton defended his claim
to a divine origin in a letter addressed to one of his
attendants.   Considering the source from which it
comes, and the light which it throws upon insane
mental action, it will repay an insertion in this place
The letter is as follows :

" SIR,—I cannot conceal from you my extreme
astonishment on learning that the cause of my de-
tention at Charenton is a suspicion of madness, on
account of my declaring myself to be the son of
Jupiter.   Very well!   You may convince yourself
of it by accompanying me to Olympus.   Do you
think that, if I were a man of ordinary birth, I
should possess all those scientific attainments which
adorn my mind and my heart with all the flowers
of the sublimest eloquence ?   Do you think I could
have related, with such vehement, impetuous, war-
like audacity, the high transactions of all the repub-
lics of Greece and Rome ?   And could I have restored to the Iliad its previous colouring, as it sprung
from the genius of Kanki, who lived many millions
of ages before the deluge of Ogyges ?

" A second hour sufficed me to make an epopée,
embracing the universal history of Greece and
Rome, and of this great and generous France ; the
same space of time to execute a painting of immense and prodigious dimensions.   I think I have
sufficiently vindicated my birth, and sufficiently established that Jupiter is my father, and the divine
Juno my tender mother.   I therefore beg, sir, that
you will have the goodness to intercede for me, to

restore me to my family and to my divine parents.
I shall cherish a divine gratitude for this favour; a
gratitude eternal as the life of the gods."*

CHAPTER V.

DISORDERED ACTION OF THE PROPENSITIES.

(IV.) IMITATIVENESS, OR THE PROPENSITY TO IMI-
TATION.

§ 187. *Evidence of the existence of this principle.*

WE next proceed to the consideration of Imitativeness, or the Propensity to Imitation.   The proof
that there is in man a principle of Imitation, which
impels him to do as others do, is so abundant as
probably to leave no reasonable doubt upon the candid mind.   We find evidence of it, not only in children, whose principal business it seems to be to repeat whatever they see others do, but also in men,
who exhibit, as a general thing, a strong tendency to
do as their fathers have done before them.   This is
an important principle of our nature; much more so
than, at first sight, would seem to be the case.   If we
examine it in its various influences and relations, it
will be found one of the great supports of society;
and if not directly, yet indirectly, a source of knowledge, happiness, and power.

* Conolly's Inquiry, Lond. ed., p. 357.

This important principle, like all the other propensities, is liable to occasional disorders. In some
individuals it is found .to exhibit, as compared with
its ordinary operation and character, a decidedly
irregular or diseased action.—Cabanis makes mention of an individual, in whom this tendency existed
in a very high degree ; so much so, that, when he
was hindered from yielding to its impulses, " he experienced insupportable suffering."—Pinel, as he is
quoted by Dr. Gall, speaks of an idiot woman,
" who had an *irresistible* propensity to imitate all
that she saw done in her presence. She repeats,
instinctively, all she hears, and imitates the gestures
and actions of others with the greatest fidelity, and
without troubling herself with any regard to propriety."*

§ 188. *Explanations in relation to sympathetic Imitation.*

There is a peculiar form of disordered Imitation,
generally known in philosophical writers under the
denomination of SYMPATHETIC IMITATION, which is
particularly worthy of attention. Of this we shall
now proceed to give some account.

It is implied, in the first place, in all cases of Sympathetic Imitation, that there is more than one person concerned in them ; and it exists in general, in
the highest degree, when the number of persons is
considerable. Some one or more of these individuals is strongly agitated by some internal emotion,
desire, or passion ; and this inward agitation is ex-

* Gall's Works, Am. ed., vol. i., p. 320.

pressed by the countenance, gestures, or other external signs.

In the second place, there is a communication of such agitation of the mind to others; they experience, as is generally the case when we witness the external signs of strong feeling, similar emotions, desires, and passions. And these new exercises of soul are expressed on the part of the sympathetic person by similar outward signs.—In a single word, when we are under the influence of this form of imitation, we both act and feel as others. There is an imitation of the feelings as well as of action, a sympathy of the mind as well as of the body.

§ 189. *Familiar instances of Sympathetic Imitation.*

Abundance of instances (many of them frequent and familiar) show the existence of SYMPATHETIC IMITATION ; in other words, that there is in human feelings, and in the signs of those feelings, a power of contagious communication, by which they often spread themselves rapidly from one to another.

" In genr al, it may be remarked" (says Mr. Stewart), " that whenever we see, in the countenance of another individual, any sudden change of features ; more especially such a change as is expressive of any particular passion or emotion, our own countenance has a tendency to assimilate itself to his. Every man is sensible of this when he looks at a person under the influence of laughter or in a deep melancholy. Something, too, of the same kind takes place in that spasm of the muscles of the jaw which we experience in vawning ; an action which

is well known to be frequently excited by the contagious power of example. Even when we *conceive,*
in solitude, the external expression of any passion,
the effect of the conception is visible in our own appearance. This is a fact of which every person
must be conscious, who attends, in his own case, to
the result of the experiment; and it is a circumstance which has been often remarked with respect
to historical painters, when in the act of transferring
to the canvass the glowing pictures of a creative imagination."*

To these statements, illustrative of sympathetic
imitation, may be added the fact that, if there are
a number of children together, and one of them suddenly gives way to tears and sobs, it is generally
the case that all the rest are more or less affected in
the same manner. Another case, illustrative of the
same natural principle, is that of a mob, when they
gaze at a dancer on the slack-rope. They seem not
only to be filled with the same anxiety which we
may suppose to exist in the rope-dancer himself, but
they naturally writhe, and twist, and balance their
own bodies as they see him do. It has also been
frequently remarked, that, when we see a stroke
aimed and just ready to fall upon the leg or arm of
another person, we naturally shrink, and slightly
draw back our own leg or arm, with a sort of pro-
phetic or anticipative imitation of the person on
whom the blow is about to be inflicted. Hysterical
paroxysms are said to have been sometimes produced at witnessing the exhibition of the pathetic parts

* Stewart's Elements, vol. iii., chap. ii.

of a drama. And even the convulsions of epilepsy have been excited by the mere sight of a person afflicted with them.

§ 190. *Of Sympathetic Imitation in large multitudes.*

It has been often noticed, that the power of sympathetic imitation has been rendered intense, nearly in proportion to the numbers assembled together.— In a large army, if the voice of triumph and joy be raised in a single column, it immediately extends through the whole. On the other hand, if a single column be struck with panic, and exhibit external signs of terror by flight or otherwise, the whole army is likely to become rapidly infected. The tremendous power of the mobs, which are often collected in large cities, may be explained in part on the same principle. The dark cloud that is standing upon the brow of one, is soon seen to gather in darkness on the brow of his neighbour ; and thus to propagate itself rapidly in every direction, till one universal gloom of vengeance settles broadly and blackly upon the moving sea of the multitude.

Similar results are sometimes witnessed in large deliberative assemblies. The art of the orator introduces a common feeling, which glows simultaneously in their bosoms. Soon some one, either sustained by weaker nerves or under the influence of stronger internal impulses, gives signs of bodily.agitation. Those who sit nearest will probably next imbibe the contagion, which spreads and increases until the whole assembly is in a tumult. The spread of this sympathetic communication will be particularly rapid if the first instances of emotion and action are of a decided and strong character.— The statements which have been made are matters of common observation, and can hardly be supposed to have escaped the notice of any. But there are various other facts on record of a less common character, although involving essentially the same principles ; some of which we shall now proceed to mention.

§ 191. *Of the Animal Magnetism of M. Mesner in connexion with this subject.*

About the year 1784, M. Mesner, of Vienna, professed to perform various and important cures by what he called animal magnetism. As this new mode of healing was introduced into France, and much interest was felt on the subject, Louis the Sixteenth appointed a number of persons to examine into it ; among whom were Lavoisier, Bailly, and Dr. Franklin, at that time American minister at Paris. On inquiry, it appeared that it was common in the process to assemble a considerable number of patients together. The patients were placed round a circular box or bucket of oak, the lid of which was pierced with a number of holes, through which there issued moveable and curved branches of iron. These branches were to be applied by the patient to the diseased part. The commissioners, who were witnesses to these proceedings, found that no effect was produced at first. The patients usually sat an hour, and sometimes two, before the crisis came on ; being connected with each other meanwhile by means of a cord passed round their bodies. At length some one, wearied and nervous, and with feelings evidently much excited, was thrown into extraordinary convulsions; and in a short time the whole body of patients became similarly affected, in a greater or less degree. But the commissioners themselves, after having witnessed these singular results, consented to become the subjects of these experiments in their own persons. But they testify that no effect was produced upon them. They also aver, when the process was gone through on persons alone, the same effects were not produced as when a number were together, provided the attempt were made for the first time. In the following extract they seem to attribute the results partly to imagination and partly to sympathy; that is to say, to Sympathetic Imitation.

"The magnetism, then" (the commissioners remark), " or, rather, the operations of the imagination, are equally discoverable at the theatre, in the camp, and in all numerous assemblies, as at the bucket; acting, indeed, by different means, but producing similar effects. The bucket is surrounded with a crowd of patients; the sensations are continually communicated and recommunicated; the nerves are at last worn out with this exercise, and the woman of most sensibility in the company gives the signal. In the mean time, the men who are witnesses of these emotions partake of them in proportion to their nervous sensibility; and those with whom this sensibility is greatest and most easily excited, become themselves the subjects of a crisis.

"This irritable disposition, partly natural and partly acquired, becomes in each sex habitual. The sensations having been felt once or oftener nothing is now necessary but to recall the memory of them, and to exalt the imagination to the same degree in order to operate the same effects. The public process is no longer necessary. You have only to conduct the finger and the rod of iron before the countenance, and to repeat the accustomed ceremonies. In many cases the experiment succeeds, even when the patient is blindfolded, and, without any actual exhibitions of the signs, is made to believe that they are repeated as formerly. The ideas are re-excited; the sensations are reproduced; while the imagination, employing its accustomed instruments, and resuming its former routes, gives birth to the same phenomena."*

§ 192. *Instances of Sympathetic Imitation at the poorhouse of Haerlem.*

Multitudes of other facts, equally well attested, show the sympathetic connexion between mind and mind, and the sympathy between the mind and the nervous and muscular system. Few are more interesting and decisive than what is stated to have occurred at Haerlem under the inspection of Boerhave.—"In the house of charity at Haerlem" (says the account), " a girl, under the impression of terror, fell into a convulsive disease, which returned in regular paroxysms. One of the by-standers, intent

* Rapports des Commissaires chargés par le Roi, de l'Exa men du Magnetisme Animal (as quoted by Stewart)

upon assisting her, was seized with a similar fit, which also recurred at intervals; and, on the day following, another was attacked; then a third, and a fourth; in short, almost the whole of the children, both girls and boys, were afflicted with these convulsions. No sooner was one seized, than the sight brought on the paroxysm in almost all the rest at the same time. Under these distressing circumstances, the physicians exhibited all the powerful antepileptic medicines with which their art furnished them, but in vain. They then applied to Boerhave, who, compassionating the wretched condition of the poor children, repaired to Haerlem; and, while he was inquiring into the matter, one of them was seized with a fit, and immediately he saw several others attacked with a species of epileptic convulsion. It presently occurred to this sagacious physician, that. as the best medicines had been skilfully administered, and as the propagation of the disease from one to another appeared to depend on imagination [the sympathy of imagination], by preventing this impression upon the mind the disease might be cured; and his suggestion was successfully adopted. Having previously apprized the magistrates of his views, he ordered, in the presence of all the children, that several portable furnaces should be placed in different parts of the chamber, containing burning coals, and that irons, bent to a certain form, should be placed in the furnaces; and then he gave these farther commands: that all medicines would be totally useless, and the only remedy with which he was acquainted was, that the first who should be seized

B b

with a fit, whether boy or girl, must be burned in the arm to the very bone by a red-hot iron. He spoke this with uncommon dignity and gravity; and the children, terrified at the thoughts of this cruel remedy, when they perceived any tendency to the recurrence of the paroxysm, immediately exerted all their strength of mind, and called up the horrid idea of the burning; and were thus enabled, by the stronger mental impression, to resist the influence of the morbid propensity."

§ 193. *Other instances of this species of imitation.*

It would not be difficult to multiply cases similar to those which have been mentioned. A few years since, there was a man in Chelmsford, Massachusetts, who had a family of six children, one of whom became affected with the CHOREA or St. Vitus's dance. The others, in the indulgence of that thoughtless gayety which is natural to children, amused themselves with imitating his odd gestures, until, after a time, they were irresistibly affected in the same way. At this state of things, which seems to be susceptible of an explanation in no other way than on the principles of sympathetic imitation, the family, as may naturally be supposed, were in great affliction. The father, a man of some sagacity as well as singularity of humour, brought into the house a block and axe, and solemnly threatened to take off the head of the first child who should hereafter exhibit any involuntary bodily movements, except the child originally diseased. By this measure, which proceeded on the same view of the human mind as the experiment of Boerhave just mentioned, a new train of feeling was excited, and the spell was broken.*

It may be added, that not only those in the same family and in the same building have been seized, but the contagion has sometimes spread from one to another (by the mere influence of sympathetic imitation, as we suppose), over whole towns, and even large districts of country. This was the case in a part of the island of Anglesey in 1796; and still later in this country, in some parts of Tennessee. When the disease appeared in Tennessee, which was essentially of the nature of the CHOREA, although it had its origin in connexion with religious excitement, it is the statement of a writer who seems to have had good opportunities of information (Felix Robertson, of Tennessee, author of an Essay on Chorea Sancti Viti), "that it spread with rapidity, through the medium of the principle of imitation. Thus it was not uncommon for an affected person to communicate it to a greater part of a crowd, who, from curiosity or other motives, had collected around him."†

§ 194. *Additional and striking facts on this subject.*

This subject, which, after what has been said, we shall certainly be justified in considering a very important one, might be pursued to much greater length. We shall dismiss it, however, with a very few facts and remarks more.

A few years since a female in France, Henriette

---

* Powers's Essay on the Influence of the Imagination, p. 32
† See Edinburgh Med. and Surg. Journal, vol. iii., p. 446.

Cornier, under the influence, probably, of an insane impulse, put to death a young child, of which she had always appeared to be fond. She made no attempt to escape or defend herself after having committed the deed, but calmly, and even with indifference, awaited her arrest. The conduct of this unfortunate woman, and the trial which took place, occupied much of public attention, and caused a general and deep sensation.—At a sitting of the French Academy of Medicine, which took place soon after, M. Esquirol made the statement, which cannot well be explained except in connexion with the principle under consideration, that six cases had occurred of persons having been seized with the propensity to destroy their children since the trial of Henriette Cornier for a similar crime.

At the same meeting of the Academy, M. Costel made a statement, in connexion with the same subject, which is still more to our present purpose. He stated that a soldier at the Hotel des Invalides hung himself on a certain post. In a very short time afterward twelve other invalid soldiers hung themselves in the same place. And the suicidal epidemic was stopped only by removing the post.

It is stated that thirteen hundred people destroyed themselves at Versailles in the year 1793; a fact which finds its explanation partly in the atrocities of that remarkable period, and partly in the strong tendencies of the principle under examination. In the year 1806, sixty persons destroyed themselves in the city of Rouen in the months of June and July; an event striking as it was melancholy, and which cannot well be explained, except in connexion with the same principle.   In 1813, in the little village of St. Pierre Monjau, in the Valais, one woman hung herself; and it is stated that many others followed her example.   So that it required the interposition of the civil authorities to prevent the spreading of this suicidal contagion.

Says Dr. Burrows, in connexion with these and other similar statements, " There is also a favourite method, or a fashion in the choice of death sometimes prevailing.   When a person of note has rushed on a voluntary death, the majority of succeeding suicides will be marked by the selection of a similar instrument or mode of immolation, whether it be a halter, a pistol, a razor, or by drowning, or by asphyxia from the fumes of carbon, which is now common in France."[*]

§ 195. *Application of these views to the Witchcraft Delusion in New-England.*

The doctrines of this chapter furnish, in part at least, an explanation of the witchcraft delusion which prevailed in New-England about the year 1690.   In the first place, it is to be recollected that the existence of witches and wizards, possessing a powerful but invisible agency, was a part of the popular creed, and was generally and fully believed.   It is further to be recollected, that the people were, as a general thing, very ignorant at that time, a state of mind exceedingly favourable to any superstition or delusion of that sort; and also that their minds were kept in

[*] Commentaries on Insanity, p. 438.

a state of constant and high excitation, not only in consequence of living scattered abroad and remote from each other, but by residing, in many cases, in the midst of dense and dark forests.

Under these circumstances, certain individuals, under the influence of some form of nervous disease, as we have already suggested and explained in a former chapter, became affected with pains in certain parts of the body, resembling the pain occasioned by the pricking of pins, or by sudden and heavy blows; and in some cases became subject to certain involuntary motions of the body, similar to those of the CHOREA or St. Vitus's dance. Of course, in accordance with the common belief, those mysterious personages, popularly denominated witches, were at their work; and the whole country was at once thrown into a ferment. It is not easy to conceive a more favourable basis than this for the operations of the powerful principle of Sympathetic Imitation. The few cases of nervous and muscular disease which existed at first, were rapidly propagated and multiplied on every side; and, as the popular belief ascribed them to the agency of Satan, manifested in the subordinate agency of witchcraft, the infatuation soon arose to the highest point. The accusations of innocent individuals as exercising the art of witchery, and the scenes of blood which followed, were the natural consequence.—Similar views will probably apply to the witchcraft delusions which, to the ruin of thousands of individuals have prevailed in other periods and countries.

§ 196. *Practical results connected with the foregoing views.*

As sympathetic imitation, if it be correctly considered as a modification of the more ordinary form
of Imitativeness, is to be regarded as, in its basis at
least, an original part of our mental constitution, we
may well suppose it has its beneficial ends. But it
is evident, from the facts which have been given,
that it may also be attended, and, under certain circumstances, is very likely to be attended, with results
of a different kind. Hence the direction has sometimes been given by physicians, that a free intercourse with persons subject to convulsive attacks
ought not to be unnecessarily indulged in, especially
by such as are inclined to nervous affections. And
this precautionary rule might be extended to other
cases : for instance, of madness. "It is a question" (says Mr. Stewart, in the chapter already referred to) "worthy of more attention than has yet
been bestowed upon it by physicians, whether certain kinds of insanity have not a contagious tendency, somewhat analogous to that which has just been
remarked. That the incoherent ravings and frantic
gestures of a madman have a singularly painful effect in unsettling and deranging the thoughts of
others, I have more than once experienced in myself; nor have I ever looked upon this most afflicting of all spectacles without a strong impression of
the danger to which I should be exposed if I were
to witness it daily. In consequence of this impression, I have always read, with peculiar admiration,

the scene in the tragedy of Lear, which forms the transition from the old king's beautiful and pathetic reflections on the storm, to the violent madness in which, without any change whatever in his external circumstances, he is immediately after represented. In order to make this transition more gradual, the poet introduces Edgar, who, with a view of concealing himself from Lear, assumes the dress and behaviour of a madman. At every sentence he utters, the mind of the king, '*whose wits*' (as we are told in the preceding scene) were '*beginning to turn*,' becomes more and more deranged, till at length every vestige of reason vanishes completely."

§ 197. *Application of these views to Legislative and other Assemblies.*

We have already had occasion to intimate that the effects of sympathetic imitation have been strikingly experienced in public assemblies; and we may here add, when those effects have been strongly marked, they have seldom been beneficial. In all political deliberative assemblies, it is a reasonable suggestion that all violent external signs of approbation and disapprobation should be, in a great degree, suppressed. There is generally enough in the subjects which are discussed to excite the members, without the additional excitement (to use a phrase of Buffon) of " *body speaking to body.*" It is said of the famous Athenian tribunal of the Areopagus, that they held their deliberations in the night, in order that their attention might not be diverted by external objects. And, without expressing an opinion on this practice, it is certainly not unwise to guard against the terrible influences under consideration ; otherwise truth, honour, and justice will often be sacrificed to feeling.   Every public deliberative assembly has probably furnished facts illustrative of the propriety of this caution.

Similar remarks will apply to religious assemblies, and perhaps with still more force, as religious subjects are more important, and, in general, more exciting than any other.   If, in such an assembly, the feelings of a few individuals become so strong as to show themselves very decidedly in the countenance and the movements of the body, and particularly by sobs and loud outcries, it will not be surprising if this state of things should quickly spread itself through the whole body.   In this way it is probable that serious evils have sometimes been experienced, and that true and false religious feelings have been confounded.   It is true that people may sometimes be led, by the mere power of sympathy, to attend to religious things ; and so far, if there are no collateral evils, the result may be regarded as favourable ; but, at the same time, it should be kept in recollection, that the feelings, which are really propagated from one to another by mere sympathy, are not in themselves religious feelings in any proper sense of the terms, though they are often confounded with them.

C c

CHAPTER VI.

DISORDERED ACTION OF THE PROPENSITIES

(v.) THE DESIRE OF ESTEEM.

§ 198. *The desire of Esteem susceptible of a disordered action.*

THERE may be a disordered action of the desire o.
Esteem. This principle is not only an original one,
but, as a general thing, it possesses, as compared
with some of the other propensities, a greater and
more available amount of strength. It is a regard
for the opinion of others (a sense of character, as we
sometimes term it), which, in the absence or the too
great weakness of higher principles, serves to restrict the conduct of multitudes within the bounds of
decency and order. This principle is good and important in its place and under due regulation ; but
it is exceedingly apt to become irregular, unrestrained, and inordinate in its exercise. This view throws
light upon the character of many individuals. It is
here, probably, that we may discover the leading defect in the character of Alcibiades, a name of distinguished celebrity in the history of Athens. His
ruling passion seems to have been not so much the
love of POWER as the love of APPLAUSE. In other
words, his great desire was, as has been well re

marked of him, "to make a noise, and to furnish matter of conversation to the Athenians."

Pope, in the first of his Moral Essays, illustrates this subject, in his usual powerful manner, in what he says of the Duke of Wharton ; the key to whose character he finds in the excessive desire of human applause.

> " Search then the ruling passion. There alone
> The wild are constant and the cunning known ;
> This clew, once found, unravels all the rest,
> The prospect clears, and Wharton stands confess'd.
> Wharton, the scorn and wonder of our days,
> Whose ruling passion was the LUST OF PRAISE.
> Born with whate'er could win it from the wise,
> Women and fools must like him, or he dies."

§ 199. *Further explanatory remarks on this subject.*

The inordinate exercise of this propensity, as is correctly intimated by Mr. Stewart, tends to *disorganize* the mind. It cannot well be otherwise. The man who is under the influence of such an excessive appetite for the world's smiles and flatteries, has no fixed rule of conduct ; but the action of his mind, his opinions, desires, hopes, and outward conduct, are constantly fluctuating with the changing tide of popular sentiment. It is nearly impossible that the pillars of the mind should remain firm, and without more or less undermining and dislocation, under the operations of such a system of uncertainty and vicissitude. Hence the disorganization which Mr. Stewart speaks of; not merely in the power primarily affected, but also in other parts of the mind.

Nor is this all.—When persons who are under

the influence of this excessive desire are disappointed in the possession of that approbation and applause which are its natural food, they are apt to become melancholy, misanthropic, and unhappy in a very high degree. In fact, numerous cases of actual Insanity, using the term in distinction from the more ordinary forms of irregularity and disorder, may probably be traced to this source. Various statements of writers on the subject of Mental Alienation evidently support this view.

§ 200. *Incidents illustrative of this form of Alienation.*

Pinel mentions a young man who, under the influence of an overweening vanity, which is one of the excessive or disordered exercises of the implanted Desire of Esteem, resolved at all hazards to become distinguished ; at least, like Alcibiades, so far as to be talked about. He studied natural philosophy, chymistry, and the fine arts. He travelled in unknown regions, which his ample fortune enabled him to do; and published his discoveries with superb plates, and in a style of great elegance. He kept artists with him to aid him in his plans. In imitation of other celebrated names, he stimulated his faculties, already over-excited, by the free use of strong coffee and ardent spirits. He endeavoured to do without sleep, hurrying from place to place night and day. And finally, as might be expected, became furiously insane.

An instance very recently occurred in Paris, which may be regarded, on the whole, as rather a striking illustration of the shape which mental disorder assumes when originating in the propensity which we are examining. A journeyman printer, in a joke, threw something at one of his companions, which broke the glass of his spectacles, and slightly wounded him. The feelings of the sufferer were so severely excited by what he considered a premeditated insult, that he insisted upon having his injured honour healed by a mortal duel. The thoughtless offender protested his innocence of any intended outrage. The infatuated man, nevertheless, continued to urge his hostile appeal till he found it totally in vain. Conceiving himself thus degraded for ever, he shut himself up in his room, in the Rue de Foin, and there at length did, as he madly supposed, justice to himself by cutting his throat. His father is said to have put an end to his life in a similar fit of monomania.

§ 201. *Other instances still further illustrative of the subject.*

And where Insanity or the highest form of disorder does not supervene, there are sometimes consequences scarcely less unfavourable. It is well known, that within a few years a number of gifted individuals have been hurried to an early grave, in consequence of being held up to public contempt and ridicule in anonymous Reviews. The principle which led them to seek the sympathy and the favourable opinion of others was too exquisitely susceptible to be treated with that severity and roughness of manners which it experienced.

The case of Henry Kirk White, too keenly alive to the frowns and favours of popular sentiment, notwithstanding his great and unquestionable excellences, will illustrate what we mean. Keats, also, the gifted author of Endymion, may probably be regarded as another victim of the severity of criticism, operating upon a mind too eagerly desirous of popular approbation, and too susceptible to the influences of popular aversion and reproof.

The circumstance that the inordinate exercise of the Desire of Esteem is sometimes connected with distinguished vigour of intellect and purity of moral sentiment, does not necessarily secure the disappointed and calumniated individual who is the subject of it against great anguish of mind ; so great in some instances as not only to destroy happiness, but life itself.

CHAPTER VII.

DISORDERED ACTION OF THE PROPENSITIES.

(VI.) SOCIALITY, OR THE DESIRE OF SOCIETY.

§ 202. *Origin of the propensive principle of Sociality.*

THERE are yet other propensive principles which may properly be considered under this general head. Nothing is more obvious than that men naturally (not moved to it primarily by the influences of education, or considerations of interest, or anything of that kind, but of themselves and *naturally*) have a desire of the company or society of their fellow-men; a tendency of the mind expressed by the term SOCIALITY or SOCIABILITY.

We are aware that some writers take a different view, and endeavour to resolve this principle, as well as some others, into the principle of self-love. But when we consider the evident importance of this principle to man in his present situation; when we take into account its early appearance, and its immense strength in childhood as well as in later years, together with various other circumstances which would be properly adduced in a full inquiry into this topic, we cannot hesitate to speak of the social principle as an original or implanted one. This propensity, implanted within us for the most useful purposes, may exist with such a degree of weakness on the one hand, or with such a degree of intensity on the other, as justly to entitle its action in either of these forms to be called a disordered, and even, in some cases, an alienated or insane one.

§ 203. *True idea of Alienation, or Insanity of the Sensibilities.*

And here it may be proper to revert briefly once more to the precise idea which we attach to the term Alienation, considered as expressive of a state or condition of the Sensibilities. There may be an imperfection of mental action; there may be a disorder of mental action, which is not, nevertheless, an absolute alienation or insanity of mental action. The term alienation, and the same may be said of the term insanity, properly applies to those forms of mental action (we speak now particularly of the sensibilities) which are so much disordered as to set at defiance any efforts of the Will to control them; in a word, they are involuntary. So that, in accordance with this statement, there may be either a disordered state of the principle of sociality or of any other principle (that is to say, one which is irregular, but still is susceptible of correction under the efforts of the will); or there may be, when this disorder is found to exist beyond certain limits, an alienated, an insane state. But although this distinction ought to be clearly understood, it is not necessary, in the remarks which for the most part we have occasion to make, that we should always keep it distinctly in view.

§ 204. *The irregular action of the Social principle exists in two forms.*

But to return to our subject. An irregular action of the social principle, whether it be truly alienated or exist in some lighter form of disorder, may show itself in two aspects, which are entirely diverse from each other, viz., either in a morbid aversion to society, or in a desire of society inordinately intense.

Persons to whom the first statement will apply are generally, and for the most part justly, designated as misanthropes. There are some cases, it is true, where the character of being misanthropic does not, in strictness of speech, appear to be applicable.   Individuals may be found, although it is not often the case, in whom the social principle is naturally so very weak that they shun all intercourse with their fellow-men, and yet without hating them. They live apart, but not in opposition.   They have no enmity to their fellow-men, although they do not seek their company.

The more frequent and decided cases are those which have their origin, not in nature, but in circumstances.   Under the influence of some sudden revulsion of the mind, of some great disappointment, of some ill-treatment on the part of near relatives and supposed friends, or of some other powerful cause, the natural tie of brotherhood, which binds man to his fellow-man, is snapped asunder, and the unhappy individual flees to the rock and the desert, never more to return.   Such instances (the Timon of Athens of Shakspeare, the Black Dwarf of Walter Scott, and numerous others) are frequently found, not only on the recorded annals of human nature, but in almost every one's personal experience.

The views which have now been presented appear to be rather remarkably illustrated in the case of Henry Welby, who died in London in 1639, in the eighty-fourth year of his age.   This individual was a man of good education and of some wealth; charitable to others, and happy in the esteem and love of his friends.   When he was about forty years of age, his brother, a man without affection or principle, attempted to shoot him with a pistol double charged with bullets.

The attempt was unsuccessful ; but the result upon his own mind was such as to fill him with horror and disgust of the human race. He resolved, from that time, to seclude himself from society. He ever afterward lived alone, avoiding, as far as possible, the sight of every human being, and spending his time in reading, meditation, and prayer. And although he seems to have had but one child, an amiable daughter, who was happily married, he could never, after having been affected with this disordered mental bias, be persuaded to see her or any of her family.

§ 205. *Further remarks on the disordered action of the Social propensity.*

There is another class of cases, which in their character appear to be directly the reverse of those which have just been mentioned.—Individuals, when they are cut off from society, particularly the society of their friends, are sometimes the subjects of a misery inexpressibly intense. In these persons the social principle is, perhaps, too strong. It is, at least, subjected to too severe a trial. Deprived of its natural food, it disorganizes, in the intensity of its grief, the whole mind.

Such was the case, perhaps, with the unfortunate Foscari, whose sad story is so well known. Having been banished from Venice, he took measures to return again, to see once more his beloved parents and family, at the evident hazard of his life. On being again banished from his country, he died in a short time of pure anguish of heart.

In this place, and as illustrating the connexion which the social principle has in various ways with soundness of mind, we may briefly refer to certain psychological and disciplinary experiments which have been made in this country.—In the year 1821, the Legislature of New-York directed the Superintendent of the Auburn State Prison to select a number of the most hardened criminals, and to lock them up in solitary cells, to be kept there day and night, without any interruption of their solitude, and without labour. This order, which was regarded, and was designed to be regarded, in the light of an experiment, was carried into effect in September of that year, by confining eighty criminals in the manner prescribed. On this experiment, Messrs. Beaumont and Toqueville, who were recently commissioned by the French government to examine and to report on the American system of Prison Discipline, make the following remarks: "This trial, from which so happy a result had been anticipated, was fatal to the greater part of the convicts; in order to reform them, they had been subjected to complete isolation; but this absolute solitude, if nothing interrupt it, is beyond the strength of man; it destroys the criminal without intermission and without pity; it does not reform, it kills.—The unfortunates on whom this experiment was made fell into a state of depression so manifest, that their keepers were struck with it; their lives seemed in danger if they remained longer in this situation; five of them had already succumbed during a single year; their moral state was not less alarming; one of them had become

insane ; another, in a fit of despair, had embraced
the opportunity, when the keeper brought him something, to precipitate himself from his cell, running
the almost certain chance of a mortal fall.—Upon
these and similar effects the system was finally
judged. The Governor of the State of New-York
pardoned twenty-six of those in solitary confinement.
The others, to whom this favour was not extended,
were allowed to leave the cells during the day, and
to work in the common workshops of the prison."

§ 206. *Of the disease founded on the Social propensity termed Nostalgia.*

There is an exceedingly painful disease, founded,
in a great degree, upon the disordered action of the
social principle, which is termed by physicians Nostalgia, but which is more commonly known under
the familiar designation of HOME-SICKNESS. This
disease, which is sometimes fatal, is said to have
frequently prevailed among the Swiss when absent
from their native country. The beautiful sky which
shone over them in their absence from their native
land, the works of art, the allurements of the highest forms of civilization, could not erase from their
hearts the image of their rugged mountains and their
stormy heavens. They had society enough around
them, it is true ; but it was not the society which
their hearts sought for, or in which, in existing circumstances, they could participate. They bowed
their heads under the influence of a hidden and irrepressible sorrow ; and in many cases not merely
pined away, but died in the deep anguish of their
separation.

In the year 1733, a Russian army, under the command of General Praxin, advanced to the banks of the Rhine. At this remote distance from their native country, this severe mental disease began to prevail among the Russians; so much so, that five or six soldiers every day became unfit for duty ; a state of things which threatened to affect the existence of the army. The progress of this home-sickness was terminated by a severe order from the commander (designed probably, and which had the effect to produce a strong counteracting state of mind), that every one affected with the sickness should be buried alive.*

§ 207. *Disordered action of the principle of Veracity.*

We close these remarks on the alienated action of the Propensities, although we do not profess to have fully exhausted the subject, by a brief reference to another important principle, that which is the natural basis of the utterance of the truth.

The principle of Veracity, or the tendency of mind which leads men to utter the truth, appears to be an original or implanted one. This principle, either through habit or by natural defect, sometimes exhibits itself in strangely perverted forms.—In accordance with this view, Dr. Rush speaks of a LYING disease.

"It differs" (he says) "from exculpating, fraudulent, and malicious lying, in being influenced by none of the motives of any of them. Persons thus

* Rush on the Diseases of the Mind, 2d ed., *p.* 113.

diseased cannot speak the truth on any subject, noi tell the same story twice in the same way, nor de scribe anything as it has appeared to other people. Their falsehoods are seldom calculated to injure anybody but themselves, being for the most part of a hyperbolical or boasting nature, but now and then they are of a mischievous nature, and injurious to the characters and property of others. That it is a corporeal disease [that is to say, in some way connected with a diseased state of the body], I infer from its sometimes appearing in mad people, who are remarkable for veracity in the healthy states of their minds, several instances of which I have known in the Pennsylvania Hospital. Persons affected with this disease are often amiable in their tempers and manners, and sometimes benevolent and charitable in their dispositions."*

Enough, perhaps, has been said on this part of our subject, although the topic is not exhausted, to give at least a general idea of it. The same train of thought, and with scarcely any modification, will apply to all the original appetites and propensities, whatever they may be, which have not been noticed. They are all implanted by the Creator of the mind ; they are all good in their place, and under proper regulation ; they are all not only morally evil when they are not properly controlled and restrained, but are liable to be attended with more or less of mental disorder, from the slightest shades of disorganization to the deep and terrible miseries of permanent insanity.

* Rush on the Diseases of the Mind, 2d ed., p. 265.

CHAPTER VIII.

DISORDERED ACTION OF THE AFFECTIONS.

§ 208. *Of the states of mind denominated Presentiments.*

WE proceed now to remark, that there may be a disordered action of the Affections or Passions, as well as of the lower principles of the Sensitive nature; and this remark is designed to apply to both classes of the Affections, the benevolent and those of an opposite kind. We do not propose, however, in this chapter to confine ourselves very strictly to the Affections, properly so called, but shall introduce some collateral or connected subjects, which may be regarded as too interesting to be omitted, and, at the same time, as too unimportant to require a distinct place. They may be expected, moreover, to throw indirectly some light upon the leading topic of the chapter. We begin with the subject of PRE-SENTIMENTS.

Many individuals have had, at certain times, strong and distinct impressions in relation to something future; so much so that not the least doubt has remained in their own minds of its being something out of the common course of nature. It is related, for instance, of the nonconformist writer, Isaac Ambrose, whose religious works formerly had some ce-

lebrity, that he had such a striking internal intimation of his approaching death, that he went round to
all his friends to bid them farewell.   When the day
arrived which his presentiments indicated as the day
of his dissolution, he shut himself up in his room
and died.   Mozart, the great musical composer,
had a strong presentiment that the celebrated Requiem which bears his name would be his last work.
Nothing could remove this impression from his mind.
He expressly said, "It is certain I am writing this
requiem for myself; it will serve for my funeral service."   The foreboding was realized.   It is stated
of Pendergrast, an officer in the Duke of Marlbo-
rough's army, that he had a strong foreboding that
he would be killed on a certain day.   He mentioned his conviction to others, and even made a written memorandum in relation to it.*   Henry the
Fourth, of France, for some weeks previous to his
being assassinated by Ravaillac, had a distinct presentiment, which he mentioned to Sully and other
men of his time, that some great calamity was about
to befall him.

Some cases of Presentiments can undoubtedly be
explained on natural principles.   Some accidental
circumstance, a mere word, the vagaries of a dream,
any trifling event which happens in the popular belief of the time and country to be regarded as a sin-
ister omen, may have been enough, in some cases,
to lay the foundation for them; and the subsequent
fulfilment may have been purely accidental.   Nor
is it necessary, so far as we are able to perceive,

* Boswell's Life of Johnson, vol. ii., p. 48.

to suppose that in any cases whatever there is any supernatural or miraculous interposition. But, if this is not the case, it is difficult to account for the deep conviction which sometimes fastens upon the mind, a conviction upon which arguments and persuasions are found to make no impression, except upon the ground that the action of the Sensibilities is in some degree disordered. But of the specific nature of that disorder, the trait or circumstance which distinguishes it from other forms of disordered mental action, it is difficult to give any account

§ 209. *Of sudden and strong impulses of Mind.*

There is another disordered condition of mind, different from that which has just been mentioned, and yet, in some respects, closely allied to it. Some persons, whose soundness of mind, on all ordinary occasions, is beyond question, find in themselves at certain times a sudden and strange propensity to do things which, if done, would clearly prove them, to some extent at least, deranged. As an illustration, a person of a perfectly sane mind, according to the common estimate of insanity, once acknowledged, that, whenever he passed a particular bridge, he felt a slight inclination to throw himself over, accompanied with some dread that his inclination might hurry him away. Such slight alienated impulses are probably more frequent than is commonly supposed. And they exist in every variety of degree, sometimes scarcely attracting notice, at others bearing the broad and fatal stamp of dangerous insanity.

Dr. Gall mentions the case of a woman in Ger-

D d

many, who, having on a certain occasion witnessed a building on fire, was ever afterward, at intervals, subject to strong impulses prompting her to fire buildings. Under the influence of these impulses, she set fire to twelve buildings in the borough where she lived. Having been arrested on the thirteenth attempt, she was tried, condemned, and executed. "She could give no other reason, nor show any other motive for firing so many houses, than this impulse, which drove her to it. Notwithstanding the fear, the terror, and the repentance she felt in every instance after committing the crime, she went and did it afresh."* Would not sound philosophy, to say nothing of the requisitions of religion, have assigned such a person to an insane hospital rather than to the block of the executioner?

The same writer, who has collected numerous valuable facts in relation to the operations of the human mind, mentions the case of a German soldier, who was subject every month to a violent convulsive attack. "He was sensible" (he proceeds to remark) " of their approach ; and as he felt, by degrees, a violent propensity to kill, in proportion as the paroxysm was on the point of commencing, he was earnest in his entreaties to be loaded with chains. At the end of some days the paroxysm and the fatal propensity diminished, and he himself fixed the period at which they might without danger set him at liberty. At Haina, we saw a man who, at certain periods, felt an irresistible desire to injure others. He knew this unhappy propensity, and had

* Gall's Works, vol. iv., Am. ed., p. 105.

himself kept in chains till he perceived that it was safe to liberate him. An individual of melancholic temperament was present at the execution of a criminal. The sight caused him such violent emotion, that he at once felt himself seized with an irresistible desire to kill, while, at the same time, he entertained the utmost horror at the commission of the crime. He depicted his deplorable state, weeping bitterly, and in extreme perplexity. He beat his head, wrung his hands, remonstrated with himself, begged his friends to save themselves, and thanked them for the resistance they made to him."*

§ 210. *Insanity of the Affections or Passions.*

From the instances which have been given, it will be seen that sudden and strong impulses, indicating a disordered state of the mind, may exist in reference to very different things, and also in very various degrees. The cases last mentioned were of such an aggravated nature, that they may properly be regarded as instances (and perhaps the same view will apply to some other cases of a less marked character) of actual alienation or insanity. And, as such, they may be correctly described as instances of the insanity of the Affections or Passions.

The insanity of the passions is a state of mind somewhat peculiar, even as compared with other forms of insanity. The powers of perception, in cases of insanity of the passions, are often in full and just exercise. The mind may possess, in a very considerable degree, its usual ability in compa-

* Gall's Works, vol. i., Am. ed., p. 329.

ring ideas and in deducing conclusions. The seat
of the difficulty is not to be sought for in what are
usually designated as the intellectual powers, in distinction from the sensitive nature, but in the passions
alone. The victim of this mental disease does not
stop to reason, reflect, and compare ; but is borne
forward to his purpose with a blind, and often an irresistible impulse.

Pinel mentions a mechanic in the asylum BICE-
TRE who was subject to this form of insanity. It
was, as is frequently the case, intermittent. He
knew when the paroxysms of passion were coming
on, and even gave warnings to those who were exposed to its effects to make their escape. His powers of correctly judging remained unshaken, not
only at other times, but even in the commission of
the most violent and outrageous acts. He saw
clearly their impropriety, but was unable to restrain
himself ; and, after the cessation of the paroxysms,
was often filled with the deepest grief.

§ 211. *Of the mental disease termed Hypochondriasis.*

The seat of the well-known mental disease termed Hypochondriasis is to be sought for in a disordered state of the Sensibilities. It is, in fact, nothing more or less than a state of deep depression,
gloom, or melancholy. This is the fact ; and we
never apply the term hypochondriasis to a state of
the mind where such gloom or melancholy does not
exist ; but it is nevertheless true, that the occasion
or basis of the fact may sometimes be found in a

disordered condition of some other part of the mind. One or two concise statements will illustrate what we mean.

One of the slighter forms of hypochondriasis can, perhaps, be traced to inordinate workings of the Imagination. The mind of the sufferer is fixed upon some unpromising and gloomy subject; probably one which has particular relation either to his present or future prospects. He gives it an undue place in his thoughts, dwelling upon it continually. His imagination hovers over it, throwing a deeper shade on what is already dark. Thus the mind becomes disordered; it is broken off from its ordinary and rightful mode of action, and is no longer what it was, nor what nature designed it should be.

§ 212. *Of other forms of Hypochondriasis.*

There is another and still more striking form of hypochondriasis, which is connected in its origin with an alieration of the power of belief. As in all other cases of hypochondriasis, the subject of it suffers much mental distress. He is beset with the most gloomy and distressing apprehensions, occasioned, not by exaggerated and erroneous notions in general, but by some fixed and inevitable false belief.—One imagines that he has no soul; another, that his body is gradually but rapidly perishing; and a third, that he is converted into some other animal, or that he has been transformed into a plant. We are told in the Memoirs of Count Maurepas, a fact which we have already had occasion to refer to, that this last idea once took possession of the mind of

one of the princes of Bourbon.   So deeply was he
infected with this notion, that he often went into his
garden, and insisted on being watered in common
with the plants around him.   Some have imagined
themselves to be transformed into glass, and others
have fallen into the still stranger folly of imagining
themselves dead.—What has been said confirms
our remark, that although hypochondriasis is, in itself considered, seated in the sensibilities, yet its
origin may sometimes be found in a disordered state
of some other part of the mind.

It is also sometimes the case that this disease
originates in a violation of some form of sensitive
action.   It is not only, as its appropriate position,
seated in the sensibilities, but it sometimes has its
origin there.   We have already mentioned the case
of a certain Englishman, a man of generous and
excellent character, whose life was once attempted
by his brother with a pistol.   On wresting the pistol
from his brother's hand and examining it, he found
it to be double charged with bullets.   This transaction, as might be expected in the case of a person
of just and generous sentiments, filled him with such
horror, and with such disgust for the character of the
man, that he secluded himself ever after from human
society.   He never allowed the visits even of his
own children.   It is certainly easy to see, that under such circumstances the sensibilities may receive
such a shock as to leave the subject of it in a state
of permanent dissatisfaction and gloom.   In other
words, he may in this way, and for such reasons,
become a confirmed hypochondriac.

§ 213. *Of intermissions of Hypochondriasis, and of its remedies.*

The mental disease of hypochondriasis is always understood to imply the existence of a feeling of gloom and depression ; but this depressed feeling does not exist in all cases in the same degree. In all instances it is a source of no small unhappiness, but in some the wretchedness is extreme. The greatest bodily pains are light in the comparison. It is worthy of remark, however, that the mental distress of hypochondriasis is in some persons characterized by occasional intermissions. An accidental remark, some sudden combination of ideas, a pleasant day, and various other causes, are found to dissipate the gloom of the mind. At such times there is not unfrequently a high flow of the spirits, corresponding to the previous extreme depression.— As this disease, even when mitigated by occasional intermissions, is prodigal in evil results, it becomes proper to allude to certain remedies which have sometimes been resorted to.

I.—The first step towards remedying the evil is to infuse health and vigour into the bodily action, especially that of the nervous system. The nerves, it will be recollected, are the great medium of sensation, inasmuch as they constitute, under different modifications, the external senses. Now the senses are prominent sources of belief and knowledge. Consequently, when the nervous system (including, of course, the senses) is in a disordered state, it is not surprising that persons should have wrong sen-

sations and external perceptions, and, therefore, a
wrong belief.   If a man's nerves are in such a state
that he feels precisely as he supposes a man made
of glass would feel, it is no great wonder, when we
consider the constitution of the mind, that he should
actually believe himself to be composed of that substance.   But one of the forms of the disease in
question is essentially founded on an erroneous but
fixed belief of this kind.   Hence, in restoring the
bodily system to a right action, we shall correct the
wrong belief, if it be founded in the senses ; and, in
removing this, we may anticipate the removal of that
deep-seated gloom which is characteristic of hypochondriasis.

§ 214.   *Further remarks on the remedies of Hypo-*
chondriasis.

II.—As all the old associations of the hypochondriac have been more or less visited and tinctured
by his peculiar malady, efforts should be made to
break them up and remove them from the mind, by
changes in the objects with which he is most conversant, by introducing him into new society, or by
travelling.   By these means his thoughts are likely
to be diverted, not only from the particular subject
which has chiefly interested him, but a new impulse
is given to the whole mind, which promises to interrupt and banish that fatal fixedness and inertness
which had previously encumbered and prostrated it.

III.—Whenever the malady appears to be founded on considerations of a moral nature, the hypochondriasis may sometimes be removed, or, at least,

alleviated, by the suggestion of counteracting moral motives. If, for instance, the despondency of mind has arisen from some supposed injury, it is desirable to suggest all well-founded considerations which may tend to lessen the sufferer's estimate of the amount of the injury received. When the injury is very great and apparent, suggestions on the nature and duty of forgiveness may not be without effect. —But, whatever course may be taken, it is desirable that the attention of the sufferer should be directed as little as possible to his disease, by any direct remarks upon it. It was a remark of Dr. Johnson, whose sad experience enabled him to judge, that conversation upon melancholy feeds it. Accordingly, he advised Boswell, who, as well as himself, was subject to melancholy of mind, " Never to speak of it to his friends, or in company."

§ 215. *Disordered action of the passion of Fear.*

The passion of FEAR, inasmuch as there are various objects around us which are or may be dangerous, is obviously implanted in us for wise purposes. But it not unfrequently exhibits an irregular or disordered action. This disordered state of the affection may discover itself, when considered either in reference to the occasion on which it exists, or in reference to the degree in which it exists. In some cases, for instance, it is connected with objects which, in the view of reason and common sense, ought not to excite it. Some persons are afraid to be alone in the dark; it is exceedingly distressing to them. Others are afraid (so much so, perhaps, as to be thrown into convulsions by their presence) of a mouse, or a squirrel, or an insect. It will be necessary to refer to, and to give some explanation of cases of this kind, under the head of Casual Associations.

Sometimes the disordered action of the passion of fear is not so restricted and shut up, as it were, to a particular thing ; but takes a wider range, attaching itself to all objects which can possibly excite the idea of danger, even in the slightest degree. Pinel, who, more than any other writer, is the great source of facts on this part of our subject, mentions an individual who was so subject to fears that he could scarcely get a few moment's repose, "not lying down till four or five o'clock in the morning. He passed the night in a state of constant fear ; imagined he heard a voice speaking in a low tone ; carefully shut his door ; a moment after, feared that he had not closed it tight, and continually returned, and continually discovered his mistake. Another idea took possession of his mind ; he would rise from his bed to examine his papers ; he would separate them one after another ; collect them again ; believe that he had forgotten something ; and be afraid of the very dust on the furniture. He would evince the greatest instability in his thoughts and intentions ; would wish and not wish ; constantly tormented by suspicion and gloom ; he even feared to breathe the external air, and always kept himself within doors."

§ 216. *Other illustrations of the disordered action of this passion.*

Again, fear may exist with such an intensity as essentially to affect the very structure of the mind, and even cause insanity in the higher sense of the term. Probably the power of this passion is not well understood. Certain it is, that terrible results have often followed from the attempts of persons, particularly of children, to excite it in others, even in sport. Many instances are on record of individuals who have been permanently and most seriously injured, either in mind or body, or both, by a sudden fright. It is somewhere stated in the writings of Pinel, that he received into the hospital of which he had charge three insane persons within a very short time, whose insanity was caused in this way.

Sometimes, especially when connected with permanent causes, it gradually expands and strengthens itself, till it is changed into DESPAIR. The distinctive trait of Despair, in distinction from all other modifications of fear, is, that it excludes entirely the feeling of hope, which exists in connexion with fear in other cases. Despair may exist, therefore, in a greater or less degree, and with a greater or less amount of mental anguish, in accordance with the nature of the thing, whatever it is, which occasions it. When great present or future interests are at stake, and the mind, in relation to those interests, is in a state of despair, the wretchedness which is experienced is necessarily extreme.

§ 217. *Perversions of the Benevolent Affection.*

The general division of the Affections, as is well understood, is into the Benevolent and Malevolent. There are some singular perversions of the benevolent affections, as well as those of an opposite kind, which are worthy of notice here.—It is not unfrequently the case, that persons in a state of mental alienation are entirely indifferent to, and sometimes they even hate those whom, at.other times, they love most sincerely and deeply. It is, perhaps, difficult to explain this, although it is practically important to know the fact.

Dr. Rush, in speaking of a singular apathy or torpor of the passions, which is sometimes found to exist, says : " I was once consulted by a citizen of Philadelphia, who was remarkable for his strong affection for his wife and children when his mind was in a sound state, who was occasionally afflicted with this apathy ; and, when under its influence, lost his affection for them all so entirely, that he said he could see them butchered before his eyes without feeling any distress, or even inclination to rise from his chair to protect them."

II.—There are other cases where there seems to be not merely an extinction of the benevolent affection, but its positive conversion into hatred. The same philosophic physician mentions the case of a young lady, who was confined as a lunatic in the Pennsylvania Hospital in the year 1802. One of the characteristics of her insanity was hatred for her father. She was gradually restored ; and, for several weeks before she was discharged from the hospital, discovered all the marks of a sound mind, excepting the continuance of this unnatural feeling of hatred. On a certain day she acknowledged with pleasure a return of her filial attachment and affection, and soon after was discharged as cured.*

§ 218. *Other cases of perverted Benevolent Affections.*

III.—There are other cases where insanity is the indirect result of the mere intensity of the benevolent affections. In cases of this kind, the affections are so strong, so intense, that they are unable to withstand the shock of sudden and great opposition and disappointments.—" A peasant woman" (says Dr. Gall) " became insane three times ; the first, at the death of her brother ; the second, at the death of her father ; and the third, at that of her mother. After she had recovered the third time she came to consult me. As she was very religious, she complained to me of her unfortunate disposition to be afflicted, at the loss of persons who were dear to her, more than religion permits ; an evident proof that she had yielded to grief, although she had combated it by motives which were within her reach." Pinel also mentions the case of a young man, who became a violent maniac a short time after losing a father and mother whom he tenderly loved. It is true that in these cases the proximate cause of the insanity is sorrow or grief ; but the remote cause, and that without which the unfortunate result would not have existed,

* Rush on the Diseases of the Mind, p 255, 345.

is an unrestrained and excessive position of the be
nevolent affections.

It may be proper to add here, that sudden and
strong feelings of joy have, in repeated instances,
·caused a permanent mental disorganization, and
even death itself.—" The son of the famous Leibnitz died from this cause, upon his opening an old
chest, and unexpectedly finding in it a large quantity
of gold.   Joy from the successful issue of political
schemes or wishes has often produced the same effect.   Pope Leo the Tenth died of joy, in consequence of hearing of a great calamity that had befallen the French nation.   Several persons died
from the same cause, Mr. Hume tells us, upon witnessing the restoration of Charles the Second to the
British throne ; and it is well known that the door-
keeper of Congress died of an apoplexy, from joy,
upon hearing the news of the capture of Lord Corn-
wallis and his army during the American revolution-
ary war."*

CHAPTER IX.

DISORDERED ACTION OF THE MORAL SENSIBILITIES.

§ 219. *Nature of voluntary Moral Derangement.*

THE moral, as well as the natural or pathematic
Sensibilities, the Conscience as well as the Heart,

* Rush on the Diseases of the Mind, p. 339.

may be the subject of a greater or less degree of disorder and alienation. There are probably two leading forms, at least, of moral derangement, viz., VOLUNTARY, and NATURAL or CONGENITAL.—In regard to voluntary moral derangement we remark, as an interesting and practically important fact, that man may virtually destroy his conscience. There is sound philosophy in the well-known passage of Juvenal, " NEMO REPENTE FUIT TURPISSIMUS." The truth implied in this passage is unquestionably applicable to all persons, with the exception of those few cases where the moral derangement is natural or congenital. A man is not, in the first instance, *turpissimus* or a villain, because his conscience makes resistance, and will not let him be so. But if the energies of the will are exercised in opposition to the conscience; if, on a systematic plan, and by a permanent effort, the remonstrances of conscience are unheeded, and its action repressed, its energies will be found to diminish, and its very existence will be put at hazard. There is no doubt that in this way the conscience may be so far seared as to be virtually annihilated. Multitudes have prepared themselves for the greatest wickedness, and have become, in fact, morally insane, by their own voluntary doing. There is a passage in Beaumont, in his " King and no King," which strikingly indicates the progress of the mind in such cases.

> " There is a method in man's wickedness;
> It grows up by degrees. I am not come
> So high as killing of myself; there are
> A hundred thousand sins 'twixt it and me,
> Which I must do. *I shall come to 't at last.*"

We say in such cases the conscience is virtually annihilated. And by this remark we mean that it .s inert, inefficient, dormant, paralyzed. We do not mean that it is dead. The conscience never dies. Its apparent death is impregnated with the elements of a real and terrible resurrection. It seems to gather vivification and strength in the period of its inactivity; and at the appointed time of its reappearance inflicts a stern and fearful retribution, not only for the crimes which are committed against others, but for the iniquity which has been perpetrated against itself.

§ 220. *Of Accountability in connexion with this form of Disordered Conscience.*

If the moral sensibility, under the system of repression which has been mentioned, refuses to act, the question arises whether, at such a time, a person is morally accountable for his conduct. As his conscience does not condemn him in what he does, is the transaction, whatever its nature, a criminal one? There can be but one answer to this question. It the individual is not condemned by his conscience, it is the result of his own evil course. We may illustrate the subject by a case which is unhappily too frequent. A man who commits a crime in a state of drunkenness may plead that he was not, at the time, aware of the guilt of his conduct. And this may be true. But he was guilty for placing himself in a situation where he knew he would be likely to injure others, or in some other way commit unlawful acts. His crime, instead of being diminished, is, in fact, increased. It is twofold. He is guilty of drunkenness, and he is guilty of everything evil, which he knew, or might have known, would result from his drunkenness.

In like manner, a man is not at liberty to plead that he was not, in the commission of his crimes, condemned by conscience, if it be the fact that he has, by a previous process, voluntarily perverted or hardened the conscience. On the contrary, it would be fair to say, as in the case of drunkenness, that he has increased his guilt; for he has added to the guilt of the thing done the antecedent and still greater crime of aiming a blow at the mind, of striking at the very life of the soul. Practically he is not self-condemned, for the mere reason that he has paralyzed the principle by which the sentence of self-condemnation is pronounced. But, in the eye of immutable justice, there is not only no diminution of his guilt, but it is inexpressibly enhanced by the attempts to murder, if we may so express it, the principle which, more than anything else, constitutes the dignity and glory of man's nature.

§ 221. *Of natural or congenital Moral Derangement.*

The other form of moral derangement is NATURAL or CONGENITAL. We do not know that we are authorized to say that men are by nature, in any case whatever, absolutely destitute of a conscience; nor, on the other hand, have we positive grounds for asserting that this is not the case. There is no more inconsistency or impossibility in a man's com-

E e

ing into the world destitute of a conscience, than there is in his being born without the powers of memory, comparison, and reasoning, which we find to be the case in some idiots. But certain it is, that there are some men who appear to have naturally a very enfeebled conscience; a conscience which but very imperfectly fulfils its office; and who, in this respect at least, appear to be constituted very differently from the great body of their fellow men. They exhibit an imbecility, or, if the expression may be allowed, an *idiocy* of conscience, which unquestionably diminishes, in a very considerable degree, their moral accountability. A number of those writers who have examined the subject of Insanity have taken this view, and have given instances in support of it.

"In the course of my life" (says Dr. Rush), "I have been consulted in three cases of the total perversion of the moral faculties. One of them was in a young man, the second in a young woman, both of Virginia; and the third was in the daughter of a citizen of Philadelphia. The last was addicted to every kind of mischief. Her wickedness had no intervals while she was awake, except when she was kept busy in some steady and difficult employment." He refers also to instances in other writers.

§ 222. *Further illustrations of congenital Moral Derangement.*

Dr. Haslam, in his Observations on Madness has given two decided cases of moral derangement. One of these was a lad about ten years of age.

Some of the traits which he exhibited were as follows. He early showed an impatience and irrita-
bility of temper, and became so mischievous and
uncontrollable that it was necessary to appoint a
person to watch over him. He gave answers only
to such questions as pleased him, and acted in opposition to every direction.   " On the first interview
I had with him" (says Dr. Haslam), " he contrived,
after two or three minutes' acquaintance, to break a
window and tear the frill of my shirt. He was an
unrelenting foe to all china, glass, and crockery
ware. Whenever they came within his reach, he
shivered them instantly. In walking the street, the
keeper was compelled to take the wall, as he uniformly broke the windows if he could get near them ;
and this operation he performed so dexterously, and
with such safety to himself, that he never cut his
fingers. To tear lace and destroy the finer textures
of female ornament seemed to gratify him exceedingly, and he seldom walked out without finding an
occasion of indulging this propensity. He never
became attached to any inferior animal, a benevolence so common to the generality of children. To
these creatures his conduct was that of the brute ;
he oppressed the feeble, and avoided the society of
those more powerful than himself. Considerable
practice had taught him that he was the cat's master; and, whenever this luckless animal approached
him, he plucked out its whiskers with wonderful rapidity ; to use his own language, ' *I must have her
beard off*.' After this operation he commonly
threw the creature on the fire or through the win-

dow. If a little dog came near him, he kicked it;
if a large one, he would not notice it. When he
was spoken to, he usually said, 'I do not choose to
answer.' When he perceived any one who appeared to observe him attentively, he always said, 'Now
I will look unpleasant.' The usual games of children afforded him no amusement; whenever boys
were at play he never joined them; indeed, the
most singular part of his character was, that he appeared incapable of forming a friendship with any
one; he felt no considerations for sex, and would
as readily kick or bite á girl as a boy. Of any
kindness shown him he was equally insensible; he
would receive an orange as a present, and afterward
throw it in the face of the donor."

This unfortunate lad seems sometimes to have
been sensible of his melancholy condition. When,
on a certain occasion, he was conducted through an
insane hospital, and a mischievous maniac was
pointed out to him who was more strictly confined
than the rest, he said to his attendant, " This would
be the right place for me." He often expressed a
wish to die, and gave as a reason "that God had
not made him like other children."

§ 223. *Facts in relation to an individual in the
Lunatic Asylum in Dublin.*

There was recently an individual in the Richmond
Lunatic Asylum in Dublin, in whom the moral sense
seems to have been naturally paralyzed, or, perhaps,
extinct. Some account is given of him by Dr.
Crawford, the physician of that asylum, in a letter

to Mr. George Combe.—"It is one of those cases"
(says Dr. Crawford) "where there is great difficulty
in drawing the line between extreme moral depravi-
ty and insanity ; and in deciding at what point an
individual should cease to be considered as a re-
sponsible moral agent, and amenable to the laws.
The governors and medical gentlemen of the asylum have often had doubts whether they were justified in keeping E. S. as a *lunatic*, thinking him a
more fit subject for a Bridewell. He appears, however, so totally callous with regard to every moral
principle and feeling ; so thoroughly unconscious of
ever having done anything wrong ; so completely
destitute of all sense of shame or remorse when reproved for his vices or crimes ; and has proved himself so utterly incorrigible throughout life, that it is
almost certain that any jury before whom he might
be brought would satisfy their doubts by returning
him *insane*, which in such a case is the most humane
line to pursue.

"He was dismissed several times from the asylum, and sent there the last time for attempting to
poison his father. And it seems fit he should be
kept there for life as a *moral lunatic*. But there
has never been the least symptom of *diseased* action
of the brain, which is the general concomitant of
what is usually called insanity."

§ 224. *Of Moral Accountability in cases of natural
or congenital Moral Derangement.*

The question recurs here, also, whether persons
who are the subjects of a natural or congenital mor-

al derangement are morally accountable, and in what degree. If there is naturally an entire extinction of the moral sense, as in some cases of idiocy there is an entire extinction of the reasoning power, which, although it may not frequently happen, is at least a supposable case, there is no moral accountability. A person in that situation can have no distinct perception of what right and wrong are ; nor can he be conscious of doing either right or wrong in any given. case ; and, consequently, being without either merit or demerit, in the moral sense of the terms, he is not the proper subject of reward and punishment. He is to be treated on the principles that are applicable to idiots and insane persons generally.

In other cases, where the mental disorder is not so great, but there are some lingering rays of moral light, some feeble capability of moral vision, the person is to be judged, if it is possible to ascertain what it is, according to what is given him. If he has but one moral talent, it is not to be presumed that the same amount of moral responsibility rests upon him as upon another who possesses ten. The doctrine which requires men, considered as subjects of reward and punishment, to be treated alike, without regard to those original diversities of structure which may exist in all the departments of the mind, not only tends to confound right and wrong, but is abhorrent to the dictates of benevolence. Many individuals, through a misunderstanding of this important subject, have suffered under the hands of the executioner, who, on principles of religion and strict justice, should have been encircled only in the arms of compassion, long-suffering, and charity.

CHAPTER X.

CASUAL ASSOCIATIONS IN CONNEXION WITH THE
SENSIBILITIES.

§ 225. *Frequency of Casual Associations, and some
instances of them.*

WE propose to conclude this part of our subject
by giving some instances of Casual Associations.
Such associations, deeply affecting the whole character, are not unfrequent. By a thousand circumstances, and in thousands of instances, the feelings
are wrenched from their natural position, and shoot
forth and show themselves in misplaced and disproportionate forms. Casual associations, in the shape
of antipathies, fears, aversions, prepossessions, remorse, &c., are found seated in many a mind, which
is otherwise unembarrassed and unexceptionable in
its action ; they have established their empire there
on immoveable foundations, and are incorporated
with the whole mental nature.

If it were otherwise, how could a man, who would
willingly face a thousand men in battle, tremble at a
mouse, a squirrel, a thunder-shower, at the trivial
circumstance of placing the left slipper on the right
foot, or any other very trifling thing ! And yet such
instances are without number.—It may be considered singular enough, but so it is, that some men

cannot endure the sight of a fish, eel, or lobster ;
another person is disgusted at the sight of cheese,
honey, eggs, milk, or apples ; another is exceedingly distressed, and even convulsed, at the sight of
toad or a cat, a grasshopper or a beetle.

§ 226. *Of Association in connexion with the Appetites.*

In proceeding to give some illustrations of this
interesting subject, which has hitherto received but
little attention, we begin with the Appetites, which
are subject to strong Associative influences, as will
appear by some statements.

I.—Almost every article which is capable of being
masticated and digested is made, in one country or
another, an article of food. It is the case, at the
same time, that there are many articles used as food
in one country which are not used as food in another. This difference in the manner of living is to
be ascribed, in many cases, to some early and fixed
association. In some countries the people eat rats,
mice, frogs, lizards, horseflesh, dogs, locusts, cater-
pillars, &c.* In other countries, in our own for
instance, the associations adverse to the use of such
kinds of food are so strong that it is next to impossible to overcome them.

II.—There are appetitive associations of a different kind. It is well known, for instance, that the
appetite for drink may be inflamed by a mere name,
or the sight of a particular building or place, or the

* Lander's Niger, vol. i., Am. ed., p. 170, 179.—Lives of Celebrated Travellers, vol. i., Am. ed., p. 102, 215.

return of a certain hour of the day. This unquestionably is the result of a casual association. And
the association may have become so strong, that the
appetite is rendered wholly irrepressible whenever
such objects recur.—This is particularly true when
the liquor itself, the rum, gin, wine, or brandy, is
placed directly before the thorough-going drunkard.
The appetite in a moment becomes so strong as to
convulse the whole soul. He is agitated and rent
with a sort of madness; and rushes upon the object
before him, much as the furious lion seizes and
rends his keeper when he has accidentally seen and
tasted his blood.

§ 227. *Of Casual Associations in connexion with the Propensities.*

As we pass on from the Appetites to the consideration of that part of our Sentient nature which, in
distinction from the appetites on the one hand and
the affections on the other, is known as the Propensities, we find some instances of the power of association, both in strengthening and in annulling them.
—Among other Propensities, which have a distinct
and natural origin, is the desire of society; but it is
undoubtedly the case, that peculiar circumstances
may operate either to increase this desire or to an-
nul it altogether. All cases of decided and permanent Misanthropy, for instance, are the work, with
perhaps a few exceptions of congenital alienation,
not of nature, but of circumstances. If a man of
kind and benevolent feelings is exceedingly ill-treated by one whom he has often favoured, it is possi-
F f

ble, at least, that it will result in a fixed aversion to that person, which nothing can afterward overcome.

If a deep and permanent injury were inflicted, not merely by a friend, but a brother, the effect on the mind might be so great as not only to break up the original principle of sociability, but implant a decided and unchangeable hostility to the whole human race. Such treatment would be so contrary from what the injured person had a right to expect, that the mind would be thrown entirely out of its original position, and with such force as to be unable to recover it.

§ 228. *Other instances of Casual Association in connexion with the Propensities.*

The desire of power, in the remarks which were formerly made upon that subject, was regarded as an original propensity. This principle may become disordered in its action by becoming inordinately intense, and also in connexion with some casual association. Mr. Locke, in his Letters on Toleration, mentions the case of an individual (the case already instanced under the head of inordinate desire of power) whose mind was so long and intently fixed upon some high object, that he became partially insane. He was, for the most part, rational at other times, but whenever the object he had so earnestly pursued was mentioned, it brought into exercise so many intense associations that he immediately became deranged.

Although we might find it difficult to illustrate this subject from the ordinary forms of the propensity to

Imitation, the power of casual associations may distinctly be shown in *sympathetic* imitation. If a person's feelings be, from any cause, so strongly excited as to show themselves in involuntary bodily action, subsequently the mere sight of the person, place, or instrument that was prominently concerned in the original excitement of the mind, will generally be attended with a recurrence of the sympathetic bodily action. After such results have followed a number of times, the association will become so strong, that it will be very difficult, if not impossible, for the sympathetic person to repress the outward bodily signs, in all cases, coming within the reach of the association.

§ 229. *Inordinate fear from Casual Associations.*

The same views may undoubtedly be carried into the higher department of the Affections or Passions. It is sufficiently evident, for instance, that the passion of FEAR is an attribute of man's nature ; and, in ordinary cases, it is susceptible of being subjected to the control of reason and the sentiments of duty. But this is not always the case. Casual associations are sometimes formed which no effort of reason and no calls of duty can rend asunder.— We will endeavour to illustrate this subject by some familiar instances.

Some persons have been exceedingly frightened by thunder and lightning at early periods of life. The fright may have been occasioned either directly, or by the actual terrific power and nearness of the explosion, or by merely seeing an exhibition of great fear in parents or others more advanced in years. And from that hour to the end of life they have never been able, with all possible care and anxiety, to free themselves from the most distressing fear on such occasions.

Casual associations, occasioned by some unfortunate circumstances in early life, have been the source of very great and irrepressible fears in respect to death. The fear of death is natural; and, perhaps we may say, is instinctive; but it does not ordinarily exist in such intensity as essentially to interrupt one's happiness. And yet, from time to time, we find unhappy exceptions to this statement. Miss Hamilton, in her Letters on Education, gives an interesting account of a lady who suffered exceedingly from such fears. She was a person of an original and inventive genius, of a sound judgment, and her powers of mind had received a careful cultivation. But all this availed nothing against the impressions which had been wrought into her mind from infancy. The first view which she had of death in infancy was accompanied with peculiar circumstances of terror; and the dreadful impression which was then made was heightened by the injudicious language of the nursery. Ever afterward, the mere mention or idea of death was attended with great suffering; so much so, that it was necessary, by means of every possible precaution, to keep her in ignorance of her actual danger when she was sick; nor was it permitted, at any time, to mention instances of death in her presence. So that the estimable writer of this statement asserts, that she often suffered mcre from the apprehension than she could have suffered from the most agonizing torture that ever attended the hour of dissolution.*

§ 230. *Casual Associations in respect to persons.*

That the Affections may be more or less disordered by means of casual associations, is further evident from what we notice in the intercourse of individuals with each other. Men sometimes form such an aversion to others, or associate with them such sentiments of dread, that the connexion of the persons and the feelings becomes permanent and unconquerable.—It has sometimes been the case, that a man of distinguished talents has been defeated and prostrated by another, in an argument, perhaps, on some public occasion; and although he harbours no resentment against his opponent, and has no sense of inferiority, yet he never afterward meets him in company without experiencing a very sensible degree of uneasiness and suffering.

Persons have sometimes been ill-treated by others; and this occasionally forms the basis of an invincible association, either of aversion or of dread. The poet Cowper, in early life, suffered in this way. A boy of a cruel temper, his superior in age, made him the object of long-continued ill-treatment and persecution. "This boy" (he remarks) "had impressed such a dread of his figure upon my mind, that I well remember being afraid to lift my eyes upon him higher than his knees; and that I knew him by his shoebuckles better than by any other part of his dress."

* Elementary Principles of Education Letter III.

An individual was once perfectly cured of madness by a very harsh and offensive operation.   During all his life after, he acknowledged, with the most sincere gratitude, that he could not have received a greater benefit; and still he was utterly unable to bear the sight of the operator, it suggested so strongly the dreadful suffering which he underwent.*

Some men have an exceeding and unaccountable aversion to the mere features and countenance of another, and cannot bear to be looked upon by them. A statement is somewhere given of a person of a noble family, who was not able to bear that an old woman should look upon him.   Certain persons, in a season of merriment, which is not always wisely directed towards these humbling infirmities of our nature, succeeded in suddenly and unexpectedly introducing him into the presence of one such, but the shock to his feelings was so great as to terminate in his death.

§ 231. *Casual Association in connexion with objects and places.*

The mental operations, in consequence of strong casual associations, may be perplexed in their action in connexion with particular places and objects. " Some persons" (says Dr. Conolly, in reference to this subject) " are mad and unmanageable at home, and sane abroad.   We read in Aretæus of a carpenter who was very rational in his workshop, but who could not turn his steps towards the Forum without beginning to groan, to shrug his shoulders,

* Locke's Essay, book ii., ch. xxxii.

and to bemoan himself. Dr. Rush relates an instance of a preacher in America, who was mad among his parishioners except in the pulpit, where he conducted himself with great ability ; and he also speaks of a judge who was very lunatic in mixed society, but sagacious on the bench."

" I have known patients" (says the same writer in another place) " in whom there was a tendency to mania, complain of the difficulty they found in guarding against dislike, not only of particular individuals, but of particular parts of a room, or of the house, or of particular articles of furniture or dress ; those momentary feelings of uneasiness or antipathy to which all are subject, becoming in them aggravated or prolonged."* In connexion with the facts just stated, he mentions the case of an individual who could not bear the sight of white stockings ; and of a certain Russian general who entertained a singular antipathy to mirrors ; so much so, that the Empress Catharine always took care to give him audience in a room without any.

§ 232. Of Casual Association in connexion with particular days.

The same marked tendencies of mind may sometimes be discovered in connexion with particular days or other periods of time. Pinel mentions a lady who fancied that Friday was a day of ill omen and ill luck. " She at length carried this notion so far, that she would not leave her room on that day. If the month began on a Friday, it rendered her ex-

* Conolly on Insanity, London ed., p. 98, 218.

tremely fearful and miserable for several days.   By
degrees, Thursday, being the eve of Friday, excited
similar alarms.   If ever she heard either of those
days named in company, she immediately turned
pale, and was confused in her manner and conver
sation, as if she had been visited by some fatal mis
fortune."*

Statements, much to the same effect, have been
made of an individual no less distinguished than
Lord Byron.   From some circumstance or other,
he became deeply impressed with the belief that
Friday was destined to be, in relation to himself, an
unlucky or ill-omened day.   This was not a mere
transitory feeling, which was under the control of his
philosophy, but was deeply seated and operative.
And, with his characteristic frankness, he did not
hesitate to declare, or, rather, he took no pains to
conceal, that his mind was actually under the des-
potism of this strange influence.†

We will subjoin here, as bearing some affinity to
the cases which might properly be arranged under
this head, an instance mentioned in the Encyclopæ-
dia Americana, by the author of the article on Memory.   The statement is as follows : " How strange
are the associations of ideas which often take place
in spite of us.   Every one must have experienced
such.   The writer recollects a melancholy instance
in the case of an insane boy in an hospital, whose
derangement was referred to an irreverent association with the name of God, which occurred to him

* Treatise on Insanity, p. 140.
† Moore's Life of Byron, vol. ii., p. 458.

while singing a hymn in church, and of which he could not divest himself, the painfulness of the impression making it occur to him more forcibly every time he sung in church, till his reason became unsettled."

§ 233. *Antipathies to Animals.*

Nothing but the fact of the existence and great power of casual associations can explain the circumstance, that individuals have, from time to time, discovered a very great antipathy to certain animals. Tasso, according to his biographers, would fall into convulsions at the sight of a carp. Henry the Third, of England, could not be persuaded to sit in the room with a cat. Admiral Coligni, a name justly renowned in the history of France, was so afraid of a mouse, that he could not be induced to admit one to his presence unless he had his sword in his hand.

No man ever gave more decided proofs of courage than the celebrated Marquis de la Roche Jacqueline; but it is a singular fact (although no account is given of the origin of this strange association), that he could not look in the face of a squirrel without trembling and turning pale. He himself ridiculed his weakness in this respect; but, with all his efforts, he could not prevent the physical effects which have been referred to, whenever he was in the presence of that harmless animal.

But we have an incident nearer home, which appears the less surprising, because we know the origin of it. The late Governor Sullivan, of Massachusetts, when a boy, fell asleep under a tree, and was awakened by a serpent crawling over him. He arose in great terror, ran towards the house, and fell down in a convulsive fit. Afterward, through life, he retained such aversion for everything of the serpent kind, that he could not see one, or even the picture of one, without falling into convulsions.

Peter the Great, of Russia, who certainly was not wanting in expansion and force of mind, was subject to a strong and invincible aversion of this kind. His biographer, without giving any explanation of it, merely mentions the facts as follows.—" Nothing was sò much the object of the Czar's antipathy as a black insect of the scarabeus or beetle kind, which breeds in houses that are not kept clean, and especially in places where meal and other provisions are deposited. In the country the walls and ceilings of the peasant's houses are covered with them, particularly in Russia, where they abound more than in any other part of the world. They are there called *taracan;* but our naturalists give them the name of *dermeste,* or dissecting scarabeus.

" Although the Russian monarch was far from being subject to childish fears or womanish fancies, one of these insects sufficed to drive him out of an apartment, nay, even out of the house. In his frequent journeys in his own dominions, he never went into a house without having his apartment carefully swept by one of his own servants, and being assured that there were no taracans to fear. One day he paid a visit to an officer, who stood pretty high in his esteem, at his country house, which was built of wood, at a little distance from Moscow. The Czar expressed his satisfaction with what was offered him, and with the order he observed in the house. The company sat down to table, and dinner was already begun, when he asked his landlord if there were taracans in his house.

" ' Not many,' replied the officer, without reflecting ; ' and, the better to get rid of them, I have pinned a living one to the wall.' At the same time he pointed to the place where the insect was pinned, and still continued to palpitate. Unfortunately, it was just beside the Czar, in whom the unexpected sight of this object of his aversion produced so much emotion, that he rose instantly from table, gave the officer a violent blow, and left his house with all his attendants."*

* Stælhim's Original Anecdotes of Peter the Great

IMPERFECT AND DISORDERED

MENTAL ACTION.

DIVISION THIRD.

DISORDERED ACTION OF THE WIL

DISORDERED ACTION

OF THE

WILL.

CHAPTER I.

NATURE OF THE WILL.

§ 234. *On the relation of the Will to the other parts of the Mind.*

IT cannot fail to have been noticed, that our inquiries hitherto have proceeded upon the important principle, which is now generally acknowledged to be a correct one, of a threefold division of the mind, viz., the Intellect, the Sensibilities, and the Will. Having considered the subject before us, very briefly, it is true, in connexion with the two first-mentioned departments, we proceed now to the only remaining topic, viz., the Disordered Action of the Will.

The Will is a department of the Mind, evidently standing by itself; having its distinct nature and attributes, as well as its appropriate laws. The purely intellectual acts have something peculiar and characteristic, which shuts them out, as it were, from the region of the Sensibilities. The Sensitive action, as well as the Intellectual, has its specific nature ; something by which it is known and distinguished from other forms of mental movement. The Will also stands apart, having its appropriate sphere and its allotted duties ; holding, as it were, the place of keystone to the arch, and exercising a sort of supervisory and authoritative power over the other departments of the mind.

The philosophy of the Will, considered in its regular or normal action, is a subject of great importance and interest ; nor will it be found wholly wanting in interest when considered in reference to those irregularities of action of which it is sometimes the subject.

§ 235. *Of the attribute of Power as existing in the Will.*

The subject of the disordered action and insanity of the Will will be found, in its basis or origin, to have relation, in nearly all cases, to the attribute of Power.—It will be noticed, that we take it for granted that there is such a thing as power. In other words, that power, notwithstanding the fact of its not being directly cognizable by the outward senses (as it is not), is something positive and real ; something which can be estimated to some extent, and which can be made a subject of examination, reasoning, and opinion. Accordingly, every man is supposed to know what power is, although it may be very true that it is not a direct object of the sight or hearing, or any of the outward senses.

And not only this. It is a fact also, for which we have the testimony of our consciences, that, although it does not exist in the form of a separate faculty analogous to perception or memory, it exists, nevertheless, as an attribute of the whole mind, and is diffused, in a greater or less degree, through all its faculties. In other words, we have an original feeling or conviction, originating in the facts of our consciousness, that in every exercise or operation of the mind there is, and must be, power.

And this is not all. Power is not only, in general terms, predicable of the mind as a whole, but it is particularly and emphatically so of the department of the Will. If the other mental acts clearly indicate to us the existence of an innate energy, certainly we should not expect to find less of energy, less of power, existing as the basis of acts of the will. When a person wills to go to a certain place, or wills to do a certain thing, it requires no train of reasoning to convince him that power is the basis of the volition, and, consequently, that power truly exists as an attribute of the voluntary or volitive nature.

§ 236. *Of the degree of Power existing in the Will.*

We are not to suppose that the power which exists in the Will is unlimited in degree. The degree of power is different in different minds ; but in all cases it may be regarded as a fixed and definite thing ; capable of a certain amount of action, or of sustaining a certain degree of pressure, but utterly inefficient beyond that amount or degree.

The Will, therefore, may, under certain circum-

G g

stances, be overburdened and oppressed in its action. We may expect too much from it ; and it may not answer to our requisitions, merely because it is unable to. It may be thrown into a wrong position by the excited state and the inordinate action of other parts of the mind. It may be undermined by a crazy belief, or trammelled by an invincible association. For these and for other reasons, it may fail (and, in point of fact, this is not unfrequently the case) to discharge successfully its appropriate offices.

§ 237. *Of Positive in distinction from Relative disorder of the Will.*

Accordingly, a disordered or alienated condition of the Will is as frequently relative as positive. That is to say (and this is an important consideration, which it may be well to keep in mind), it fails to fulfil the duties which pertain to it as a voluntary power, as frequently, and probably more so, in consequence of the disordered action of other parts of the mind, as in consequence of any absolute defect inherent in itself. Nevertheless, there are some cases where it is evident that the defective voluntary action is to be ascribed, not so much to any perplexities and hinderances which lay out of the will, as to something which nature herself may be said to have wrought into it.

CHAPTER II.

IMBECILITY OF THE WILL.

§ 238. *Of natural weakness or imbecility of the Will.*

ONE of the forms in which a disordered will developes itself is that of Imbecility or inordinate Weakness.—We not unfrequently see persons who develope this trait of mind ; men who are easily intimidated, vacillating, who affirm when they should deny, and deny when they should affirm ; who, in common parlance, and almost in strict truth, " have no will of their own."

Their minds are essentially in the condition of a paralytic limb, that may be acted upon, but without giving any signs of vitality in itself. Sometimes these persons possess a considerable share of natural intellectual vigour ; but it is almost of no avail, since their voluntary energy is not sufficient to bring it into permanent action. They sometimes form plans, but generally exhaust themselves in the incipient efforts, and the execution is a NON SEQUITUR ! They would be wholly useless in society, were it not that they can be acted on by others, and thus be kept in a sort of automatic movement by means of other person's wills substituted in the place of their own.

§ 239. *Consideration of the foregoing statements in connexion with Power.*

The statements which have just been made illustrate a leading remark in the preceding chapter to this effect, that the subject of disordered action existing in the Will will be found, in nearly all cases, to have a relation to the attribute of Power.   A normal or right Will may, of course, be expected to have power enough to secure the great objects for which the Will obviously exists, viz., the exercise of a supervisory control, and the enforcement of that control upon the other parts of the mind, as well as upon the body.   This is the true idea of a perfectly regular or sane state of the Will.   Consequently, every deviation from this state, when, for instance, there is not power enough to secure these great objects, and the man is governed by the impulses of association and feeling rather than by the great regulator, necessarily implies, to some extent, an imperfect or disordered state.

And this is precisely the case which was considered in the preceding section.   The Will fails of its object, and, therefore, is not such as it should be. It does not exhibit the great requisite and characteristic of its own nature, viz., the element of authoritative control, and, therefore, cannot escape the imputation, according to the degree in which the defect exists, either of disorder short of insanity, or of positive alienation.

Of this form of disordered Will some illustrations might properly be given in this place, additional to the facts and instances given in the chapters on Abstraction and Attention, which will help to communicate some idea of it.

§ 240. *Illustration of natural imbecility of the Will.*

Pinel states, that he had frequent opportunities of seeing a person, whose conduct, as it seems to us, rather strikingly illustrates this form of mental disorder.—After stating that his ideas appeared to be insulated, and to rise one after the other without connexion, he goes on to remark as follows : " His motions, his ideas, his broken sentences, his confused and momentary glimpses of mental affection, appeared to present a perfect image of chaos. He came up to me, looked at me, and overwhelmed me with a torrent of words, without order or connexion. In a moment he turned to another person, whom, in his turn, he deafened with his unmeaning babble, or threatened with an evanescent look of anger. But, as incapable of determined and continued excitement of the feelings, as of a just connexion of ideas, his emotions were the effects of a momentary effervescence, which was immediately succeeded by a calm.

" If he went into a room, he quickly displaced or overturned the furniture, without manifesting any direct intention. Scarcely could one look off before he would be at a considerable distance, exercising his versatile mobility in some other way. He was quiet only when food was presented to him. He rested, even at nights, but for a few moments."*

* Pinel's Treatise on Insanity, Davis's Translation, p. 163.

It is very evident that the power of Will existed in this person in a very limited degree. Indeed, it is not easy to perceive how his conduct could be very much different, if the faculty of the Will had been entirely erased from his mind, and he had been left without any controlling principle at all.

§ 241. *Further remarks on imbecility of Will.*

There are some important applications which may be made of the view that has now been taken. There are some men, for instance, who, under the influence of some more or less slightly excited passion, commit crimes which we should certainly suppose they would not do if they had the least power of self-restraint. They go forward much as do some children, in whom the volitive power is but little developed, and whose constantly varying acts seem to originate exclusively in mere sensitive, passionate impulses. In other words, their conduct is very much such as we should suppose it would be if the outward action were based directly upon the sensibilities, without the suspensive and regulative faculty of the Will intervening. They feel, they have an impulse, and they go and do accordingly, without any interrogatory being put or any restraint being exercised by the higher regulating power. In all such cases, where we do not see occasion for great excitement of the passions, and where, in point of fact, although there is some, there is yet no very great excitement, it seems impossible to explain the facts that present themselves, except on the ground of inordinate weakness of the Will.

I am inclined to the opinion, that in many cases
of murder, if we could analyze perfectly the mental
structure of those who commit this crime, we should
find these individuals differing from a multitude of
other persons less in the positive malignity of the
passions than in a great weakness of the will, which
renders them unable to control their passions.   It
is probable that, in most cases, this is not the only
ground of difference, as there may, for instance, be
combined with the weakness of the will an inordinate feebleness of the moral power; but it is one,
and a very important one. The persons in question are the subjects of excited feeling and passion
in a greater or less degree ; sometimes in rather a
small degree. They have, however, something, and
evidently *must* have something, to move them on in
the course which they take ; but they would probably do otherwise than they do, in fact, and would
frequently repress their emotions and passions, which
have put them on a wrong direction, if they were not
greatly deficient in the superintending and controlling principles of the mind.

These remarks will perhaps apply to the case of
an individual by the name of Prescott, who was recently executed in New-Hampshire for the crime of
murder. The case is given at some length, and
with appropriate remarks, in the work of Dr. Ray
on Medical Jurisprudence.

§ 242. *Of alienation of the Will termed* INCON-
STANTIA.

Imbecility of the will is sometimes connected with

an irregular action of the power of Association ; and it seems to be the peculiar modification of mental disorder which the mind then assumes, which is known in medical writers under the name of INCONSTANTIA. The instances which illustrate this form of mental disorder might many times be arranged, according to the view which is taken of them, eithei as instances of alienated will or alienated association. The persons who are subject to this form ol perplexed and disordered mental action are designaled by various epithets, such as fickle, flighty, light-headed, hair-brained. The thoughts of these persons, as we have already described them undei the head of Association, fly from one subject to another with great rapidity ; their bodies are almost always in motion, and their volubility of speech is excessive.

M. Pinel mentions an instance (a gentleman who had been educated in the prejudices of the ancient noblesse of France) which illustrates this singular condition of mind. " He constantly bustled about the house, talking incessantly, shouting, and throwing himself into great passions for the most trifling causes. He teased his domestics by the most frivolous orders, and his neighbours by his fooleries and extravagances, of which he retained not the least recollection for a single moment. He talked with the greatest volatility of the court, of his periwig, of his horses, of his gardens, without waiting for an answer, or giving time to follow his incohe rent jargon."

§ 243. *Of superinduced weakness of Will, or that which is occasioned by wrong mental training.*

We are not always to infer, however, from the mere fact of the existence of a weakness of the Will, that it is in all cases natural, and, consequently, something for which the individual is not accountable.—The Will admits of its appropriate exercise, and its nature requires such exercise. And, if it is denied what its nature thus requires ; if it is never placed in difficult positions, and never permitted to exert itself, the necessary result is, that it will lose in a considerable degree, and sometimes almost entirely, the amount of power, whether more or less, which it naturally had.

There are sometimes whole classes of people, in whom, not so much by nature as by circumstances, the faculty of the Will, which ought ever to show itself as a decisive and leading principle, appears inert and feeble.—Dr. Rush intimates that slaves are very apt to exhibit this trait of mind ; not, however, in consequence of natural imbecility so much as a feebleness and uncertainty of purpose, gradually superinduced by being constantly under the direction of others, and not being called upon to exercise their own wills.

It may be added also, that these views may essentially aid, in some cases at least, in the explanation of that weakness and uncertainty of purpose which we not unfrequently notice in old people, and which forms an important element in that complex trait of character which we denominate the childishness of old age. Their wills grow weak from the want of exercise ; and their passions, showing themselves in the forms of peevishness and fickle ill-humour, grow strong for the opposite reason.

CHAPTER III.

DISORDERED ACTION OF THE WILL IN CONNEXION WITH OTHER POWERS.

§ 244. *The action of the Will may be perplexed through the medium of the other faculties.*

SOMETIMES the perplexed and disordered action of the Will is relative rather than positive. It stands well in itself. It bears the stamp and gives the evidence of entire soundness, when considered apart from the other powers. Nevertheless, in consequence of its connexion with other parts of the mind its action may be interrupted and perplexed, and sometimes in the very highest degree. We do not, however, mean to say that it is perplexed and hindered in its action in all respects, which is not the fact ; but only when it comes within reach of the influence of this connexion.

§ 245. *Disordered Action of the Mind in connexion with Casual Associations.*

As an illustration of this matter, we may very

properly refer to some of those striking facts which
were introduced in the chapter on Casual Associations. Peter the Great, for instance, in whom energy of the will was unquestionably a very conspicuous characteristic, was utterly unable to bear the
sight of a certain insect. La Roche Jacqueline, another individual mentioned in the chapter just refer-
ed to, was brave and chivalric in the very highest
degree. Few names among the numberless renowned men of France stand higher on the heroic
and patriotic list than his. And yet it appears, from
the accounts which are given of him, that he always
lost all courage, and was entirely unmanned in the
presence of a harmless squirrel. In these, and a
multitude of other cases like them, we have instances of men who possessed, in general, great energy
and decision, but who displayed in certain very trivial conjunctures the greatest imbecility.

In all cases of this kind, we may probably regard
the origin, the *seat* of the disorder, as existing in the
associating principle. This principle calls up, from
time to time, certain very unpleasant feelings, which,
in the history of the individual, are found to be connected with certain objects. And it does it with
great force and distinctness; so much so as to set
the regulating power of the will entirely at defiance.
Consequently, the individual, apparently without any
adequate cause, is thrown into great agitation; his
fears, or, perhaps, some other passion, are greatly
excited; his will is, as it were, taken captive; and
his conduct at once assumes an aspect which can

not be explained in accordance with the ordinary results of a sound mind.

We assert, therefore, that the action of the will in these cases is a disordered one, although the cause of the disorder lays out of itself, because it does not act, and is not able to act, in accordance with the original tendencies and constitution of its own nature. It is not what it should be, and what a truly sound and unperplexed will always is, viz., capable of regulating the feelings and actions, so far as is suitable and proper, or, in other words, so far as is required by a true view of the nature and relations of things.

§ 246. *Additional illustration of the preceding view.*

Perhaps we have, in the personal history of Dr. Johnson, an instance of alienation of will, based on a disordered casual association.—" He had another particularity" (says his biographer), " of which none of his friends ever ventured to ask him an explanation. It appeared to me some superstitious habit, which he had contracted early, and from which he had never called upon his reason to disentangle him. This was his anxious care to go out or in at a door or passage by a certain number of steps from a certain point, or, at least, so that as either his right or left foot (I am not certain which) should constantly make the first movement when he came close to the door or passage. Thus I conjecture : for I have, upon innumerable occasions, observed him suddenly stop, and then seem to count his steps with a deep earnestness ; and, when he had neglected or gone wrong in this sort of magical movement, I have seen him go back again, put himself into a proper posture to begin the ceremony, and, having gone through it, break from his abstraction, walk briskly on, and join his company."—With such clearness of perception, with such vast powers of understanding as Dr. Johnson possessed, we cannot suppose that he would ever have submitted to the utter folly of such a practice, if his will had not entirely lost its power in that particular, in consequence of some early association, which had fastened itself in the mind too deeply for eradication.

§ 247. *Of alienation of the Will as connected with a disordered state or alienation of Belief.*

There are yet other cases of a disordered action of the Will, resulting from its connexion with other parts of the mind. There is a close connexion, for instance, between the faculty of the Will and that state of the mind which is termed Belief. And this connexion appears, among other things, in this way. It will be found, on examination, that the strength of the will's acts or volitions will become diminished more and more in conformity with the diminution of belief; and that, by the original constitution of the mind itself, there is not even a possibility of putting forth the mental exercise of volition when there is no belief that the thing to which it relates is in our power. Hence it follows as a general truth, that a disordered or alienated state of belief will be followed by a corresponding alienation of the will.

Accordingly, if a man, in the condition of insanitv of belief, truly looks upon himself as made of glass, it is just as difficult for him to *will* to move himself about rapidly, and to throw himself suddenly and violently in contact with solid and hard bodies, as it is for a man in a sane mind to *will* to thrust his hand or foot into the fire or boiling water, which, with many persons, would be found to be an utter impossibility. His will is in such cases enslaved (not in the more common and ordinary form of enthralment, which is fully consistent with moral accountability), but to the degree of *insanity.*

We will suppose, as a further illustration of this view, that a man in the state of insanity of belief has a firm and unalterable conviction, as much so as of his own existence, that he has, by amputation or in some way, lost an arm or a leg ; and it will be found, just so long as he remains the subject of this alienation of belief, impossible for him to put forth a single volition having a relation to the action of those parts of the body. To that extent the power of willing is entirely lost. If his physician, or any one else, should require him to put forth such volition, it would appear to him (and necessarily so, from the constitution of the mind itself) not only impossible, but as supremely ridiculous as for a man of sound mind to will to walk upon the ocean or to fly in the air.

§ 248. *Alienation of the Will in connexion with Melancholy.*

Furthermore, the will is sometimes alienated (that is to say, is in that state which is usually indicated by the term INSANITY) in cases where there is a deeply-rooted and permanent melancholy. The mind of the person is fixed upon some gloomy subject; it remains the object of contemplation day after day and hour after hour; a thick, impenetrable cloud seems to invest every prospect, whether present or future. It seems to the spectator that there is nothing wanting but a mere act of the will, a resolution, a mere decision, in order to bring the person out of this state of gloomy inactivity, and carry him once more into the discharge of the duties of life. And this is true, if the will could be made to act. But the gloom spreads itself from the understanding to the heart, and from the heart to the region of the voluntary power; and the will, invested on every side by the darkness of this dense and impenetrable atmosphere, remains closed up and fixed, as if imbedded in a mass of ice. When the gloom is deepened to a certain degree, although the power of the will is not entirely gone, it is impossible for it to put forth any effective action.

The English poet Collins is an instance of this unhappy state of mind. "He languished some years" (says his biographer) "under that depression of mind which enchains the faculties without destroying them, and leaves reason the knowledge of right *without the power of pursuing it.* These clouds, which he perceived gathering upon his intellects, he endeavoured to disperse by travel, and passed into France; but found himself constrained to yield to his malady, and returned. He was for some time confined in a house of lunatics."* Well might this

* Johnson's Lives of the English Poets, art. *Collins.*

genuine poet have adopted the language, afterward
so feelingly applied to himself by his biographer,

> " Canst thou not minister to a mind diseased ?
> Pluck from the memory a rooted sorrow ?"

In all cases of this kind, whatever may be the
cause of them, the will has obviously lost its power;
it has ceased, and apparently without the possibility
of doing otherwise, to exercise that authority over
the other powers of the mind to which it is, by its
nature, entitled.

§ 249. *Of Accountability in connexion with Alienation or Insanity of the Will.*

It will be seen, from what has been said, that the
particular form or aspect of disorder and insanity of
the will is very various; sometimes consisting of the
entire or almost entire abstraction of its own power;
sometimes in an immovable fixedness, either occasioned by its own imbecility or the undue prepon-
derance of some other principle; sometimes in an
action, powerful enough, perhaps, but urged on, and
wholly shut up in one direction, and not in possession of an adequate degree of liberty; sometimes
in a fickleness approaching to entire contingency,
occasioned by the suspension or violation of those
general laws by which the action of the will is ordinarily restrained and regulated.—In all cases of actual insanity, under whatever aspect or form it may
appear, the person who is the subject of it is free
from moral accountability, to the degree or extent
in which the insanity exists; for it has now become
a settled principle on the subject of mental aliena-

tion, and one which is perfectly well understood, that not unfrequently the insanity extends to a particular power or a particular subject, and that beyond that particular power or subject the ordinary degree of perception and action remains.

But the question here presents itself to us, How can we ascertain the existence of insanity? By what rule can it be discovered or known to exist in a particular case? How can the line of demarcation be detected between that pressure of the will known as mere temporary enthralment, which exists in such a limited degree as to be consistent with moral accountability, and actual insanity of the will, which wholly destroys it?—On this subject we do not feel called upon to lay down any general rule; nor, if we were, should we be able to do it. The Supreme Being alone can tell, with entire certainty, when the limit is passed beyond which moral accountability ceases to exist. Men can do nothing more than approximate to such certainty of decision, determining, according to the best of their judgment, on the circumstances of individual cases.

THE END.

MENTAL ILLNESS AND SOCIAL POLICY
THE AMERICAN EXPERIENCE

AN ARNO PRESS COLLECTION

Barr, Martin W. Mental Defectives: Their History, Treatment and Training. 1904.

The Beginnings of American Psychiatric Thought and Practice: Five Accounts, 1811-1830. 1973

The Beginnings of Mental Hygiene in America: Three Selected Essays, 1833-1850. 1973

Briggs, L. Vernon, et al. History of the Psychopathic Hospital, Boston, Massachusetts. 1922

Briggs, L. Vernon. Occupation as a Substitute for Restraint in the Treatment of the Mentally Ill. 1923

Brigham, Amariah. An Inquiry Concerning the Diseases and Functions of the Brain, the Spinal Cord, and the Nerves. 1840

Brigham, Amariah. Observations on the Influence of Religion upon the Health and Physical Welfare of Mankind. 1835

Brill, A. A. Fundamental Conceptions of Psychoanalysis. 1921

Bucknill, John Charles. Notes on Asylums for the Insane in America. 1876

Conolly, John. The Treatment of the Insane Without Mechanical Restraints. 1856

Coriat, Isador H. What is Psychoanalysis? 1917

Deutsch, Albert. The Shame of the States. 1948

Dewey, Richard. Recollections of Richard Dewey: Pioneer in American Psychiatry. 1936

Earle, Pliny. Memoirs of Pliny Earle, M. D. with Extracts from his Diary and Letters (1830-1892) and Selections from his Professional Writings (1839-1891). 1898

Galt, John M. The Treatment of Insanity. 1846

Goddard, Henry Herbert. Feeble-mindedness: Its Causes and Consequences. 1926

Hammond, William A. A Treatise on Insanity in Its Medical Relations. 1883

Hazard, Thomas R. Report on the Poor and Insane in Rhode-Island. 1851

Hurd, Henry M., editor. The Institutional Care of the Insane in the United States and Canada. 1916/1917. Four volumes.

Kirkbride, Thomas S. On the Construction, Organization, and General Arrangements of Hospitals for the Insane. 1880

Meyer, Adolf. The Commonsense Psychiatry of Dr. Adolf Meyer: Fifty-two Selected Papers. 1948

Mitchell, S. Weir. Wear and Tear, or Hints for the Overworked. 1887

Morton, Thomas G. The History of the Pennsylvania Hospital, 1751-1895. 1895

Ordronaux, John. Jurisprudence in Medicine in Relation to the Law. 1869

The Origins of the State Mental Hospital in America: Six Documentary Studies, 1837-1856. 1973

Packard, Mrs. E. P. W. Modern Persecution, or Insane Asylums Unveiled, As Demonstrated by the Report of the Investigating Committee of the Legislature of Illinois. 1875. Two volumes in one

Prichard, James C. A Treatise on Insanity and Other Disorders Affecting the Mind. 1837

Prince, Morton. The Unconscious: The Fundamentals of Human Personality Normal and Abnormal. 1921

Putnam, James Jackson. Human Motives. 1915

Russell, William Logie. The New York Hospital: A History of the Psychiatric Service, 1771-1936. 1945

Sidis, Boris. The Psychology of Suggestion: A Research into the Subconscious Nature of Man and Society. 1899

Southard, Elmer E. Shell-Shock and Other Neuropsychiatric Problems Presented in Five Hundred and Eighty-Nine Case Histories from the War Literature, 1914-1918. 1919

Southard, E[lmer] E. and Mary C. Jarrett. The Kingdom of Evils. 1922

Southard, E[lmer] E. and H[arry] C. Solomon. Neurosyphilis: Modern Systematic Diagnosis and Treatment Presented in One Hundred and Thirty-seven Case Histories. 1917

Spitzka, E[dward] C. Insanity: Its Classification, Diagnosis and Treatment. 1887

Supreme Court Holding a Criminal Term, No. 14056. The United States vs. Charles J. Guiteau. 1881/1882. Two volumes

Trezevant, Daniel H. Letters to his Excellency Governor Manning on the Lunatic Asylum. 1854

Tuke, D[aniel] Hack. The Insane in the United States and Canada. 1885

Upham, Thomas C. Outlines of Imperfect and Disordered Mental Action. 1868

White, William A[lanson]. Twentieth Century Psychiatry: Its Contribution to Man's Knowledge of Himself. 1936

Willard, Sylvester D. Report on the Condition of the Insane Poor in the County Poor Houses of New York. 1865